ANALECTA BIBLICA

INVESTIGATIONES SCIENTIFICAE IN RES BIBLICAS

122

BARBARA A. BOZAK, c.s.j.

LIFE 'ANEW'

A Literary-Theological Study of Jer. 30-31

EDITRICE PONTIFICIO ISTITUTO BIBLICO – ROMA 1991

IMPRIMI POTEST
Romae, die 13 Julii 1991

R. P. KLEMENS STOCK, S.J.
Rector Pontificii Instituti Biblici

ISBN 88-7653-122-X

EDITRICE PONTIFICIO ISTITUTO BIBLICO
Piazza della Pilotta, 35 - 00187 Roma

To my mother and the memory of my father

PREFACE

This volume is a slightly revised version of a doctoral dissertation defended at the Gregorian University in May 1988. The research and writing were directed by Charles Conroy, m.s.c., whose encouraging support, careful reading and critical comments were invaluable in the shaping and refining of both the original idea and the final work.

While the responsibility of a work such as this is ultimately the burden of the author, many persons and groups have given both economic and moral support, without which this book could never have been published. To all these I owe a debt of gratitude. My religious community, the Sisters of St. Joseph of Chambery and in particular those of the generalate, have lightened the weight of my task by their constant support and encouragement. The professors of the Pontifical Biblical Institute not only introduced me to biblical exegesis and gave me the tools to work independently, but also opened new vistas to me. In particular I would like to mention Dennis McCarthy, s.j., for the countless ways in which he has opened my eyes and my mind and whose memory continues to be an inspiration. A word of thanks is also owed to John Welch, s.j., who has challenged me to ever new scholarly heights. I undertook doctoral studies at the encouragement of the theology faculty of St. Paul University, Ottawa, Canada, which sustained me with both economic and moral support during the writing of the dissertation.

Several individuals cannot go unrecognized for their contributions to the final redaction of this book. Normand Bonneau, o.m.i., suggested many stylistic improvements to the original manuscript and Nina Rusko-Berger gave excellent editorial advice. Proof-reading was aided by Louise Pambrun whose eagle eye caught innumerable errors. Many of the more practical details were taken in hand by Graziano Tassello, c.s., who took time from his very demanding work to deal directly with the editors in Rome. The recognition of these few persons is not meant to exclude the many others who have contributed in ways small or great to the formation and publication of this book and to whom I owe thanks.

The support of St. Paul University, Ottawa, where I have been a professor since 1981, has been extraordinary including, most recently, a generous grant from the Research Centre which has, in part, made this publication possible.

Due in large measure to my responsibilities on the theology faculty of St. Paul University, a few years have elapsed between the writing and the publication of this book. During that time other articles and books have appeared that might have been included. However since the validity of this study does not rely on one or another piece of secondary literature I make no apologies for presenting it as it stands, in the hope that it will make a small contribution to the ongoing discussion of Hebrew poetic literature.

Table of Contents

Abbreviations

Ab	'Aboth
AB	Anchor Bible
AJSL	*American Journal of Semitic Literature and Languages*
AnBib	Analecta Biblica
ANE	Ancient Near East(ern)
ANET	*Ancient Near Eastern Texts Relating to the Old Testament*, J.B. Pritchard, ed., 3rd ed., with Supplement. Princeton: Princeton University Press, 1969
AnOr	Analecta Orientalia
AOAT	Alter Orient und Altes Testament
Ar	ʿArakhin
ASTI	*Annual of the Swedish Theological Institute*
ATD	Das Alte Testament Deutsch
b	*The Babylonian Talmud*
BBB	Bonner Biblische Beiträge
Ber	Berakhot
BEThL	Biblioteca Ephemeridum Theologicarum Lovaniensium
BEvTh	Beiträge zur evangelische Theologie
BDB	*The New Brown, Driver, and Briggs Hebrew and English Lexicon of the Old Testament*, F. Brown, S.R. Driver, C.A. Briggs, eds. Lafayette, Indiana: Associated Publishers and Authors, Inc., 1981. (Reprint, with corrections, of 1907 ed.)
Bib	*Biblica*
BibOr	Bibliotheca Orientalis
BW	*Biblical World*
BWANT	Beiträge zur Wissenschaft vom Alten und Neuen Testament
BZ	*Biblische Zeitschrift*
BZAW	Beihefte zur Zeitschrift für die Alttestamentliche Wissenschaft
CBC	Cambridge Bible Commentaries
CBQ	*Catholic Biblical Quarterly*
DBS	*Dictionnaire de la Bible. Supplément*. L. Pirot, *et al*., eds., 10 vols. Paris: Letouzey & Ané, Editeurs, 1928-85
EncJud	*Encyclopedia Judaica*, 16 vols., C. Roth, *et al*., eds. Jerusalem: Keter Publishing House, Ltd., 1972
EstBib	*Estudios Biblicos*
EvQ	*Evangelical Quarterly*
EvTh	*Evangelische Theologie*
ExR	*Midrash Rabbah: Exodus*
FRLANT	Forschungen zur Religion und Literatur des Alten und Neuen Testament
Fs.	Festschrift

G-K	*Gesenius' Hebrew Grammar as Edited and Enlarged by E. Kautzsch*, 2nd English ed., rev. according to 28th German ed. (1909) by A. E. Cowley. Oxford: Clarendon Press, 1910 (1983 reprint)
GenR	*Midrash Rabbah: Genesis*
Greg	*Gregorianum*
HAL(AT)	*Hebräisches und aramäisches Lexikon zum Alten Testament*, 3 Lfg., L. Köhler u. W. Baumgartner, 3. Aufl., neu bearbeitet v. W. Baumgartner, J. J. Stamm *et al.* Leiden: E. J. Brill, 1967-83
HAT	Handbuch zum Alten Testament
HKAT	Handkommentar zum Alten Testament
HSM	Harvard Semitic Monographs
HUCA	*Hebrew Union College Annual*
IB	*The Interpreter's Bible*, 12 vols., G. Buttrick, *et al.*, eds. New York, Nashville: Abingdon, 1952-57
IDB	*The Interpreter's Dictionary of the Bible*, G. A. Buttrick, *et al.*, eds., 4 vols., Nashville: Abingdon, 1962
IDBS	*The Interpreter's Dictionary of the Bible. Supplementary Volume*, K. Crim, *et al.*, eds., Nashville: Abingdon, 1976
Int	*Interpretation*
JAOS	*Journal of the American Oriental Society*
JBL	*Journal of Biblical Literature*
JESHO	*Journal of Economic and Social History of the Orient*
JNES	*Journal of Near Eastern Studies*
JQR Supp	Jewish Quarterly Review, Supplement
JSOT	*Journal for the Study of the Old Testament*
JSOTS	Journal for the Study of the Old Testament, Supplement
JSS	*Journal of Semitic Studies*
JThS	*Journal of Theological Studies*
KAT	Kommentar zum Alten Testament
KHAT	Kurzer Hand-Kommentar zum Alten Testament
M	Midrash
m	Mishnah
NICOT	New International Commentary on the Old Testament
Nid	Niddah
OBO	Orbis Biblicus et Orientalis
OTS	Oudtestamentische Studiën
RB	*Revue Biblique*
RevHPhRel	*Revue d'Histoire et de Philosophie Religieuses*
RSPhTh	*Revue des Sciences Philosophiques et Théologiques*
SBLDS	Society of Biblical Literature Dissertation Series
SBS	Stuttgarter Bibelstudien
SBT	Studies in Biblical Theology
s.d.	No publication date
StMiss	*Studia Missionalia*
SVT	Supplements to Vetus Testamentum
Taan	Taʿanit

TDNT *Theological Dictionary of the New Testament*, 10 vols., G. Kittel, *et al.*, eds., G.W. Bromiley, trans. Grand Rapids: Wm. B. Eerdmans, 1964-76

THAT *Theologisches Handwörterbuch zum Alten Testament*, 2 Bde., E. Jenni u. C. Westermann, Hrsg. München: Chr. Kaiser Verlag; Zürich: Theologisches Verlag, 1971-76

ThL *Theologische Literaturzeitung*

TWAT *Theologisches Wörterbuch zum Alten Testament*, 5 Bde., G.J. Botterweck u. H. Ringgren, *et al.*, Hrsg. Stuttgart, Berlin, Köln, Mainz: Verlag W. Kohlhammer, 1973-86

UF *Ugarit-Forschungen*

VT *Vetus Testamentum*

ZA *Zeitschrift für Assyriologie*

ZAW *Zeitschrift für die Alttestamentliche Wissenschaft*

ZKTh *Zeitschrift für Katholische Theologie*

Foreword

Until very recently, most biblical scholarship (including Jeremiah studies) has focused on historical-critical questions, which, for the book of Jeremiah, have been translated primarily into determining which portions of the book are 'authentic' (i.e., the words of the prophet himself) and which are from other sources or later redactors. Of late, however, many biblical scholars have applied methods of literary criticism to biblical texts, following the lead of those contemporary literary critics who view a piece of literature as art to be studied in and for itself, rather than for its philological or historical value. The present study of Jer 30-31 can be counted among this latter group for it is an application of literary analysis to the Little Book of Consolation, with special emphasis given to the technique of 'close reading' popularized by the New Critics.

This volume has three main parts: introductory (Chapters 1 and 2), analytical (Chapter 3), and synthetic (Chapters 4 and 5). The first two chapters, which deal with introductory material, give a brief overview of the state of research on Jer 30-31 and its connection with Jeremiah studies in general, and then prepare the ground for a literary analysis by situating biblical poetic analysis and setting out the literary presuppositions of the author. The analytical portion (Chapter 3) is the longest part of the book and the foundation for the synthesis which follows. After determining the limits of the smaller text units (six poems with a prose introduction and a prose conclusion), Chapter 3 analyzes the text in terms of its diction, prosody, syntax and imagery, with a view to understanding each unit in its historical and literary contexts. This lengthy analysis leads to consideration of Jer 30-31 as a whole. Chapter 4 first considers the connective devices among the sections and then goes on to indicate how the poetic cycle is unified around seven motifs (feminine imagery; voice and listening; suffering and punishment; turn and return; city and settlement; mountain and Sion; covenant) and three themes (transformation of reality; gratuitousness of Yhwh's salvific deed; a future based upon, yet different, from the past). Chapter 5 focuses on a single motif, the feminine image and address as used in Jer 30-31, with a view to its literary, historical and psychological contexts and proposes some hypotheses for its use in this particular text.

Although the approach taken is essentially synchronic it is a valid method for exegesis since it does not consider the text either anachronistically or ahistorically nor does it deny the validity of more traditional methods of analysis. What it does do is concentrate attention on the meaning of the existing text as a whole at a given historical moment (the time of the final redaction) and interpret all references in that light. Thus it gives grist for the mill of the redaction-critic and all those who are concerned with the final text as a source for other information. It also approaches exegesis at the level where it touches theology — an understanding of the relationship between God and humanity at a given historical moment which can then become universalized and shed light on another, contemporary, reality.

Chapter 1

JEREMIAH 30-31 IN EXEGESIS

1.1 SEARCH FOR THE HISTORICAL JEREMIAH

To begin a study of any portion of the book of Jeremiah is to be thrown immediately into the problematic of the "search for the historical Jeremiah."[1] This is not surprising since the same historical-critical questions which were the foundation of exegesis in general during the nineteenth and twentieth centuries have shaped the fundamental concern of Jeremiah scholars: to discover the oldest and most original portions of the text and to ascertain the historical circumstances of their composition as well as their *Sitz-im-Leben*. For Jeremiah scholars this concern took the form of distinguishing the 'authentic' from the inauthentic words of the prophet, determining the provenance of the inauthentic words, and establishing the audience and the historical circumstances of those that were authentic.[2] The same interest in the authentic words is evident in the importance given to distinguishing the prose from the poetry, a topic which has occupied Jeremiah scholars since the beginning of the century. Duhm was the first to focus on the issue by dividing the text into jeremianic poetry, biographical material attributed to Baruch and later editorial additions.[3] Within a few years, Mowinckel, following Duhm's

---

[1] This expression, reminiscent of Schweitzer's search for the historical Jesus, is widely used, as reflected in the first chapter of R. Carroll's *From Chaos to Covenant*, New York: The Crossroad Publishing Company, 1981, "The Quest of the Historical Jeremiah," 5-30, and the article by D. Jobling "The Quest of the Historical Jeremiah: Hermeneutical Implications of Recent Literature" in L. G. Perdue and B. W. Kovacs, eds., *A Prophet to the Nations: Essays in Jeremiah Studies*, Winona Lake: Eisenbrauns, 1984, 285-98 (reprinted from USQR 34 [1978] 3-12), as well as in the introductions to many commentaries.

[2] Cf. S. Herrmann, "Forschung am Jeremiabuch: Probleme und Tendenzen ihren neueren Entwicklung" *ThL* 102 (1977) 481-90; J. Crenshaw, "A Living Tradition: the Book of Jeremiah in Current Research" *Int* 37 (1983) 117-29 and L. G. Perdue, "Jeremiah in Modern Research: Approaches and Issues" in L. G. Perdue and B. W. Kovacs, eds., *A Prophet to the Nations*, 1, who note the fundamental issue of contemporary Jeremiah research as the recognition of the authentic Jeremianic material.

[3] B. Duhm, *Das Buch Jeremia*, KHAT XI, Tübingen und Leipzig: J. C. B. Mohr (Paul Siebeck), 1901, x. (Because of the constant reference to several major commentaries on Jer, after the first citation, the commentaries will be referred to by using only the author's last name.)

lead, developed his theory of four sources[4] which has remained the foundation for most subsequent Jeremiah studies. Even the contemporary attention given to the prose-poetry distinction[5] reflects an interest in the authentic words since they are most often seen as limited to the poetic portions.[6]

Janzen's recent study of the relationship between the MT and the LXX of Jeremiah seeks also to uncover the more original text, the one which carries the earliest tradition and is thus closest to Jeremiah's *ipsissima verba*.[7] Janzen's argument, while convincing on first reading, is systematically refuted by Soderlund.[8] In similar fashion Soderlund discredits the theory of Tov who is more concerned with inner LXX problems of the Jeremiah text.[9]

Whether in the last century or in this, scholars who have attempted to determine the authenticity of Jer 30-31 have come up with results which are as widely divergent and at times as contradictory as those of Soderlund, Tov and Janzen. In the nineteenth century Movers argued for Deutero-Isaianic authorship of Jer 30-31,[10] Graf proposed that Jeremiah alone speaks in 30:1-31:34,[11] while Cornill held a middle

---

[4] In his influential *Zur Komposition des Buches Jeremia*, Kristiania: Jacob Dybwad, 1914, 47, S. Mowinckel tightened Duhm's text divisions, noting as sources for the book of Jeremiah: A = Jeremianic poetry; B = biographical prose; C = stereotyped prose sermons; D = ch. 30-31, an anonymous collection, non-Jeremianic, added by a later editor.

[5] Cf., e.g., W. Holladay, "Prototype and Copies: A New Approach to the Poetry-Prose Problem in the Book of Jeremiah" *JBL* 79 (1960) 351-67; *ibid.*, "The Recovery of the Poetic Passages of Jeremiah" *JBL* 85 (1966) 401-35; W. McKane, "Relations between Poetry and Prose in the Book of Jeremiah with Special Reference to Jeremiah III 6-11 and XII 14-17" in J. A. Emerton, ed., *Congress Volume: Vienna 1980*, SVT 32, Leiden: E. J. Brill, 1981, 220-37; W. Brueggemann, "The Book of Jeremiah: Portrait of the Prophet" *Int* 37 (1983) 130-45.

[6] Cf., e.g., J. Bright, *Jeremiah*, AB 21, Garden City: Doubleday, 1965, LXIII-LXX; E. W. Nicholson, *Jeremiah 26-52*, CBC, Cambridge: Cambridge University Press, 1975, 10; D. N. Freedman, "Pottery, Poetry, and Prophecy: An Essay on Biblical Poetry" *JBL* 96 (1977) 5-26; W. Brueggemann, "The Book of Jeremiah: A Portrait of the Prophet" 134-37.

[7] J. G. Janzen, *Studies in the Text of Jeremiah*, HSM 6, Cambridge: Harvard University Press, 1973, proposes that the LXX of Jeremiah is based on a Hebrew *Vorlage* which is older than the MT and is thus closer to the original prophetic words.

[8] S. Soderlund, *The Text of Jeremiah: A Revised Hypothesis*, JSOTS 47, Sheffield: JSOT Press, 1985.

[9] E. Tov, *The Septuagint Translation of Jeremiah and Baruch: A Discussion of an Early Revision of the LXX of Jeremiah 29-52 and Baruch 1:1-3:8*, HSM 8, Missoula: Scholars Press, 1976.

[10] C. F. Movers, *De Utriusque Recensionis Vaticiniorum Ieremias, Graecae Alexandrinae et Hebraicae Masorethicae, Indole et Origine Commentatio Critica*, Hamburgi: Fridericum Perthes, 1837, 38.

[11] K. H. Graf, *Der Prophet Jeremia*, Leipzig: T. O. Weigel, 1862, 366.

position[12] following Giesebrecht,[13] who asserted that the text was composed of a Jeremianic core with some interpolations.

In this century the two extreme positions are perhaps best represented by Carroll and Weiser. Since he maintains that the views in 30-31 are foreign to the spirit of Jeremiah in the rest of the book, Carroll attributes these two chapters to the same anonymous circles which developed the Hosea-Deutero-Isaiah outlook on the future during the Persian period.[14] Weiser, while accepting the redactional character of the text, considers all of 30-31 authentic with the sole exception of two short prose passages: 30:1-4 and 31:38-40.[15] The middle position is represented by Rudolph, who accepts a large Jeremianic core with later additions and expansions.[16]

The most recent studies of Jer 30-31 reflect, either directly or indirectly, this same interest in sources and authenticity. Böhmer, with great care and precision, considers the authenticity of these oracles by comparing each one in turn with authentic *Heilswörte* from elsewhere in the Jeremianic corpus. As a result of his research on Jer 30-31 he proposes that 30:12-15, 23f.; 31:2-6, 15-20 alone are authentic. After determining which are the authentic words, Böhmer discusses the formation, origin, and redaction of these chapters and finally gives a brief theological interpretation of the whole in light of the different strata.[17]

Böhmer's analysis, as precise as it is, is not definitive. Lohfink, in his 1981 article, establishes as authentic a greater part of the poetry of Jer 30-31 than did Böhmer. Lohfink maintains that what is found in Jer 30-31 is not merely a collection of originally short units but a unified Jeremianic text which includes 30:5-7, 12-15, 18-21; 31:2-6, 15-22. His analysis of this 'original' poem leads to the conclusion that Jeremiah himself pronounced these words early in his prophetic career as a

---

[12] C.H. Cornill, *Einleitung in das Alte Testament*, 1891, 161 (quoted in S. Böhmer, *Heimkehr und neuer Bund: Studien zu Jeremiah 30-31*, Göttingen: Vandenhoeck & Ruprecht, 1976, 112, n. 15), a book unavailable to me in the 1891 edition, accepted the greater part of Jer 30-31 as authentic. In his later commentary (*Das Buch Jeremia*, Leipzig: Chr. Herm. Tauchnitz, 1905) he limits the authentic elements to 31:2-6, 15-20, 27-34.

[13] Cornill makes reference to Giesebrecht's first (1897) edition of his Jeremiah commentary, which was not available to me. In his second (1907) edition (*Das Buch Jeremia*, HKAT, Göttingen: Vandenhoeck & Ruprecht, 2. völlig umgearbeitete Aufl., 1907), F. Giesebrecht accepts as authentic only 31:2-6, 15-20, 29-34.

[14] R. Carroll, *Jeremiah*, London: SCM Press, Ltd., 1986, 570.

[15] A. Weiser, *Das Buch Jeremia. Kapitel 25,15-52,34*, ATD 21, Göttingen: Vandenhoeck & Ruprecht, 1966, 265-89.

[16] W. Rudolph, *Jeremia*, HAT 12, Tübingen: J.C.B. Mohr (Paul Siebeck), 3., verbesserte Auflage, 1968, 188-207.

[17] S. Böhmer, *Heimkehr*.

propagandist for king Josiah and his policies.[18] Fohrer, writing in the same year as Lohfink, accepts a still larger portion of the text as a unified poem (30:5-7, 10-11, 16-21; 31:2-22, 31-37) but denies it Jeremianic authorship. He, rather, attributes these lines to an unknown prophet, a precursor of Deutero-Isaiah.[19]

In a more recent article on these chapters, Lohfink studies the text strata and how they interact, indicating the importance of how the later additions are interpretive of the earlier.[20] He investigates the received text in view of a diachronic understanding and a deuteronomistic re-interpretation of the earlier strata. Schröter responds to Lohfink's analysis in an article which eliminates 30:18-21 from the authentic poem because of its 'late' and 'cultic' terminology, and develops the theological interpretation of the resultant poem which is comprised of 30:5-7, 12-15; 31:2-6, 15-22. Schröter's analysis is thus limited to these twenty verses which he studies as a unified whole, making no mention of the rest of chapters 30 and 31.[21]

Although these authors are concerned with the Little Book of Consolation, they reflect the direction of Jeremiah studies in general as well as research on Jer 30-31 in particular. It is hardly necessary to repeat the already excellent summary available in Böhmer's introduction, which traces the development and changing attitudes toward Jer 30-31 in German scholarship from Movers in 1837 to Thiel in 1973.[22]

A glance at non-German and more recent works does not give a different perspective on the issues. Most commentaries show a similar interest in authenticity and datation as the focus of exegesis of Jer 30-31.

Condamin follows the lead of Cornill and Giesebrecht, accepting a large portion of Jer 30-31 (including what has most often been noted as Deuteronomistic prose in 31:23-40) as an authentic Jeremianic poem.[23] Hyatt admits 30:5-7, 12-15; 31:2-6, 15-22 and the ideas of 31:31-34 as

---

[18] N. Lohfink, "Der junge Jeremia als Propagandist und Poet. Zum Grundstock von Jer 30-31" in P.-M. Bogaert, éd., *Le livre de Jérémie: Le prophète et son milieu, les oracles et leur transmission*, BEThL 54, Leuven: Leuven University, 1981, 351-68.

[19] G. Fohrer, "Der Israel-Prophet in Jeremia 30-31" in A. Caquot et M. Delcor, éds., *Mélanges bibliques et orientaux en l'honneur de M. Henri Cazelles*, AOAT 212, Kevelaer: Butzon & Berker; Neukirchen-Vluyn: Neukirchener Verlag, 1981, 135-48.

[20] N. Lohfink, "Der Gotteswortverschachtelung in Jer 30-31" in L. Ruppert, *et al.*, Hrsg., *Künder des Wortes*, Fs. Josef Schreiner, Würzburg: Echter Verlag, 1982, 105-20.

[21] U. Schröter, "Jeremias Botschaft für das Nordreich, zu N. Lohfink's Überlegungen zum Grundbestand von Jeremia xxx-xxxi" *VT* 35 (1985) 312-29.

[22] S. Böhmer, *Heimkehr*, 11-20.

[23] A. Condamin, *Le livre de Jérémie*, Paris: J. Gabalda et Cie., Editeurs, 3me édition corrigée, 1936, 235-39, sets out in strophic arrangement the 'authentic' poem which consists of 30:5-9, 12-21; 31:1-34, 38-40.

authentic but dates the composition as post-exilic.[24] Bright, on the other hand, dates this text no later than the middle of the Exile. Although he limits the genuine portion to 30:5-7, 10-11, 23-24; 31:2-6, 15-22, 31-34 and possibly 30:12-17; 31:35-37, he does concede that the whole of chapters 30-31 contains Jeremiah's ideas, if not always in his words.[25] Thompson does not distinguish between the authentic and the inauthentic words of Jer 30-31 despite his admitted interest in the authenticity and origin of these two chapters.[26] Carroll considers the sources of Jer 30-31 to be a non-issue since he sees nothing in the cycle of poems, apart from 30:1-3, which would connect it with the prophet Jeremiah himself. From Carroll's perspective only a few editorial elements link these two chapters to the book of Jeremiah.[27] Bracke alone has considered Jer 30-31 from a specifically theological point of view.[28]

This brief survey of the more recent exegesis gives evidence that most of the scholarship on Jer 30-31 centers on discovering the authentic words of the prophet. Yet even so critical a scholar as Carroll admits the importance of considering each passage in its literary context for, whatever the original meaning of the individual elements, they have lost most of their original force by being placed in another collection.[29] Furthermore, despite the interest in issues which necessitate independent examination of very short pericopes (as small as a single verse), Jer 30-31 is almost universally held to be a distinct and even homogeneous unit.[30]

---

[24] J. P. Hyatt, "The Book of Jeremiah" in *IB* V, New York and Nashville: Abingdon Press, 1956, 1022-23.

[25] Bright, 285.

[26] J. A. Thompson, *The Book of Jeremiah*, NICOT, Grand Rapids: Wm. B. Eerdmans Publishing Co., 1980, 552.

[27] Carroll, 569.

[28] J. M. Bracke, *The Coherence and Theology of Jeremiah 30-31*, Ann Arbor: University Microfilms International, 1983, 21, explicitly states his purpose as an "interpretation of the final form of Jeremiah" which has "as its primary focus the theological claims of Jeremiah 30-31."

[29] Carroll, 577.

[30] Duhm, 237, admits a redactional if not original unity. Cornill, 322, similarly notes a homogeneity of content, an order and association of ideas which results in a final unity. S. Mowinckel, *Zur Komposition*, 45-46, sees a single theme uniting 30:1-31:28. P. Volz, *Der Prophet Jeremia*, KAT X, Leipzig: A. Deichertsche Verlagsbuchhandlung, 1922, 283, considers the two chapters as forming a triptych. Condamin, 235, notes the fact that the two chapters are closely joined by both content and style. Rudolph, 172, follows Volz, while Bright, 284, says they form a distinct unit and thus must be treated together. Weiser, 264, agrees that "Kapitel 30 und 31 bildeten ... ursprunglich eine selbständige Einheit ..." since they are thematically united. S. Böhmer, *Heimkehr*, 88, after all his analysis of the authentic sayings concludes this part with an admission "dass die beiden Kapitel trotz der unübersehbaren Spannungen und Unausgeglichenheiten eine relative Einheit bilden ..."

Thus the existing exegetical works point to the validity of a literary analysis of Jer 30-31, an analysis which examines these two chapters as a whole.

1.2 LITERARY APPROACH TO BIBLICAL TEXTS

During the last few decades there has been a growing interest in the study of the biblical text as a literary work. This is not surprising since biblical criticism has normally appropriated methods already developed by critics of literature in general.

The literary critics of the last century reflected the questions of the 'Enlightenment' and sought to discover the genesis of the text, the background of the author, how the text reflected its own era and the author's experience. These are exactly the same questions posed by the historical-critical methods which dominated biblical exegesis in the last century and continue to do so at least in certain circles. Toward the beginning of this century most literary critics focused their attention on the text either in itself or in its ability to evoke response from the reader. By mid-twentieth century some exegetes were asking similar questions of the biblical text.[31] Thus the literary approach to biblical literature is gaining wider acceptance among exegetes of the late twentieth century, much as the historical-critical approach did a few decades ago.

For narrative biblical texts both literary critics and exegetes have turned their hand to literary analysis. On one side, literary critics and teachers of literature have directed their efforts toward an analysis of a specific text or a more global study of biblical narrative.[32] On the other side, exegetes have applied literary techniques to their analysis of the original Hebrew text.[33] The result is a large array of books and articles on narrative analysis of biblical texts.[34]

---

[31] M. Weiss, in the Introduction (1-46) to *The Bible from Within: The Method of Total Interpretation*, Jerusalem: The Magnes Press, 1984, gives an excellent overview of the development in literary criticism during the 19th and 20th centuries while in Chapter 1 (47-73) he examines biblical exegesis in light of corresponding literary criticism.

[32] K. R. R. Gros Louis, *et al.*, eds., *Literary Interpretations of Biblical Narratives*, 2 vols., Nashville: Abingdon Press, 1977 and 1982, presents a collection of short analyses of biblical narratives based on an English translation of the texts considered, with various authors using their background as teachers of literature to examine stylistic techniques. N. Frye, *The Great Code: The Bible and Literature*, London, Melbourne, and Henley: Routledge & Kegan Paul, 1981, applies his expertise as a literary critic to the consideration of language, myth and metaphor in biblical writings.

[33] Cf., e.g., C. Conroy, *Absalom Absalom!* AnBib 81, Rome: Biblical Institute Press, 1978; M. Fishbane, *Text and Texture: Close Readings of Selected Biblical Texts*, New York: Schocken Books, 1979; J.-L. Ska, *Le passage de la mer: Etude de la construction, du style et de la symbolique d'Ex 14,1-31*, AnBib 109, Rome: Biblical Institute Press, 1986.

[34] These works can be divided into two major categories: (a) those which deal with elements of style in general, represented by works such as E. Good, *Irony in the Old*

For biblical poetry a similar interest in literary analysis has been growing during the last few decades. Alonso Schökel, in his landmark volume, *Estudios de poética hebrea*, was among the first exegetes to present a formal study of the major stylistic elements of Hebrew poetic expression.[35] Fewer than ten years later, Gray's 1915 classic, *The Forms of Hebrew Poetry*,[36] which accents parallelism as the major technique of Hebrew poetry, was reprinted. This was only a beginning.

Since that time there has been a flourishing interest in the stylistic elements of Hebrew poetry and how it can be distinguished from Hebrew prose which has led to the publication of several monographs[37] and numerous articles[38] on the general aspects of Hebrew poetic analysis.

Testament, 2nd edition, Bible and Literature Series 3, Sheffield: The Almond Press, 1981; R. Alter, *The Art of Biblical Narrative*, New York: Basic Books, Inc., 1981; A. Berlin, *Poetics and Interpretation of Biblical Narrative*, Bible and Literature Series 9, Sheffield: The Almond Press, 1983; M. Sternberg, *The Poetics of Biblical Narrative: Ideological Literature and the Drama of Reality*, Bloomington: Indiana University Press, 1985; and (b) those which apply literary techniques to specific biblical texts, such as J. P. Fokkelman, *Narrative Art in Genesis: Specimens of Stylistic and Structural Analysis*, Studia Semitica Neerlandica 17, Assen/Amsterdam: Van Gorcum, 1975; C. Conroy, *Absalom Absalom!* P. D. Miller, *Genesis 1-11: Studies in Structure and Theme*, JSOTS 8, Sheffield: University of Sheffield, 1978; T. Craven, *Artistry and Faith in the Book of Judith*, SBLDS 70, Chico: Scholars Press, 1983; J.-L. Ska, *Le passage de la mer*. This is to mention only a few representative monographs whose number is far surpassed by the many articles which treat of this subject.

35 L. Alonso Schökel, *Estudios de poética hebrea*, Barcelona: Juan Flores, 1963.

36 G. B. Gray, *The Forms of Hebrew Poetry*, New York: KTAV Publishing House, 1972, reprint of 1915 edition, with prologomenon by D. N. Freedman.

37 Cf., *e.g.*, S. Geller, *Parallelism in Early Biblical Poetry*, HSM 20, Missoula: Scholars Press, 1979; M. O'Connor, *Hebrew Verse Structure*, Winona Lake: Eisenbrauns, 1980; J. Kugel, *The Idea of Biblical Poetry. Parallelism and its History*, New Haven: Yale University Press, 1983; J. Krašovec. *Antithetic Structure in Biblical Hebrew Poetry*, SVT 35, Leiden: E. J. Brill, 1984; W. G. E. Watson, *Classical Hebrew Poetry: A Guide to Its Techniques*, JSOTS 26, Sheffield: JSOT Press, 1984; R. Alter, *The Art of Biblical Poetry*, New York: Basic Books, Inc., 1985; L. Alonso Schökel, *Manual de poética hebrea*, Academia Christiana 41, Madrid: Ediciones Cristiandad, 1987.

38 Cf., *e.g.*, H. Kosmala, "Form and Structure in Ancient Hebrew Poetry (A New Approach)" *VT* 14 (1964) 423-45; *ibid.*, "Form and Structure in Ancient Hebrew Poetry" *VT* 16 (1966) 152-80; R. Gordis, "The Structure of Biblical Poetry" in *Prophets, Poets and Sages: Essays in Biblical Interpretation*, Bloomington and London: Indiana University Press, 1971, 61-94; L. Alonso Schökel, "Poésie hébraïque" in *DBS* VIII, 47-90; G. Schramm, "Poetic Patterning in Biblical Hebrew" in L. L. Orlin, *et al.*, eds., *Michigan Oriental Studies in Honor of George G. Cameron*, Ann Arbor: University of Michigan, 1976, 167-91; D. N. Freedman, "Pottery, Poetry and Prophecy" 5-26; A. Ceresko, "The Function of Chiasmus in Hebrew Poetry" *CBQ* 40 (1978) 1-9; J. S. Kselman, "Design and Structure in Hebrew Poetry" *SBL 1980 Seminar Papers*, Chico: Scholars Press, 1980, 1-16; W. G. E. Watson, "Internal Parallelism in Classical Hebrew Verse" *Bib* 66 (1985) 365-84.

The articles which apply literary methods[39] to biblical poetic texts can be divided into four groups: (a) those concerned only with the literary structure and literary figures employed[40]; (b) those using literary-stylistic analysis to answer questions of authorship, composition, or *Sitz-im-Leben*[41]; (c) those whose emphasis is on imagery and meaning[42]; (d) those taken up with meaning and its effects.[43] The few monographs which are concerned with a literary or rhetorical critical analysis of Hebrew poetry are studies of portions of the book of Isaiah[44] or the Psalms.[45]

---

[39] My interest is in literary poetic analysis, and therefore I do not include the many studies which deal with structuralist analysis or text linguistics.

[40] E.g., M. D. Coogan, "A Structural and Literary Analysis of the Song of Deborah" *CBQ* 40 (1978) 143-66; W. H. Irwin, "Syntax and Style in Isaiah 26" *CBQ* 41 (1979) 240-61; A. Ceresko, "Poetic Analysis of Ps. 105, with Attention to Its Use of Irony" *Bib* 64 (1983) 20-46.

[41] L. Alonso Schökel, "Is 10,28-32: Análisis estilístico" *Bib* 40 (1959) 230-36; L. Boadt, "Is 41:8-13: Notes on Poetic Style and Structure" *CBQ* 35 (1973) 20-34; D. N. Freedman, "The Twenty-third Psalm" in L. L. Orlin, *et al.*, eds., *Michigan Oriental Studies in Honor of G. Cameron*, Ann Arbor: Department of Near Eastern Studies, University of Michigan, 1976, 139-66; R. Clifford, "Style and Purpose in Psalm 105" *Bib* 60 (1979) 420-27; R. E. Clements, "The Unity of the Book of Isaiah" *Int* 36 (1982) 117-29; P. G. Mosca, "Psalm 26: Poetic Structure and the Form-Critical Task" *CBQ* 47 (1985) 212-37.

[42] L. Alonso Schökel, "Tres imágenes de Isaías" *Est Bib* 15 (1956) 63-84; *ibid.*, "Dos poemas a la paz: Estudio estilístico de Is 8,23-9,6 y 11,1-16" *Est Bib* 18 (1959) 149-69; S. Paul, "Amos 1:3-2:3: A Concatenous Literary Pattern" *JBL* 90 (1971) 397-403; L. Alonso Schökel, "Poetic Structure of Ps 42-43" *JSOT* 1 (1976) 4-11 (trans. from 1972 Spanish original); D. J. A. Clines, "Hosea 2: Structure and Interpretation" in E. A. Livingstone, ed., *Studia Biblica 1978 I. Papers on Old Testament and Related Themes. Sixth International Congress on Biblical Studies, Oxford, 3-7 April 1978*, JSOTS 11, Sheffield: JSOT Press, 1978, 83-103; J. C. Exum, "Isaiah 28-32: A Literary Approach" *SBL 1979 Seminar Papers*, Vol. II, Missoula: Scholars Press, 1979, 123-51.

[43] J. C. Exum, "Of Broken Pots, Fluttering Birds and Visions in the Night: Extended Simile and Poetic Techniques in Isaiah" *CBQ* 43 (1981) 331-52; N. J. Tromp, "Amos V 1-17. Towards a Stylistic and Rhetorical Analysis" in A. S. van der Woude, ed., *Prophets, Worship and Theodicy*, OTS 23, Leiden: E. J. Brill, 1984, 56-84.

[44] D. J. A. Clines, *I, He, We and They: A Literary Approach to Isaiah 53*, JSOTS 1, Sheffield: University of Sheffield, 1976; Y. Gitay, *Prophecy and Persuasion: A Study of Isaiah 40-48*, Forum Theologiae Linguisticae 14, Bonn: Linguistica Biblica, 1981; R. Clifford, *Fair Spoken and Persuading: An Interpretation of Second Isaiah*, New York, Ramsey and Toronto: Paulist Press, 1984; G. Polan, *In the Ways of Justice Toward Salvation: A Rhetorical Analysis of Isaiah 56-59*, American University Studies, Series VII: Theology and Religion Vol. 13, New York, Berne, Frankfurt am Main: Peter Lang, 1986.

[45] P. Auffret, *The Literary Structure of Psalm 2*, trans. from the French by D. J. A. Clines, JSOTS 3, Sheffield: JSOT Press, 1977; L. Alonso Schökel, *Treinta Salmos: Poesía y oración*, Valencia: Institucíon San Jerónimo, 1981; J.-N. Aletti et J. Trublet, *Approche poétique et théologique des Psaumes*, Paris: Editions du Cerf, 1983. Here it might be important to note that although the method used in these studies is literary poetic analysis, the psalms are of a different cloth from prophetic poetry and therefore these books are of limited value in work on prophetic texts.

This sample is a clear indication that literary criticism is fast becoming an alternative approach to the more traditional historical-critical methods of exegesis.

1.3 LITERARY APPROACH TO JER 30-31

The book of Jeremiah has not escaped the influence of this new approach. A few articles and monographs have appeared which favor a holistic analysis of a larger or smaller part of Jer. While earlier studies used literary or stylistic analysis more as a means of determining form or authenticity of a passage than for discerning its interpretation,[46] recent years have seen a change. In the last ten years, several examples of stylistic analysis applied to short passages of Jeremiah have appeared, studies which have focused specifically on understanding and interpretation of the existent text.[47]

The first monograph to apply literary analysis to the book of Jeremiah as a whole was Lundbom's 1975 volume. Lundbom studies the rhetorical structures of the text (especially inclusio and chiasmus) in order to determine the literary units and to arrive at an understanding of how

---

[46] Cf., e.g., W. Holladay, "Style, Irony and Authenticity in Jeremiah" *JBL* 81 (1962) 44-54; T.W. Overholt, "The Falsehood of Idolatry: An Interpretation of Jer. X. 1-16" *JThS* 16 (1965) 1-12; B.O. Long, "The Stylistic Components of Jeremiah 3:1-5" *ZAW* 88 (1976) 386-90; B. Lindars, "Rachel Weeping for Her Children—Jeremiah 31:15-22" *JSOT* 12 (1979) 47-62.

[47] Cf. B.W. Anderson, "'The Lord Has Created Something New,' A Stylistic Study of Jer 31:15-22" *CBQ* 40 (1978) 463-78, who uses stylistic analysis and examination of the literary context to arrive at the understanding of a disputed verse; M. Fishbane, "Jeremiah 20:7-12 / Loneliness and Anguish" in *Text and Texture*, 91-102, who, by analysis of language, imagery and structure, explains the inner logic and progression of what is a difficult and ambiguous text; C. Isbell and M. Jackson, "Rhetorical Criticism and Jeremiah VII 1-VIII 3" *VT* 30 (1980) 20-26, who use the analysis of vocabulary and ideas to explain the unity and sense of the present arrangement of originally independent units; G.R. Castellino, "Observations on the Literary Structure of Some Passages in Jeremiah" *VT* 30 (1980) 398-408, who, by analysis of contents and structure of five pericopes which are often seen to be composite, demonstrates the unity and coherence of each pericope and thus delivers them from that fragmentariness so often attributed to them; W.A.M. Beuken and H.W.M. van Grol, "Jeremiah 14,1-15,9: A Situation of Distress and Its Hermeneutics; Unity and Diversity of Form – Dramatic Development" in P.-M. Bogaert, ed., *Le Livre de Jérémie*, 297-342, who, through analysis of structure (form) and dynamics (themes) of the text, arrive at an explanation of the dramatic quality and development of the whole; W. Brueggemann, "The 'Uncared For' Now Cared For (Jer 30:12-17): A Methodological Consideration" *JBL* 104 (1985) 419-28, who notes the contemporary methodological shift toward holistic analysis and demonstrates this in his examination of the text, explaining it as a bearer of theological meaning in its present form.

the material engages the audience.[48] Holladay moves beyond the specificity of Hebrew rhetorical patterns studied by Lundbom and assumes a logic to the present arrangement of the MT. With this as a starting point, he shows how structure and content interact to indicate the collection process and ultimately to determine the contents of the *Urrolle*.[49] More recently, Polk, writing on the 'Confessions,' stresses the importance of the literary rather than the conjectured historical context as the locus of meaning. He proposes that the literary context is the source of understanding the persona (if not the historical person) Jeremiah.[50]

While hardly indicating the totality of research on the book of Jeremiah, this brief overview does point to the recent growing interest in holistic and stylistic studies of large sections of the book, even if the final aim is, at times, to arrive at information concerning text genesis or form.

Bracke's use of a holistic approach to Jer 30-31 is unique in its overriding theological interest. He examines these two chapters for their theological content and considers their affirmation of God's promise of restoration in its twofold literary context: the book of Jeremiah as a whole and other OT literature which speaks of restoration. After carefully determining the limits of the text, Bracke proceeds to examine the three subsections 30:5-31:1; 31:2-22; and 31:23-40, unit by unit. He maintains that the promise of restoration in Jer 30-31 is the third and last stage in the relationship between Yhwh and his people. This relationship began with Israel's faithfulness and Yhwh's care as a first step, moved to Israel's sinfulness and Yhwh's judgment as a second step, and finally arrived at the reversal of judgment and restoration of the Little Book of Consolation as the last step. Based on his study of the theme of restoration throughout the OT, Bracke posits Jer 30-31 as a primary example of the promise of restoration contained in the expression *šwb šbwt*. He effectively demonstrates the coherence of Jer 30-31 with the book of Jeremiah as a whole as well as its links with other OT literature.[51]

Bracke's thesis is valid and a first step in opening doors. He argues for coherence and unity without denying that the text is composed of several discrete units. Since his interest is largely theological rather than literary, a detailed poetic analysis which focuses on literary figures as well as on themes remains to be done. Thus the following poetic analysis builds on the work of Bracke and many others while at the same time filling a gap in Jeremiah studies.

---

[48] J. Lundbom, *Jeremiah: A Study in Ancient Hebrew Rhetoric*, SBLDS 18, Missoula: Scholars Press, 1975.

[49] W. Holladay, *The Architecture of Jeremiah 1-20*, Cranberry, N.J., and London: Associated University Presses, 1976.

[50] T. Polk, *The Prophetic Persona: Jeremiah and the Language of the Self*, JSOTS 32, Sheffield: JSOT Press, 1984.

[51] J.M. Bracke, *The Coherence and Theology of Jeremiah 30-31.*

CHAPTER 2

NEW CRITICISM AND BEYOND

2.1 NEW CRITICISM

The decision to use literary criticism as a basic methodology for text analysis is not as simple as might appear at first glance, for it is a decision to enter a vast territory filled with claims and counterclaims concerning the validity and utility of one approach over another. This confusion arises because literary criticism is not a single approach but rather a variety of approaches, each having its specific emphasis.[1] The aspect that unites them all under the umbrella of literary criticism is their concern with the text itself, a concern which is especially marked among the New Critics.

The New Critics, in reaction to the then prevalent attitude which limited literary scholarship to philological and historical interests, considered the poem as a work of art in its own right since, in the words of Cleanth Brooks, "... if poetry exists as poetry in any meaningful sense, the attempt [to view it *sub specie aeternitatis*] must be made. Otherwise the poetry of the past becomes significant merely as cultural anthropology, and the poetry of the present, merely as a political, or religious or moral instrument."[2]

---

[1] M.H. Abrams (*A Glossary of Literary Terms*, 4th ed., New York, Chicago, San Francisco, Dallas, Montreal, Toronto, London and Sydney: Holt, Rinehart and Winston, 1981, s.v. 'Criticism') discriminates among different literary theories according to whether they relate the work primarily to the outer world (Mimetic Criticism), to the reader (Pragmatic Criticism), to the author (Expressive Criticism), or consider it as an entity unto itself (Objective Criticism). It suffices to glance at the way three authors organize this vast territory to realize the numerous ways of viewing the same subject. W.S. Scott (*Five Approaches of Literary Criticism. An Arrangement of Contemporary Critical Essays*, New York: Collier Books, 1962) organizes contemporary literary criticism around five general categories: moral, psychological, sociological, formalist and archetypal approaches. R. Wellek, in several of the essays in *The Attack on Literature and Other Essays* (Chapel Hill: University of North Carolina Press, 1982) speaks of schools or distinct groups: New Critics, Chicago Aristotelians, Myth-critics, Structuralists, the Geneva School, Existentialists, Text-linguists and Russian Formalists. A. Jefferson and D. Robey, eds., (*Modern Literary Theory. A Comparative Introduction*, London: Batsford Academic and Educational, Ltd., 1982) divide contemporary literary criticism into six major areas: Russian Formalism, Linguistic Theory, New Criticism, Structuralism, Post-Structuralism, Psychoanalytic Criticism, and Marxist Theory.

[2] C. Brooks, *The Well Wrought Urn. Studies in the Structure of Poetry*, New York: Harcourt, Brace and World, 1947, x-xi.

New Criticism in its extreme form has been accused of denying the importance of any context for the work under consideration[3] because historical locus, authorship and audience are not deemed to be the subject matter of criticism. Yet such extremism is not of the essence of their theory. René Wellek defends the New Critics against such attacks, noting that they did grant the importance of historical background and knowledge of the author, although never as the fundamental concerns of criticism.[4] Thus New Criticism, despite the accusations of isolationism, shallowness and ahistoricism leveled against it, is a valid approach insofar as it is concerned with literature as literature rather than literature as a source for history, anthropology, sociology or other similar disciplines.

In their concern for the literary work of art in and of itself, the New Critics reject anything that smacks of dualism, anything which separates form from meaning, style from content, for they recognize and respect the essential unity of these two aspects of the literary entity.[5] New Critics reject the idea of a paraphrase as a substitute for the individual poem,[6] as well as any theory of stylistics or text linguistics as an adequate explanation of how meaning is conveyed. (This, however, is not to deny the importance of paraphrase or stylistics in the task of understanding.) It is because of its focus on the text that New Criticism has been chosen as a basic methodology for this study. This choice is not meant to negate the value of other literary-critical approaches (e.g., sociological, moral,

---

[3] A similar attitude can be attributed to all formalists, i.e., those who view the literary work as a "self-sufficient object," as Abrams notes in *A Glossary of Literary Terms*, s.v. 'Russian Formalism.'

[4] R. Wellek, "The New Criticism: Pro and Contra" in *The Attack on Literature*, 87-103.

[5] Among the New Critics, C. Brooks (*The Well Wrought Urn*, 74) gives expression to this idea in his statement that "the poem is not only the linguistic vehicle which conveys the things communicated most 'poetically' but it is also the sole linguistic vehicle which conveys the things communicated accurately." Yet it is not only the New Critics who manifest an interest in the integrity of the literary artifact. A. Cluysenaar (*Introduction to Literary Stylistics. A Discussion of Dominant Structures in Verse and Prose*, London: B. T. Batsford, Ltd., 1976, 19) with her interest in linguistic features says: "No act of communication, much less the subtle uses of language we tend to call 'literature,' can be treated dualistically, as if 'form' and 'meaning' were not merely separately *describable* (up to a point) but actually separable." Similarly, the exegete M. Fishbane (*Text and Texture*, 8) notes that "any attempt to ... distinguish between 'objective' facts of form and subjective interpretations of meaning is singularly misguided."

[6] In *The Well Wrought Urn*, C. Brooks dedicates a whole chapter (Ch. 11: "The Heresy of Paraphrase") to this topic. D. Robey ("Anglo-American New Criticism" in A. Jefferson and D. Robey, eds., *Modern Literary Theory*, 80) notes: "The error of so many critics and scholars is to write as if the paraphrasable elements in literature constituted its substance, whereas the value of literature is to be found not in propositions, but in relationships, and these relationships are not logical but imaginative."

anthropological, or psychological) or the importance of historical-critical questions.[7]

2.2 BEYOND CLOSE READING

Just as recent biblical scholars, seeking answers to historical questions such as authorship and text genesis, have used literary analysis as a tool to move 'beyond' the text or 'through' it[8] to specific information, so literary critics can and must keep in mind other approaches and what their results bring to bear on understanding the text.[9] It is, for example, only by knowing (or hypothetically establishing) a certain historical context that one can hope to understand certain references within an ancient text. Similarly, classifying a text according to a specific genre contextualizes it by helping to explain the presence of certain forms and thus clarify the terms of understanding the text.[10]

Clearly, the New Critic by the very nature of his/her inquiry is drawn outside the confines of close reading because the text itself calls for the consideration of many other questions.[11] Even R. S. Crane, member of the Chicago School who advocates Aristotle's *Poetics* as the only adequate analytical tool for poetry, sees the major problem in criticism to be "the spirit of exclusive dogmatism" which keeps one school or group of critics from listening to and learning from another.[12] It becomes clear that to arrive at the fullest understanding of a given text, a certain eclecticism is needed.

---

[7] R. W. L. Moberly, *At the Mountain of God. Story and Theology in Exodus 32-34*, JSOTS 22, Sheffield: JSOT Press, 1983, 22, gives a good example of a careful use of literary analysis, seeing its value yet also noting the danger which arises when it becomes an exclusivist approach: "The phoenix of conservatism which simply studies the final text and eschews any kind of historical criticism might swiftly arise from the ashes. The responsible interpreter must deal with every aspect and dimension of the text he is seeking to interpret." J. Barr, "Historical Reading and Theological Interpretation of Scripture" in *The Scope and Authority of the Bible*, Explorations in Theology 7, London: SCM Press, 1980, 47, admits that any reading which is completely ahistorical would in fact lead to a literal historicity, a negative consequence, indeed.

[8] M. Savage has used this differentiation in "Literary Criticism and Biblical Studies: A Rhetorical Analysis of the Joseph Narrative" in C. D. Evans, *et al.*, eds., *Scripture in Context. Essays on the Comparative Method*, Pittsburgh Theological Monograph Series 34, Pittsburgh: The Pickwick Press, 1980, 79.

[9] K. R. R. Gros Louis, *Literary Interpretations of Biblical Narratives* II, 13, says that even those studying the Bible as literature cannot be ignorant of biographical, historical and other critical information.

[10] A letter, for example, calls for a different attitude than does a poem.

[11] D. Daiches, *Critical Approaches to Literature*, New York: W. W. Norton and Co., 1956, 175, and W. S. Scott, *Five Approaches*, 11, both note this fact.

[12] R. S. Crane, *The Languages of Criticism and the Structure of Poetry*, Toronto: University of Toronto Press, 1953, 193.

This study, then, besides its main focus on form and content which are internal to the text, considers the historical context as a key to better understanding the text and uses psychological information as another means to elucidate it. Throughout, attention is given to other contemporary or near-contemporary texts which may have a bearing on understanding Jer 30-31.

2.3 PRESUPPOSITIONS

Since a literary approach is the foundation of the following study, it is important to clarify certain presuppositions on which such a literary analysis is based.

The first is that biblical writings are indeed literature[13] and that Jer 30-31 unquestionably falls into this category.[14] As is important for any literary analysis, the following study of Jer 30-31 begins with a formal textual analysis based on that of the New Critics' "close reading"[15] (which in fact is what every careful reading of a text is) but does not remain limited to the text itself. Rather, it considers historical and other factors in order to understand better the context within which the text exists and out of which it came.

A second presupposition on which this work is based is that Jer 30-31 is essentially poetry, although there are prose elements included, specifically 30:1-4, 8-9; 31:23-34, 38-40.

The prose vs. poetry problem has been an important topic of discussion in recent years in both the secular and biblical fields. In general literary criticism, it has become clear after much discussion that at the extremes prose and poetry are easily distinguished. When, however, the work studied is free verse or highly literary prose, judgment is often based entirely on how the piece is set down on the page.[16]

---

[13] Most scholars are in general agreement on this point, though admitting that perhaps the genealogies and laws fall outside this category. On the other hand J. Kugel, *The Idea of Biblical Poetry*, 303-04, denies the validity of any literary reading of the Bible on the premise that literature is a category which is not applicable to "legal, historical, sermonic, wisdom or oracular genres" and the fact that nowhere does the Bible define itself as literature, as artful composition.

[14] I will not get involved in the fascinating but difficult question of what makes a given text literature. This issue has been discussed by many scholars and critics including: R. Wellek and A. Warren, *Theory of Literature*, 3rd ed., San Diego, New York, London: Harcourt Brace Jovanovich, 1977, 20-28; A. Jefferson and D. Robey, *Modern Literary Theory*, 4-5, 8; as well as R. Wellek, "The Attack on Literature" in *The Attack on Literature*, 3-18.

[15] M.H. Abrams (s.v. "New Criticism", *A Glossary of Literary Terms*) sees the distinctive approach of the New Critic as "explication, or close reading: the detailed and subtle analysis of the complex interrelations and ambiguities (multiple meanings) of the component elements within a work."

[16] The question of distinguishing prose and poetry has been treated by many scholars

The discussions concerning the differentiation of Hebrew poetry from Hebrew prose have also been many, but the results remain as indefinite as those concerning Anglo-American literature. Determining poetry on the basis of meter appears hopeless since there is no agreement on how a Hebrew metric system might work.[17] The earliest definition of poetry as parallel structure (synonymous, antithetic, synthetic)[18] is hardly adequate since such parallelism is found frequently in Hebrew narrative.[19] The recent efforts to define Hebrew poetry along the lines of text linguistics or syntactic form give similarly inconclusive results.[20]

---

including: C. Brooks and R. Warren, *Understanding Poetry*, 3rd ed., New York, Chicago, San Francisco, Toronto: Holt, Rinehart and Winston, 1960, 120-22, and M.K. Danziger and W.S. Johnson, *An Introduction to Literary Criticism*, Boston: D.C. Heath and Company, 1961, 64-66. The former demonstrate the problem in their analysis of W.C. Williams' "Red Wheelbarrow" (p. 172). C.T. Scott, "Typography, Poems, and the Poetic Line" in M.A. Jazayery, *et al.*, eds., *Linguistic and Literary Studies*, Fs. A.A. Hill, Linguistic and Literary Studies IV, Trends in Linguistics 10, The Hague, Paris, New York: Mouton Publishers, 1979, 156, argues against using typographical conventions as the basis of a prose-poetry distinction.

[17] D.N. Freedman ("Pottery, Poetry, and Prophecy," 10) states that "The quest [for the key to Hebrew metrics] has proved futile..., no such magic key has ever been found, or is likely to be." W.G.E. Watson (*Classical Hebrew Poetry*, Ch. 5: Metre, 86-113), on the other hand, personally affirms the presence of meter based on stress, yet also gives a summary of the several theories of meter proposed for biblical poetry (alternating stress, word-feet, thought-unit, syllable-count), thus demonstrating the wide variety of opinions in this area. T. Longman ("A Critique of Two Recent Metrical Systems" *Bib* 63 [1982] 230-54) considers and actually applies two methods, that of syllable counting and that of a syntactic accentual system, with the conclusion that neither gives unequivocal results. In the end, he advocates no metrical system but syntactic or linguistic parallelism as the key to the structure of biblical poetry. Thus the lack of agreement on this issue is easily demonstrated.

[18] G.B. Gray, *The Forms of Hebrew Poetry*, has been followed by many books including: S. Geller, *Parallelism in Early Biblical Poetry*; J. Kugel, *The Idea of Biblical Poetry*; R. Alter, *The Art of Biblical Poetry*, all of which hold that parallelism is the foundational element of biblical poetry.

[19] J. Kugel, *The Idea of Biblical Poetry*, 59-63, shows how parallelism, which is most often linked to biblical poetry, is also found in so-called prose. In fact he sees the prose-poetry distinction for biblical texts as an imposition of Hellenistic categories which are not native to the texts themselves (p. 85). A. Berlin, *The Dynamics of Biblical Parallelism*, Bloomington: Indiana University Press, 1985, 6, notes that Hebrew poetry does indeed use parallelism but this is a figure which is also found in prose.

[20] T. Collins, *Line Forms in Hebrew Poetry. A Grammatical Approach to the Stylistic Study of the Hebrew Prophets*, Studia Pohl: Series Maior 7, Rome: Biblical Institute Press, 1978, and M. O'Connor, *Hebrew Verse Structure*, both use text linguistic approaches but both examine only relatively small portions of the poetic corpus and neither does a comparative study with prose portions of the Bible. Thus, although their theories are very interesting, their accuracy for actually distinguishing prose from poetry has yet to be established.

It is, however, widely accepted that poetry is recognizable by its heightened language and more clipped and concise style.[21] Moreover, Hebrew poetry also relies heavily on parallelism[22] as well as the avoidance of articles, relative pronouns and direct object markers.[23] Based on these criteria, most of 30:5-31:22 and 31:35-37 can be classified as poetry (as most scholars do). On the other hand, a more discursive style including the use of articles, relative pronouns and direct object markers leads to the identification of 30:1-4,8-9; 31:1,23-34,38-40 as prose, although some exegetes have considered 30:8-9; 31:1,31-34 and 38-40 to be poetic.[24]

Because of the predominance of poetic elements, this analysis approaches Jer 30-31 as poetry rather than prose, for even the prose portions use heightened language and are clearly not in prose narrative style.

2.4 AN ECLECTIC APPROACH

This study begins with a close reading à la New Criticism but does not remain confined therein. It is divided into three parts: Close Reading, Motifs and Themes, and Hypotheses concerning the use of the Feminine Imagery and Address.

The first, and longest, part of this investigation is dedicated to a close reading of Jer 30-31. After establishing the limits of the smaller units (poem or prose section) it examines each in detail, paying attention to language, stylistic and poetic devices and imagery. Special concern is given to the diction of the text (i.e., the choice of words with their denotation, connotation and plurisignation), its imagery (understood both as evocation of a sense experience and as the tropes used to convey

---

[21] This is also the basis for a linguistic approach to poetry, which presupposes that poetry differs from formal discourse in the way in which it uses language. Cf. S. Levin, *Linguistic Structures in Poetry*, Janua Linguarum, Series Minor 23, The Hague, Paris, New York: Mouton Publishers, 1962, 59.

[22] Parallelism exists in the deep structure as well as in the surface structure of Hebrew poetry according to E. L. Greenstein, "How Does Parallelism Mean?" in *A Sense of Text. The Art of Language in the Study of Biblical Literature*, JQR Supp 1982, Winona Lake: Eisenbrauns, 1983, 41-70.

[23] This is the basis on which W. F. Albright determined (and emended) poetic texts, an hypothesis taken up and promulgated by his student D. N. Freedman (cf. "Pottery, Poetry, and Prophecy," 2-3). It has become the most generally held mode of differentiating the two types of text according to A. Berlin, *The Dynamics of Biblical Poetry*, 5-7. G. Schramm, "Poetic Patterning in Biblical Hebrew," 174, distinguishes the two simply by the criterion of "tightness in structure."

[24] Condamin, 216-33, includes 30:8-9; 31:1,23-34 and 38-40 among the poetic portions. Volz, 279, 293, accepts 31:31-34 as poetry. Thompson, 556, indicates a possible metrical structure for 30:8-9. Giesebrecht, 160-74, moves to the other extreme, accepting only 31:2-20, 31-37 as poetic.

the same), syntax (both those patterns used and those rules stretched or broken), and prosody (sound patterns of the poem).[25] The terms of poetic analysis are taken to a great extent from W. G. E. Watson's *Classical Hebrew Poetry*, but never to the exclusion of other authors.

This close reading focuses on both the smaller elements (words and grammar) and the larger structure of each individual poem or section, always with a view to understanding the meaning of the unit in its literary and historical contexts.

The second part of the study gives particular attention to those aspects of the text which indicate its unity. After the elements which connect each poem or prose section with the following one are noted, there is a discussion of seven motifs (the feminine image, voice and listening, suffering and punishment, turn and return, city and settlement, mountain and Sion, covenant) and three themes (transformation of reality; gratuitousness of Yhwh's salvific deed; future as based upon, yet different from, the known, both past and present) which are threads running through the whole. In this way an actual (if redactional) unity is established for the Little Book of Consolation.

The final part consists in a careful analysis of a single motif, the feminine imagery, in order to discover how and why it was used in Jer 30-31. Along with a brief survey of the social situation and status of woman in both Israel and Babylon of the exilic period, the last chapter proposes three hypotheses, literary, historical and psychological, for the use of the remarkable feminine image. It moves beyond the more limited literary analysis to raise questions of how this particular literary artifact is a response to or a reflection of specific historical and socio-religious concerns.

The validity of the method will be demonstrated if it gives a coherent reading of the text.[26] No single approach can hope to arrive at a complete understanding. Wheelwright saw this clearly yet encouraged even faltering attempts to arrive at truth when he said: "The truest explanation of anything is not necessarily the one that is the most efficient or that is most free from incidental error. Perhaps truth, like certain precious metals, is presented best in alloys. In that case the way toward it will be through a guided succession of tentative errors."[27]

Whatever the factor of error in the ʿalloy' of this work, this study will have been a success if it contributes even minimally to a deeper understanding of the riches and truth of Jer 30-31.

---

[25] This terminology is taken from M. K. Danziger and W. S. Johnson, *An Introduction to Literary Criticism*, 33-54.

[26] Cf. C. Brooks and R. Warren, *Understanding Poetry*, 56, for a discussion of coherence as a criterion of interpretation.

[27] P. Wheelwright, *Metaphor and Reality*, Bloomington and London: Indiana University Press, 1962, 173.

CHAPTER 3

CLOSE READING OF JER 30-31

3.1 TEXT DIVISION

As already noted in the introduction, scholars generally agree that Jer 30-31 forms a unit.[1] Most would concur with Bright's judgment that these two chapters are "a collection ... of originally separate sayings, the greater part of them in poetry, all of which develop the theme of comfort."[2]

Despite their acknowledgment of a unity for Jer 30-31, scholars are in general agreement that the Little Book of Consolation is a collection of sayings, both authentic (Jeremianic) and inauthentic, which originated in several distinct historical moments. Since the interest of most exegetes lies primarily in determining authenticity or a redaction history of the text, they divide the text along redactional lines, in an attempt to demarcate different sources or redactional moments.[3]

A literary rather than redactional approach also requires establishing the limits of the text and dividing it into smaller units, though the criteria for such a division are strictly literary in nature. Thus the first step in a literary analysis of Jer 30-31 is determining the boundaries of the poetic cycle. Only then can the individual poems be delimited and studied in turn.

Three criteria, two formal and one thematic, define the limits of Jer 30-31. The first is the presence of the introductory formula *hdbr 'šr hyh 'l-yrmyhw m't yhwh l'mr* of 30:1 which is repeated again in 32:1. Since this formula serves as an introduction at the beginning of major text divisions of Jer (7:1; 11:1; 18:1; 21:1; 27:1; 30:1; 32:1; 34:1; 35:1; 40:1), it demarcates Jer 30-31 as a unit distinct from what precedes and what follows.[4]

---

[1] Cf. Ch. 1, p. 5, n. 30.

[2] Bright, 284.

[3] S. Böhmer, *Heimkehr*, is an excellent example of such an approach.

[4] P. K. D. Neumann, "Das Wort, das geschehen ist ... Zum Problem der Wortempfangsterminologie in Jer I-XXV" *VT* 23 (1973) 207, considers this formula as clearly introductory, and indicative of a redactional unity for the text which follows. Th. Seidl, "Die Wortereignisformel in Jeremia. Beobachtungen zu den Formen der Redeeröffnung in Jeremia, im Anschluss an Jer 27,1.2" *BZ* 23 (N. F.) (1979) 47, agrees, noting that this formula points to a single hand for the final redaction. S. Bretón, *Vocación y misión: Formulario profético*, AnBib 111, Rome: Biblical Institute Press, 1987, 45, concurs with the previous authors.

The second formal indication that Jer 30-31 is a unit lies in its predominantly poetic form, which distinguishes it from the preceding and following chapters both of which are narrative in style.[5] Yet the unity of Jer 30-31 is not that of a single poem but of a poetic cycle which has a prose introduction and conclusion.[6] Neither the poetic nor the prose portions are stylistically integral, for a short prose element intrudes on the poetry (30:8-9) and a short poetic piece is inserted in the prose (31:35-37).

The third criterion for delimiting the unit is of a more thematic nature. The whole of Jer 30-31 is organized around a central idea which has been variously described as comfort (Bright),[7] restoration of fortunes (Weiser),[8] the restoration of the whole Israel (Duhm)[9] and the restoration of the nation (Carroll).[10] Others emphasize the compositional nature of Jer 30-31. Volz considers the organization of the unit to be that of a triptych,[11] while Giesebrecht describes it as a 'Mosaikbild.'[12]

Since this is a poetic cycle rather than a single poem, each poetic (or prose) section must be studied in its own right before the unit can be considered as a whole. But the first step in studying the individual poems is determining the limits of each section in turn. Like the criteria for delimiting the poetic cycle, those used to delimit an individual poem or prose section are both formal and thematic.

The repetition of *(ky) kh 'mr yhwh*[13] and the repeated alternation between masculine and feminine address constitute the basic formal criteria for dividing the text into single poems and prose pieces.

(ky) kh 'mr yhwh appears in 30:2, 5, 12, 18; 31:2, 7, 15, 16, 23, 35, 37, with all but two of these occurrences (31:16, 37) introducing a distinct poem or section of the text.[14] The resultant structure is a six-poem cycle with a short prose introduction and a lengthy summarizing prose conclusion:

---

[5] Internal unity and coherence of subject matter will be discussed later. What is seen here are merely the formal indications that these two chapters bear consideration as a single piece.

[6] Carroll, 568-618, uses this terminology to describe Jer 30-31.

[7] Bright, 284.

[8] Weiser, 268.

[9] Duhm, 237.

[10] Carroll, 568.

[11] Volz, 283.

[12] Giesebrecht, 161.

[13] This 'messenger formula' serves an introductory function, giving authority to both messenger and the message itself. The presence of *ky* is not of itself significant. Cf. S. Bretón, *Vocación y misión*, 83-94.

[14] In both 31:16 and 31:37 the expression is used in the middle of a short poem whose unity is clear. Cf. below, pp. 24, 125.

30:1-4	Prose Introduction	
30:5-11	Poem I	— masculine audience
30:12-17	Poem II	— feminine audience
30:18–31:1	Poem III	— masculine audience
31:2-6	Poem IV	— feminine audience
31:7-14	Poem V	— masculine audience
31:15-22	Poem VI	— feminine-masculine-feminine
31:23-34	Prose Conclusion — Part I	
31:35-40	Prose Conclusion — Part II	

3.1.1 *Prose Introduction*

After the general introductory formula for these two chapters (30:1), the prose introduction begins in 30:2 with *kh-'mr yhwh*, the expression which signals the beginning of each of the smaller units. This short introduction is distinguished from what follows by its prose style, which contrasts with the poetry of 30:5-11.

In itself it is structured by an envelope figure[15] formed by the repetition of *dbr*: *hdbrym 'šr-dbrty* (30:2) and *w'lh hdbrym 'šr dbr* (30:4). Another structural element appears in the relationship set up between Yhwh and Israel, found first in 30:2 which names the speaker as *yhwh 'lhy yśr'l* and then in 30:4 which echoes the same relationship in the expression *yhwh 'l-yśr'l*. Thus an inclusio formally delimits this introduction.

30:2	*kh-'mr*	*yhwh*	*'lhy yśr'l*
	kl-hdbrym		
	'šr-dbrty		
30:4	*w'lh hdbrym*		
	'šr dbr	*yhwh*	*'l-yśr'l*

3.1.2 *Poem I*

The first poem of this cycle, 30:5-11 begins, like the others, with the formula *ky-kh 'mr yhwh* (30:5). Directed to a masculine audience (indicated by an unspecified plural in 30:6, then specified as Jacob and Israel in 30:10 and elsewhere noted by m.s. imperatives and 2 m.s. personal pronouns), it is distinct from the following poem which uses feminine address. Although there is no repetition of specific vocabulary

[15] Cf. W. G. E. Watson, *Classical Hebrew Poetry*, 282-85.

and/or roots, there is nonetheless a thematic unity to Poem I. At the same time a change of tone and emphasis differentiates the two stanzas: 30:5-7 and 30:8-11.

30:5 opens with a cry of distress which is developed in 30:5-7a before being changed in 30:7b to a statement of promised salvation. 30:8 takes up this notion of salvation and develops it through to 30:11. Then, at the very end, with the closing line, this promised salvation is not denied but moderated by an assurance of punishment. Thus despite no verbal repetition between the two stanzas, the developed theme reflects a unity of thought:

30:5-7a	Punishment — destruction
30:7b	Salvation
- - - - - -	- - - - - - - - - - - -
30:8-11a	Salvation — freedom
30:11b	Punishment

3.1.3 *Poem II*

The second poem (30:12-17), also introduced by the formulaic *ky kh 'mr yhwh*, stands apart from both 30:5-11 and 30:18-31:1 by its use of feminine address.[16] Thematically it is, like the preceding poem, composed of two seemingly opposed ideas, which again signal the limits of the stanzas: on the one hand, Israel's deserved punishment (30:12-15) and, on the other, the punishment of her enemies and the healing of Israel (30:16-17). The whole is held together not only by the interplay between the punishment of Israel and that of her enemies, but also by the verbal inclusions found between the two stanzas:

30:13	*rp'wt*	
	t'lh 'yn lk	
30:14	. . .	*'wtk l' ydršw*
- - - - - -	- - - - - - - - - - - -	- - - - - -
30:17	*'lh 'rkh lk*	
	wmmkwtyk 'rp'k	
		drš 'yn lh

[16] Rudolph, 191, Bright, 271, Thompson, 557-58, all consider this a single unit despite the minor break between 30:15 and 30:16.

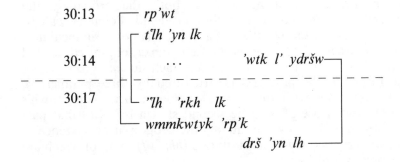

3.1.4 *Poem III*

The introductory formula *kh ’mr yhwh* in 30:18 indicates the beginning of Poem III (30:18–31:1) which, like Poem I, is addressed to a masculine audience. The end of this poem is 31:1, signaled by the *kh ’mr yhwh* found in 31:2 as well as by the change to feminine address in 31:3.

Like the preceding poems, Poem III is divided into two stanzas: 30:18-22 and 30:23–31:1, both of which begin with *hnny/hnh*, speak of the actions of Yhwh and close with the so-called covenant formula. A statement is made and developed in the first stanza and then is seemingly contradicted in the second. The first stanza presents Yhwh’s positive deeds while the second recounts his negative deeds, thus continuing the pattern established in Poems I and II.

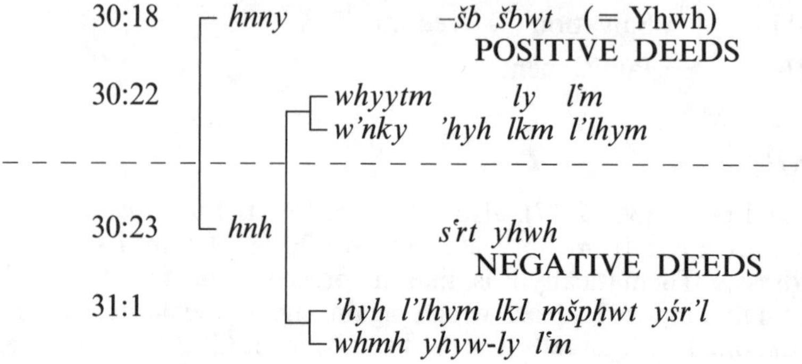

3.1.5 *Poem IV*

Poem IV (31:2-6) shifts to feminine address which, along with the formula *kh ’mr yhwh*, sets it apart from both the preceding and following poems. Like the poems already considered, Poem IV can be divided into two stanzas, though the division itself is not as immediately obvious as in the others. 31:2-3 forms the first stanza, organized around past deeds of Yhwh and marked off by the inclusio *ḥn* – *ḥsd*. 31:4-6 connects the future to the past and is structured by three parallel *ʿwd* statements. It concludes with the people’s response (*ky* ...) to Yhwh’s deeds. By the repeated use of *ʿwd*, the second stanza refers to that past which is the subject of 31:2-3 while moving the geographical reference of the text from wilderness (*bmdbr*) to mountain (*bhr[y]*), both of which are linked to the presence of Yhwh.

31:2 *ḥn*
bmdbr PAST DEEDS
31:3 *yhwh nr'h ly*
ḥsd

31:4 *'wd*
'wd FUTURE DEEDS
31:5 *'wd* *bhry šmrwn*
31:6 *ky* *bhr 'prym*
wn'lh ṣywn 'l-yhwh

3.1.6 *Poem V*

Poem V (31:7-14) once again uses masculine forms of address, an element which sets it off from the surrounding poems. It opens with the usual *ky-kh 'mr yhwh*, and its two stanzas are unified by parallelism of structure as well as by similar ideas. Both stanzas (31:7-9; 31:10-14) are introduced by a series of 3 m.pl. imperatives, each series concluding with *w'mrw* (31:7,10) and leading to an exposition of the salvific deeds of Yhwh on behalf of his people.

The repetition of *śmḥ* (31:7a,13b) as well as *'mk/'my* (*'m yhwh*) (31:7b,14) at the beginning and end forms an inclusio, while the first person speech (of Yhwh) which runs through most of 31:7-9 is taken up again in 31:13-14, adding yet another note of parallelism and unity.

31:7 *śmḥh*
w'mrw (preceded by 4 imperatives)
'mk (= *'m yhwh*)
31:8-9 SAVING DEEDS of Yhwh
(1st pers.)

31:10 *w'mrw* (preceded by 2 imperatives)
31:13-14 CARING DEEDS of Yhwh
(1st pers.)
wśmḥtym
w'my (= *'m yhwh*)

3.1.7 *Poem VI*

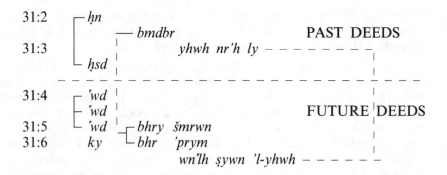

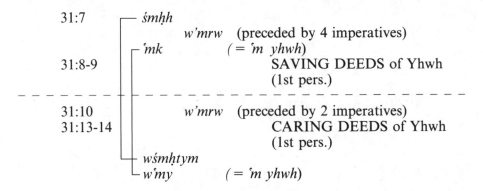

Poem VI (31:15-22), like the others, is set off from the preceding poem by a change of gender (masculine in Poem V to feminine in 31:15) and by the formulaic *kh 'mr yhwh*. Unlike the others, it is composed not of two but of three stanzas, which are differentiated among themselves by a change of gender as well as of subject or addressee: feminine (Rachel), masculine (Ephraim), and feminine (*btwlt yśr'l*) in turn.

The three stanzas are linked by the common theme of change of heart and fortunes. The first stanza (31:15-17), addressed to Rachel, calls her to a change of heart based on Yhwh's physical deed of *šwb* in favor of her sons. The second (31:18-20) speaks of Ephraim's change of heart, which is identified with Yhwh's spiritual deed of *šwb*. The final stanza (31:21-22), addressed to *btwlt yśr'l*, identifies Israel's physical action of *šwb* with her interior change. Besides their accent on the concept of *šwb* in its variety and richness of meaning, all three stanzas employ the common image of the parent-child relationship: Rachel and her sons (first stanza), Ephraim as the well-beloved son of Yhwh (second stanza), *btwlt yśr'l* as the daughter who turns from Yhwh (third stanza).

The second *kh 'mr yhwh*, found in 31:16, must not be construed as the beginning of another poem, for the first stanza is clearly united around Rachel and her weeping. The repetition of the formula (which may well be of redactional origin) serves to emphasize that it is Yhwh alone (and not another, e.g., the prophet) who guarantees a change of circumstance for Rachel.

31:15	*qwl . . . nšmʿ*		
		rḥl ʿl-bnyh	
31:16	*ky*		
			wšbw m'rṣ 'wyb
31:17			*wšbw bnym lgbwlm*

– –

31:18	*šmwʿ šmʿty*		
			hšybny w'šwbh
31:20		*hbn yqyr ly*	
		'm yld šʿšʿym	
	ky		

– –

31:21			*šwby*
31:22	*ky*	*hbt hšwbbh*	

3.1.8 *Prose Conclusion*

The prose conclusion (31:23-40) is introduced in the same way as are the poems, by the formulaic expression *kh-’mr yhwh*, though here it is extended with titles of Yhwh: *ṣb’wt ’lhy yśr’l* (31:23). It too is divided into two major sections: 31:23-34 and 31:35-40 which, while of unequal length, have a similar global structure. Both sections are organized around three common elements: the introductory formula (once in 31:23-34, twice in 31:35-40); mention of the coming days (twice in 31:23-34, once in 31:35-40); a concluding *l’... ʿwd* statement. The link between the two sections is clear since the second guarantees the promise made in the first.

31:23	*kh-’mr yhwh*	
	ʿwd y’mrw	
31:25	*ky*	
31:27	*hnh ymym b’ym*	*n’m-yhwh*
31:29	*bymym hhm*	
31:31	*hnh ymym b’ym*	*n’m-yhwh*
31:33	*’ḥry hymym hhm*	
31:34	*ky*	
	l’... ʿwd	

– –

31:35	*kh ’mr yhwh*	
31:37	*kh ’mr yhwh*	
31:38	*hnh ymym (b’ym)*	*n’m-yhwh*
31:40	*l’*	
	wl’ ʿwd	
	lʿwlm	

Having thus shown in the foregoing analysis that Jer 30-31 is a cycle of six poems with a prose introduction and conclusion, it now remains to examine the individual units in turn. The following pages, therefore, give attention to the details of each poetic (or prose) piece, focusing on the literary figures and language used, as well as on internal unity and coherence of subject matter. This detailed discussion will set the stage for the ensuing study of certain motifs and themes of Jer 30-31.

3.2 PROSE INTRODUCTION (30:1-4)

1 *hdbr 'šr hyh 'l-yrmyhw*
m't yhwh
l'mr

2 *kh 'mr yhwh*
'lhy yśr'l
l'mr

ktb-lk 't kl-hdbrym
'šr-dbrty 'lyk 'l-spr

3 *ky hnh ymym b'ym n'm-yhwh*

wšbty 't-šbwt 'my yśr'l
wyhwdh
'mr yhwh

whšbtym 'l-h'rṣ
'šr-ntty l'bwtm
wyršwh

4 *w'lh hdbrym 'šr dbr yhwh 'l-yśr'l*
w 'l-yhwdh

3.2 *Prose Introduction* — WORDS OF RESTORATION (30:1-4)

The introductory verses of this poetic cycle serve, as does every introduction, to present the major theme of what will follow, as well as to identify the figures whose relationships form the core of the dramatic dialogue contained herein.[17]

The opening expression, *hdbr 'šr hyh 'l-yrmyhw m't-yhwh*, is an introductory statement repeated eleven times in the book of Jeremiah and often considered an indication of a prose redactional unit, most frequently linked to C-material.[18] Whatever its value for redactional

[17] C. Brooks and R. Warren (*Understanding Poetry*, 20) state that every poem involves dramatic organization because it implies a speaker who, in the poem, is reacting to a situation, a scene, an idea. Jer 30-31 is considered by Volz, 284, to possess dramatic elements in its change of speakers, change of scenes, change of tone and perception.

[18] Rudolph (cf. the respective citations) maintains that the use of the formula in 7:1; 11:1; 18:1; 21:1; 34:8; and 44:1 is indicative of C-source while in 30:1; 32:1; 34:1 and 40:1 it

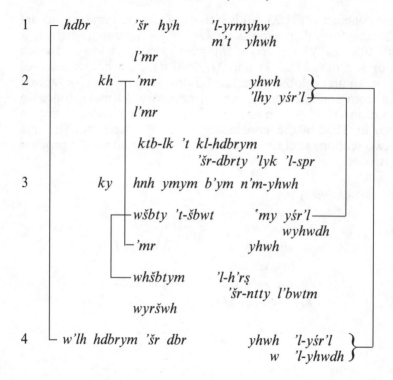

studies, as introductory it serves two functions. Being the introduction to a fairly lengthy unit, it integrates Jer 30-31 into the whole prophetic book.[19] As the opening line of a self-contained prose introduction and the first member of a concentric structure which shapes this unit, it concentrates on the word as word of Yhwh.[20] Effectively, the text does focus attention on the word (*hdbr*) whose source is Yhwh (30:1), both directly, by repetition of *dbr* (*kl-hdbrym 'šr-dbrty*, 30:2; *hdbrym 'šr dbr yhwh*, 30:4), and indirectly, by reference to Yhwh's act of speaking (*kh-'mr yhwh*, 30:2; *'mr yhwh*, 30:3).

30:1 *hdbr 'šr hyh . . . m't yhwh*
30:2 *kh-'mr yhwh* — Speech of Yhwh — Words of Yhwh
30:3 *'mr yhwh*
30:4 *hdbrym 'šr dbr yhwh*

Since *dbr*, for the Hebrew mind, is not merely a linguistic event or the expression of an intellectual idea but rather the communication or 'real-ization' of the event or object,[21] the effectiveness of the word-event (30:1,2,4) is noteworthy. As word communicated it is assured. If this is true of any human word, how much more is it true of the word whose source is Yhwh.

While *hdbr* of 30:1 refers to Yhwh's effective word which comes forth from his mouth, *hdbrym* of 30:2,4 refers to the words which follow

points to a late redaction but not C-source. S. Mowinckel (*Zur Komposition*, 31) considers as coming from source C the speeches of 7:1-8:3; 11:1-5, 9-14; 18:1-12; 21:1-10; 25:1-11a; 32:1-2, 6-16, 24-44; 34:1-7; 34:8-22; 35:1-19; 44:1-14; i.e., every locus (except 30:1) of this formulaic introduction. Jer 30-31 is, for him, part of source D, a later collection of anonymous authorship which is undatable (54-55). Cf. above, p. 2, n. 4.

[19] Rudolph, 189; Carroll, 571.

[20] J. Muilenburg ("A Study in Hebrew Rhetoric: Repetition and Style," *Congress Volume: Copenhagen 1953*, SVT 1, Leiden: E. J. Brill, 1953, 104-105) notes, though in regard to poetry, that one commonly finds repetition of the key-word at the beginning and the end of a poem, as well as repetition throughout.

[21] Even the dictionary definitions of *dbr* convey this. A glance at *HAL (AT)*, s.v. "*dbr*," makes this clear with its several translations: (1) Wort; (2) Angelegenheit, Sache; (3) Sache, Dinge; (4) Wort Gottes. Discussions of the idea and further background can be found in J. Pedersen, *Israel. Its Life and Culture I-II*, trans. by A. Møller, London: Oxford University Press: 1926, 167-68; G. von Rad, *Old Testament Theology II*, trans. by D. Stalker, New York, Evanston, San Francisco and London: Harper and Row Publishers: 1965, 81; and T. Boman, *Das hebräische Denken im Vergleich mit dem griechischen*, 4. Aufl., Göttingen: Vandenhoeck & Ruprecht, 1965, 45.

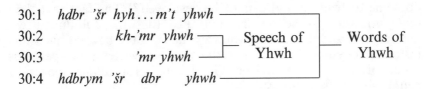

and are the content of *hdbr*.[22] These words (*hdbrym*) are for the future, and their having been set down in writing virtually guarantees their truth, for, as stated in Jer 28:9, the one who prophesies peace is recognized as a true prophet when his words are fulfilled. Hence to write down these words is to keep them for the future and to be able to judge their authenticity as well as the authenticity of the one who pronounced them. It is one way to assure that they are truly the words of Yhwh. Indeed the contrast between the word of Yhwh in 30:3 and the lying words of the false prophets recorded in the immediately preceding chapters bears this out. The words referred to as words of Yhwh in 30:3 are true, words that do come to fruition and cannot be destroyed.[23] The fact that the words (*hdbrym*) were to be written indicates that the fulfillment was not imminent[24] and that the prophecy had value beyond its immediate historical circumstances. What the prophet writes and speaks is "die geheimnisvolle Triebkraft der Geschichte," for a *dbr* spoken over a people shapes their future.[25]

Although Jeremiah is the one addressed (*'l-yrmyhw*, 30:1), the real recipient of the word-event is not the prophet but the people, for the words (*hdbrym*) are directed *'l-yśr'l w'l-yhwdh* (30:4). In 30:1 *'l-yrmyhw* means 'to Jeremiah,' 'directed towards Jeremiah' as is clear by its parallelism with *m't yhwh*; but the import of the same preposition *'l* in 30:4 is not so clear. Its relative ambiguity leaves it open to two levels of meaning. As addressed to Jeremiah (*'l-yrmyhw*), the word 'concerns' Israel and Judah,[26] yet as spoken through the prophet as mediator or messenger, the word is addressed 'to' Israel and Judah as final recipient.[27]

---

[22] G. Rinaldi, "Alcuni termini ebraici relativi alla letteratura" *Bib* 40 (1959) 271, distinguishes between the singular and plural, noting that the plural seems to have acquired a technical sense, designating a text.

[23] This is all the more striking when one considers 30-31 as the center of the larger unit 26-36. Carroll, 510, groups together chs. 26-36, based on the historical information which opens chs. 26 (the reign of Jehoiakim) and 37 (the reign of Zedekiah). He notes that ch. 36 "summarizes and acts as closure of the section," concluding what is begun in ch. 26, for "26 raises the question of turning, but 36 demonstrates the rejection of that possibility." Thus the word which is offered in 26 as the way to life and salvation is presented in 30-31 as actually effecting this salvation, before its rejection in 36 (although even here it cannot be destroyed).

[24] N. Lohfink, "Die Gotteswortverschachtelung," 111, refers to a realization of the word, soon to be accomplished.

[25] O. Grether, *Name und Wort Gottes im Alten Testament*, BZAW 64, Giessen: Alfred Töpelmann, 1934, 103.

[26] BDB, *ad loc.*; *HAL (AT)*, *ad loc.*; Joüon § 133 b.

[27] Cf. C. Westermann, *Grundformen prophetischer Rede*, München: Chr. Kaiser Verlag, 1960, 70-82.

Thus by a very simple technique these words (*hdbrym*) are both directed to and speaking about the people.

The reason for committing the words to writing is given in 30:3, a subordinate clause which could be considered grammatically extraneous and nonessential for the logical development of the argument.[28] As grammatically and logically nonessential, its importance is foregrounded, indicating that it contains essential information. It is certainly the most significant and pregnant statement of this prose introduction.

By the presence of *n'm yhwh*, a common expression in Jer,[29] 30:3 indicates what follows to be truly a revelation from Yhwh.[30] Thus it makes allusion to *dbr m't yhwh* of 30:1.

30:3 also points to an eschatological future (*hnh ymym b'ym*), the 'day of the Lord' when all will be changed,[31] yet a future which is still within history.[32] It establishes a sense of hope by mention of the

---

[28] 30:4 follows 30:2 directly, both grammatically and logically.

[29] The expression *hnh ymym b'ym* is found 15 times in Jer, of which 14 occurrences add *n'm yhwh*; in the rest of the OT there are 15 occurrences of the expression, to only two of which are added *n'm yhwh*. Cf. J. G. Janzen, *Studies in the Text of Jeremiah*, 84.

[30] S. Bretón, *Vocación y misión*, 224-25. G. Rinaldi, "Alcuni termini ebraici," 272-73, recognizes *n'm* as indicating what Yhwh communicates, i.e., accenting the act and fact of revelation by Yhwh rather than the content thereof.

[31] For C. Levin (*Die Verheissung des neuen Bundes in ihrem theologiegeschichtlichen Zusammenhang ausgelegt*, FRLANT 137, Göttingen: Vandenhoeck & Ruprecht, 1985, 22-31) this formula was originally linked to salvation promise, and thus its use here is indicative of a positive future.

[32] 'Eschatology' has been defined in two ways as noted by E. Jenni (*IDB* II, s.v. "Eschatology of OT," 126): (a) the narrow sense of an end time where there is cleavage between this world and the transcendental world of God, an almost apocalyptic vision of reality; and (b) the broader sense of a future which is so different from the present that one can speak of a change in the state of things yet always within the realm of history.

Among the proponents of the narrow interpretation are S. B. Frost, "Eschatology and Myth" *VT* 2 (1952) 70-80; and S. Mowinckel, *He That Cometh*, trans. from the Norwegian by G. W. Anderson, Oxford: Basil Blackwell, 1956, who thus consider the Jeremianic oracles not eschatological.

Among the proponents of the broader interpretation (eschatology as referring to a new world but within historical times) are J. Lindblom, "Gibt es eine Eschatologie bei den alttestamentlichen Propheten?" *Studia Theologica* 7 (1952) 79-114; Th. Vriezen, "Prophecy and Eschatology," *Congress Volume: Copenhagen 1953*, SVT 1, Leiden: E. J. Brill, 1953, 199-229, and H. Kosmala, "'At the End of the Days'" *ASTI* 2 (1963) 27-37.

G. Habets, "Die Eschatologie der alttestamentlichen Propheten" *St Miss* 32 (1983) 271, would reserve the term 'eschatology' for the notion of a complete change and use 'eschatological' for what the prophets preach.

restoration of fortunes (*wšbty 't-šbwt*), an indication that the historical locus of the text is the Exile (*hšbtym 'l-h'rṣ 'šr-ntty l'bwtm*). Throughout, it intones the alliteration of salvation in /š/ and at the end links future hope with past blessing (*wyršwh*).

The triple statement:

> *wšbty 't-šbwt*
> *whšbtym 'l-h'rṣ*
> *wyršwh*

sets the tone for the entire poetic cycle of Jer 30-31 by linking the basic content to a single sound. With its triple repetition of the root *šwb* and the addition of *yrš*, 30:3 establishes the alliteration of salvation echoed in /š/.[33]

The threefold content of the promise is linked not only by alliteration but also by the fact that each successive verbal action is the consequence of the immediately preceding one. The 'restoration of fortunes' is made concrete in the return to the land; and return means presence not only as sojourner but as the inheritor of this land.

Although the general meaning of *šwb-šbwt* is quite clear, its specific content has been disputed for some time. This expression has recently been termed enigmatic[34] due to the opposing conclusions of the two major etymological studies concerning it. Preuschen understands *šwb-šbwt* in a narrow historical context and translates it "Gefangenschaft wenden,"[35] whereas Baumann gives it a nonconcrete, ethical frame and translates it "Schuldhaft rückgängig machen."[36] Dietrich's 1925 study holds a middle position. He concludes, after a contextual study of the occurrences of the expression, that its meaning is best conveyed by "wiederherstellen wie einst," the restoration to a former situation,[37] a conclusion with which Bracke concurs in his recent article on the topic.[38] Such a generic understanding of *šwb-šbwt* seems best, for it allows the specificity of the expression to be determined by the context.[39]

---

[33] The presence of /š/ as echoing the saving deeds of Yhwh will be further elaborated below, especially with regard to Poems I and II.

[34] J. Lust, "'Gathering and Return' in Jeremiah and Ezechiel" in P.-M. Bogaert, ed., *Le livre de Jérémie. Le prophète et son milieu, les oracles et leur transmission*, BEThL 54, Leuven: Leuven University Press, 1981, 122-23.

[35] E. Preuschen, "Die Bedeutung von *šwb šbwt* im Alten Testament" *ZAW* 15 (1895) 1-74.

[36] E. L. Baumann, "*šwb šbwt*, eine exegetische Untersuchung" *ZAW* 47 (1929) 17-44.

[37] E. L. Dietrich, *šwb šbwt. Die endzeitliche Wiederherstellung bei den Propheten*, BZAW 40, Giessen: Alfred Töpelmann, 1925.

[38] J. M. Bracke, "*šwb šbwt*: A Reappraisal" *ZAW* 97 (1985) 233-44.

[39] W. Holladay, in his exhaustive study on *šwb* (*The Root ŠÛBH in the Old*

While the verbs *wšbty* and *whšbtym* of 30:3 could be a reference to the northern exiles taken to Assyria,[40] the presence in the same verse of 'Judah' together with 'Israel' (*ʿmy yśr'l wyhwdh*) indicates that the audience of the final text must be those exiled in Babylon.[41] Thus the historical context of the final redaction is seen to be the Babylonian Exile, a fact which colors the text's interpretation.

Here Yhwh's saving deed (*wšbty 't-šbwt ʿmy*...) is specified as a concrete historical action, the restoration of the people to the land (*whšbtym 'l-h'rṣ*).[42] Two literary devices present this action as both past and future. First the author identifies the land promised the people in the future with that given to their fathers in the past. Then, using a polysemantic pun based on grammatical ambiguity, the author leaves the subject of *wyršwh* unclear: is it the exilic community, or is it their fathers?

wyršwh, a perfect consecutive expressing future time, follows a participial clause which is a temporal expression (*hnh ymym b'ym*).[43] As such it both completes and is consequent upon the preceding *whšbtym*.[44] Hence its subject could well be *ʿmy yśr'l wyhwdh*, as most commentaries and recent translations interpret it. Yet the subject of *wyršwh* could just as well be not the exilic community but their ancestors, the original inheritors of the land. As a converted perfect, a form often used in the sphere of past time,[45] *wyršwh* can have the modal aspect of 'to be able to, could.'[46] In this case the action it describes would be consequent upon the preceding *ntty* and mean 'so they could inherit it.' Thus *wyršwh* would have *'bwtm*, its immediate antecedent, as subject. Grammatically, both

---

Testament with Particular References to Its Usage in Covenantal Contexts, Leiden: E. J. Brill, 1958, 87-88, 110), includes this particular passage among those which refer to return from exile, thus specifying its content by the context.

[40] The audience of the original Jeremianic oracles in 30-31 is universally accepted to be the exiles from the Northern Kingdom. Besides the commentaries, cf., S. Herrmann, *Die prophetischen Heilserwartungen im Alten Testament*, BWANT 5, Stuttgart: W. Kohlhammer Verlag, 1965, 217; N. Lohfink, "Der junge Jeremia," 366-68; S. Böhmer, *Heimkehr*, 82.

[41] It is this redactional aspect which leads many exegetes to emend the MT, eliminating *wyhwdh* as a later addition. This can be seen in BHS as well as in Volz, 281; Rudolph, 188; Weiser, 268. Carroll, 571, on the other hand, considers such emendation not only unnecessary but also unwarranted.

[42] P. Diepold, *Israels Land*, BWANT 95, Stuttgart, Berlin, Köln, Mainz: W. Kohlhammer Verlag, 1972, 134, states this clearly in his book, which seeks to understand the content of 'land' for Dtn, Jer, DtrG and Dtr-Jer: "Für Jeremia ist es offenbar selbstverständlich, dass für Israel die Heilszeit das sichere und freie Wohnen im Lande zum Inhalt hat."

[43] G-K § 112 x.

[44] G-K § 112 c.

[45] Cf. Joüon § 119 u.

[46] Cf. Joüon § 119 w.

interpretations are valid[47]; logically, they are both true. The exilic community will inherit or take possession of the land as their fathers, the Exodus community, once did. In both instances the land is the gift of Yhwh[48]: his promised gift to the exiles; his actual gift to past generations.[49]

The juxtaposition of 'give' (*ntn*) and 'inherit' (*yrš*) points to what has occurred and will occur, as a bilateral action. Although the land is Yhwh's gift (*'šr ntty*, 30:3), the act of giving requires Israel's involvement, since no gift or donation is complete without the reciprocal act of acceptance or taking into possession. This latter notion is expressed in the verb *yrš*, which refers to the taking of another's property for oneself but excludes an act of purchase.[50] Thus the deed here described is two-sided: Israel must take possession, but she cannot do so without Yhwh's prior act of giving.

The allusion to the Exodus promises, which are closely linked to obligations of the people in Deuteronomy, reflects certain consequences which flow from the inheritance of the land. According to Dt (cf., e.g., Dt 6:13-15), to possess Yhwh's land is to continue to live in communion with him, to exist as the people of Yhwh, with him alone as their Lord.[51] Thus Jer 30:3 promises not merely a renewed nationalism but a renewed relationship with Yhwh as well.

These introductory verses (30:1-4) point to the future fulfillment of a promise and set the tone for the entire poetic cycle. The united people of Yhwh, Israel and Judah together, are given a word of the Lord which assures restoration.

---

[47] L. Alonso Schökel and J.L. Sicré Diaz, *Profetas* I, Nueva Biblia Española, Madrid: Ediciones Cristiandad, 1980, 553, state this explicitly in their comment on 30:3: "El verbo final *wyršwh* puede referirse gramaticalmente a los padres o a los repatriados," while two modern translations merely make *'bwtm* the subject of *wyršwh*: " 'I will bring my people Israel and Judah back from captivity and restore them to the land I gave their forefathers to possess,' says the Lord." (*The Holy Bible: New International Version*, Grand Rapids: Zondervan, 1978) and "Ich führe sie zurück in das Land, das ich ihren Vätern zum Besitz gegeben habe." (*Die Heilige Schrift Familienbibel*, Einheitsübersetzung, Leipzig: St Benno-Verlag GmbH, 1983). N. Lohfink ("Die Gotteswortverschachtelung," 116, n. 16) recognizes the grammatical validity of *wyršwh* having as subject *'bwtm*, though he opts for Israel and Judah.

[48] For a discussion of the land as gift of Yhwh cf., e.g., H. Wildberger, "Israel und sein Land" *EvTh* 16 (1956) 405-06 and P.D. Miller, "The Gift of God, The Deuteronomic Theology of the Land" *Int* 23 (1969) 451-65.

[49] The presence of *'rṣ... ntn... yrš* recalls the Exodus promises repeated in Deuteronomy. Cf. Dt 3:18; 5:31: 9:6; 15:4; 16:20; 17:14; 19:2,14; 25:19; 26:1.

[50] F. Dreyfus, "Le thème de l'héritage dans l'Ancien Testament" *RSPhTh* 42 (1958) 5-8, gives an excellent analysis of the verb *yrš*. N. Lohfink, "*yrš*," *TWAT* III, 959, interprets this verb in a more political sense in Dt 30:5; Jer 30:3; Esr 9:10.

[51] J. Plöger, *Literarkritische formgeschichtliche und stilkritische Untersuchungen zum Deuteronomium*, BBB 26, Bonn: Peter Hanstein Verlag, 1967, 81-82, summarizes this relationship in his statement "... die Aussagen von der Landegabe und der Erwahlung Israels zu einem 'heilige,' Gott zugehörigen Volk (stehen) in innerem Zusammenhang."

3.3 POEM I — 30:5-11

5 *ky-kh ’mr yhwh*
qwl ḥrdh šmʿnw
pḥd w’yn šlwm
6 *š’lw-n’*
wr’w ’m-yld zkr
mdwʿ r’yty kl-gbr ydyw ʿl-ḥlṣyw
kywldh
wnhpkw kl-pnym lyrqwn
7 *hwy*
ky gdwl hywm hhw’
m’yn kmhw
wʿt-ṣrh hy’ lyʿqb
wmmnh ywšʿ

- -

8 *whyh bywm hhw’ n’m yhwh ṣb’wt*
’šbr
ʿlw mʿl ṣw’rk
wmwsrwtyk
’ntq
9 *wl’-yʿbdw-bw ʿwd zrym*
wʿbdw ’t yhwh ’lhyhm
w’t dwd mlkm –yšʿ
’šr ’qym lhm
10 *w’th ’l-tyr’ ʿbdy yʿqb n’m yhwh*
w’l-tḥt yśr’l
ky hnny mwšyʿ k mrḥwq
w’t zrʿk m’rṣ šbym
wšb yʿqb
wšqṭ
wš’nn w’yn mḥryd
11 *ky ’tk ’ny n’m-yhwh*
lhwšyʿk
ky ’ʿśh klh bkl-hgwym
’šr hpṣwtyk šm
’k ’tk
l’-’ʿśh klh
wysrtyk lmšpṭ
wnqh l’ ’nqk

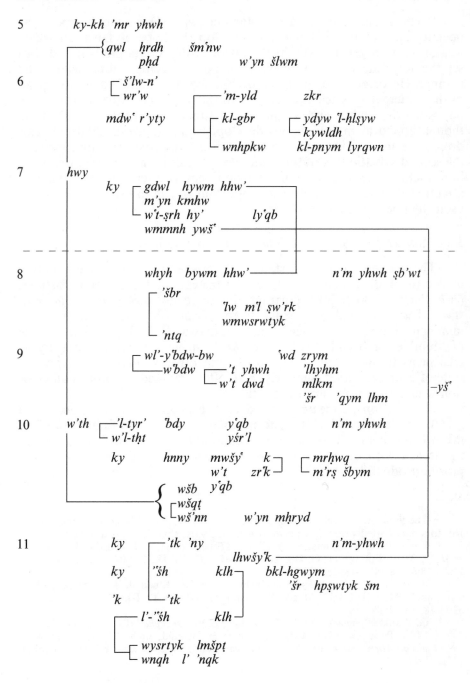

3.3 *Poem I*: A STUDY IN CONTRASTS (30:5-11)

Poem I opens in a rather startling way. One would expect the opening lines of the first poem to develop the hope of salvation which was raised in a general way in the introductory verses (30:1-4) and thus set the tone of the poetic cycle in a more specific, more determined manner. However the opening stanza[52] of Poem I (30:5-7) does not speak of the anticipated peace and security in the land, but rather portrays the opposite: the sights and sounds of distress. The expected salvation, though hinted at in 30:7, is not developed until stanza 2 (30:8-11). This divergence in tone between the two stanzas (the first accenting distress, the second salvation) is of the same type as that found between the prose introduction and the opening line of Poem I. Such contrast, with its attention-drawing effect, plays an important role in this first poem as well as in the poetic cycle as a whole.

3.3.1 Stanza 1 — *Sight and Sound of Distress* (30:5-7)

The imagery of the first stanza is overwhelmingly negative, painting a picture of distress and destruction. Instead of the restored fortunes (*šwb šbwt*) of 30:4, 30:5 portrays the opposite: *qwl ḥrdh . . . pḥd w'yn šlwm*. There is trembling, panic, terror (*ḥrdh*, *pḥd*), the reaction to an imminent destruction or one already underway.[53] With its original sense of 'tremble' or 'tremble with fear,' *ḥrdh* suggests extreme insecurity as seen in its frequent opposition to *bṭḥ* and other words which express a state of calm security.[54] Similarly, *pḥd*, often opposed to *šlwm*, is an emotion which makes one unfit for action.[55]

Desperation permeates the scene. The people have no peace (*w'yn šlwm*). The security which transforms mere existence into fullness of life is taken from them.[56] They have no tranquility, no assured future, but are threatened with destruction, in striking contrast to the promise of the prose introduction.

---

[52] The term 'stanza' refers, according to W. G. E. Watson, *Classical Hebrew Poetry*, 161, to a major subdivision of a poem. It is in this sense that the term is used here.

[53] For *ḥrdh* cf. A. Baumann, "*ḥrd*," *TWAT* III, 177-81, and its use in Is 32:11; Ez 26:16,18; 32:10. For *pḥd* cf. G. Wanke, "*phobeō*," *TDNT* IX, 203-04, and its use in Dt 11:25; 28:67; Is 24:17-18; Jer 48:43,44.

[54] P. Joüon, "Crainte et peur en hébreu biblique. Etude de lexicographie et de stylistique" *Bib* 6 (1925) 175-76; A. Baumann, "*ḥrd*," *TWAT* III, 177-81. Cf., e.g., Is 32:11-18; Ez 34:28; 39:26.

[55] G. Wanke, "*phobeō*," *TDNT* IX, 203-04; BDB, s.v. "*pḥd*." Cf. 2 Chr 17:10.

[56] Cf. J. Pedersen, *Israel* I-II, 263-335; H. H. Schmid, *šālôm. "Frieden" im alten Orient und im Alten Testament*, SBS 51, Stuttgart: Verlag Katholisches Bibelwerk GmbH, 1971, 45-90.

Through the use of alliteration and near-alliteration a sense of terror pervades this stanza. Words of similar meanings repeat similar sounds; the /ḥ/ of *pḥd* and *ḥrdh* is echoed in the similar guttural /q/ of *qwl*. A single /š/ in *w'yn šlwm* follows this triple (near) alliteration, establishing a pattern for the alliteration or sound of distress–salvation which is repeated again in 30:10.

Several poetic devices reinforce the image of distress. A complex pattern of parallelism which includes proper congruence (*ḥrdh // pḥd*) and proper anti-congruence (*ḥrdh+pḥd // w'yn šlwm*),[57] as well as triple synthetic semantic parallelism (*ḥrdh // pḥd // w'yn šlwm*), focuses attention on the experienced adversity. A pivot pattern (*qwl ḥrdh – šmʿnw – pḥd*) which uses *šmʿnw* to refer to both the preceding and the following expressions[58] is yet another device used for the same purpose.

Although these words of distress are placed, according to 30:5a, in the mouth of Yhwh (*ky-kh 'mr yhwh*), they are recounted by a 'we' (*šmʿnw*). If the speaker is Yhwh or his prophet, a 1 s. form would be logically required, and many exegetes emend *šmʿnw* to *šmʿty* so that it agrees in person and number with *r'yty* of 30:6.[59] But there is no univocal interpretation. Both Bright and Thompson understand 30:6-7 as words of the prophet alone which receive a response from Yhwh only in 30:10-11.[60] Other exegetes, however, keep the MT reading and, opting for a plural subject, construe these words as those of the people.[61] In fact, this opening statement can well be understood as words of Yhwh, but Yhwh quoting the people whom he is addressing.[62]

The final redacted text presents a single line which quotes the people's reaction to their own situation (30:5). This is followed by five lines of response to their reaction (30:6-7), placed in the mouth of the prophet or of Yhwh.[63]

---

[57] W. G. E. Watson, *Classical Hebrew Poetry*, 118-19.

[58] *Ibid.*, 214, 218-19.

[59] Volz, 281; Rudolph, 188-89; Weiser, 260, 268.

[60] Bright, 278; Thompon, 555.

[61] Giesebrecht, 161; Bright, 278; Thompson, 555. D. Barthélemy, *Critique textuelle de l'Ancien Testament* vol. 2, OBO 50/2, Fribourg: Editions Universitaires; Göttingen: Vandenhoeck & Ruprecht, 1986, 680. These are in agreement with the versions, all of which maintain a plural form, be it first person (Targum Jonathan, Peshitta, Vulgate) or second person (LXX and Arabic) (cf. B. Walton, *Biblia Sacra Polyglotta*, Tomus Tertius, London: Thomas Roycroft, 1656).

[62] H. Freedman, *Jeremiah*, Soncino Books of the Bible, London, Jerusalem and New York: The Soncino Press, 1985 (rev. ed.), 197, considers the words as those of the people placed in the mouth of Yhwh.

[63] There is no way of identifying the speaker with any certainty. If these are the words of the prophet, they are his as the messenger of Yhwh.

Such ambiguity concerning the identity of the speaker leaves interpretation open and shifts the focus to the dialogue between Yhwh and his people, a dialogue which is at times direct, at other times indirect, through the mediation of the prophet.[64] Even when present, the prophet remains in the background, thus automatically placing Yhwh's contact with Israel at center-stage. It is Yhwh who is communicating with his people, Yhwh who touches them in their crisis, be it political[65] or religious.[66]

The response in 30:6 to the sound of panic and terror is hardly consoling. Offered no hope, the people are told to open their eyes and pay attention, to consider what is occurring (*š'lw-n' wr'w*, 30:6). Distress and terror now impinge on yet another sense. This experience is not merely auditory but also visual and therefore open to more detailed description.

The reader's attention is drawn immediately to the rhetorical question (*'m yld zkr*) whose answer is generally understood to be clearly negative.[67] If the object of inquiry is beyond question, as seems to be the case, posing the question would merely be a means of emphasizing the extremity of the situation. Yet the question in and of itself is not univocal, for the verb *yld* means 'beget' (act of the male), as well as 'bear' (act of the female), a child, even though the latter is more commonly used.[68] In fact, *yld* (*qal*) is predicated of a male 22 times in the MT, with meanings both direct and metaphorical (e.g., Moses' relation to Israel as that of *yld* in Num 11:12). The question as stated is simply: "Can a male be the bearer / begetter of life?" which can be answered both positively and negatively, depending on one's understanding and interpretation of the words.[69] Giesebrecht alone of all the exegetes mentions an 'older' use of the word applied to both sexes, though his translation of this expression is the usual "ob ein Mann gebiert."[70]

---

[64] According to C. Westermann (*Das Buch Jesaja. Kapitel 40-66*, ATD 19, Göttingen: Vandenhoeck & Ruprecht, 1966, 33) Deutero-Isaiah uses the same technique (cf. Is 40:3), leaving the speaker unidentified and thus emphasizing its ultimate source which is Yhwh.

[65] Cf. Volz, 285, "sie handelt von einem ganz bestimmten einzelnen Ereignis der kommenden Zeit"; Bright, 278-79, "the destruction of Judah by the Babylonians is here understood as the day of Yahweh's judgment upon His people"; Rudolph, 189.

[66] Cf. Weiser, 268-69; Carroll, 574-75.

[67] Cf. W. Brueggemann, "Jeremiah's Use of Rhetorical Questions" *JBL* 92 (1973) 367-68, who indicates how this image in 30:6 refutes the sense of hopelessness which it conveys elsewhere in Jer.

[68] J. Schreiner, "*yld*," *TWAT* III, 634-39; J. Kühlewein, "*yld*," *THAT I, 732-36.*

[69] It is interesting to note that *tiktō*, *gennaō*, and *generāre*, the Greek and Latin words which translate *yld*, bear precisely the same ambiguity or polysemy as that of their Hebrew counterpart. For the Greek, cf. Liddell and Scott, s.v. '*gennaō*' and '*tiktō*'; for the Latin, cf. *Oxford Latin Dictionary*, s.v. '*genero*.' Thus both the LXX and the Vulgate translations are equally ambiguous.

[70] Giesebrecht, 161-62.

Although the question is startling, it is not as startling as might appear at first sight. If it were understood to say: "Can a male be the bearer of life?" the answer could be both positive and negative. Yes, he does bear life in his act of begetting; no, he cannot bear a child. This polysemantic pun[71] conveys a sense of ambiguity and uncertainty first introduced by the immediate confrontation between the promise of restoration (30:3) and a picture of terror and dread (30:5) and held in tension by the rhetorical question of 30:6.

The first stanza continues with yet more detailed description of distress presented in another rhetorical question which repeats certain aspects of the preceding one. The concrete visual image is that of a male with his hands on his loins (*kl-gbr ydyw ʿl-ḥlṣyw*, 30:6), an interesting expression whose predicate is a *hapax*.[72] Since *every* occurrence of *ḥlṣ* refers to the body of the *male* and never that of a female, the bare phrase *kl-gbr ydyw ʿl-ḥlṣyw* without the explanatory *kywldh* could portray a male preparing for work or for battle (the reasons he would gird his loins). The explanatory *kywldh* seems essential for specifying this as the distress often imaged by childbirth.[73] Those who maintain that the image of 30:6 is clear without the explanatory *kywldh* assume a context of childbirth conveyed by the preceding *yld*.[74]

This statement in 30:6 is the transformation of an image, or rather its transmogrification; what initially appears to refer to power — men begetting, men placing their hands on the locus of power (sexual and psychic insofar as it alludes to preparation for action) — turns rather into a caricature of strength. The men become like women, a typical treaty-curse of the ANE,[75] though treaty curses do not refer to pains of childbirth but merely to women as weak and helpless.

With the introduction of *kywldh* the negative picture reaches its culmination, for the context focuses on the pains and anguish and threat of death which are present in every act of giving birth. This same threat

---

71 Cf. W. G. E. Watson, *Classical Hebrew Poetry*, 241-46.

72 In no other place in the MT is *yd* found in connection with *ḥlṣ*, and *ḥlṣ* alone is found only 10 times in the MT, 5 times meaning the place of girding (often the sword) as a preparation for action (Is 5:27; 11:5; 32:11; Job 38:3; 40:7), 3 times as the place whence life comes forth (Gn 35:11; 1 Kg 8:19; 2 Chr 6:9), once as a body which needs covering (Job 31:20) and here in Jer 30:6 where the connection is with childbirth (as in Gn, 1 Kg, 2 Chr).

73 Contra Cornill, 325; Volz, 281; Weiser, 260; Bright, 269; Rudolph, 190, who consider it a gloss. Condamin, 217, opts to keep it for metric reasons; Thompson, 573, maintains the MT without explanation.

74 Cornill, 325; Volz, 281; Bright, 269; Rudolph, 190; N. Lohfink, "Der junge Jeremia," 354, n. 17.

75 For specific instances of this curse in the OT and parallel literature cf. D. Hillers, *Treaty Curses and the Old Testament Prophets*, BibOr 16, Rome: Pontifical Biblical Institute, 1964, 66-68.

of death is repeated in *wnhpkw kl-pnym lyrqwn* (30:6), which contains two *hapax*: this expression as a whole and the application of the term *yrqwn* to a human being.[76] The metaphor portrays faces drained of color, drained of life. The presence of death is pervasive.

The bleakness of the scene is emphasized by the use of oxymoron twice in this verse (*kl-gbr ... kywldh, kl-pnym lyrqwn*), both times applied to all the members of the nation (*kl*). Oxymoron, the bringing together of two concepts which are incongruous or logically incompatible,[77] is an intellectual shock technique and here describes the extremity and hopelessness of the situation.

30:6 thus presents a vivid picture of desolation and desperation: the sound of panic is heard; there is no peace; men are no longer in their role as source of life and protection but are equated with the most helpless of women; faces betray signs of death.

All these images join together to indicate the present disaster and thus offer a solution to the problematic *hwy* which opens 30:7. The use of *hwy*, an interjection which expresses pain, carries overtones of the destruction at hand. It bears the weight of a funeral lament[78] and presents the desolation in 30:5-6 as virtually assured. Rather than a prosaic *hyw*,[79] which would be merely an additional (and unnecessary) verb, *hwy* as a cry of woe or funeral lament makes better textual sense,[80] for it is a fitting response to what has just been announced.

The day described (*hywm hhw'*) is indeed great (*gdwl*) and without compare (*w'yn kmhw*, 30:7). Yet what is truly beyond compare is the pain and distress, reiterated in *'t-ṣrh*.[81] With *gdwl* in an emphatic position[82]

[76] All the other five uses of *yrqwn* (Dt 28:22; 1 Kg 8:37; 2 Chr 6:28; Am 4:9; Hag 2:17) are in parallelism with *šdpwn* and describe crop damage (blight and mildew) which is a punishment from Yhwh. This is indeed punishment for it threatens the existence of the plants, (cf. G. Dalman, *Arbeit und Sitte in Palästina* Band I, Gütersloh: C. Bertelsmann, 1928, 326, who describes both *šdpwn* and *yrqwn*) and therefore also threatens the well-being and existence of the community, as the Talmudic references indicate in citing these two scourges as sufficient threat to call a fast. (Cf. m Taan 3,5-6; m Ar 9,1.)

[77] J. T. Shipley, *Dictionary of World Literary Terms* (rev. ed.), London: George Allen & Unwin Ltd., 1970, s.v. 'oxymoron'; W. G. E. Watson, *Classical Hebrew Poetry*, 312-13.

[78] R. Clifford, "The Use of *Hôy* in the Prophets" *CBQ* 28 (1966) 458-64.

[79] Proposed by Volz, 281; Weiser, 260; Rudolph, 190, for metric reasons and following the LXX.

[80] D. Barthélemy, *Critique textuelle* II, 681.

[81] The distress of *ṣrh* is found in 5 out of 8 occurrences in Jer (4:31; 6:24; 30:7; 49:24; 50:43) to describe the pain of childbirth. Generally *ṣrh* expresses that distress which is the threat of defeat or destruction (cf. Dt 31:17,21 where it is parallel with *r'wt rbwt*; Is 46:7; 63:9; 65:16, all instances of a people in need of a saving presence). Its connection with childbirth is unique to Jer which is yet another indication of the importance of this image.

[82] The predicate, here an adjective, is emphatic when in P-S structure, according to T. Muraoka, *Emphatic Words and Structures in Biblical Hebrew*, Jerusalem: The Magnes Press, 1985, 15.

and the emphatic addition of *hy'* pointing back to *wʿt-ṣrh*,[83] the greatness of the distress can be neither doubted nor denied. The poem uses every means at its disposal to portray an image of desolation and hopelessness for Jacob.

Even if the use of 'Jacob' in 30:7 indicated the N. Kingdom in the original poem,[84] the term is used in prophetic literature to refer to the people as the community of Yhwh, as a group who were the recipients of Yhwh's blessings.[85] Thus the one who had not only been promised but actually enjoyed the presence and blessings of Yhwh ('Jacob') is now facing a time of desolation and distress (which the Exile certainly was for the Israelites). The picture could not be bleaker.

Then suddenly at the end of 30:7 there is an assurance, even if somewhat tentative, of salvation: *wmmnh ywšʿ*. Although several scholars have noted an (original) irony in the expression,[86] in its present context, it is at best ambiguous. At first reading it might appear to be a statement of incredulity that salvation could even be thought of in the present circumstances. Yet it raises a note of hope which, though unexpected in the immediate literary context, is consistent with the larger context.

The tension between the well-developed imagery of distress and the closing assurance of salvation is reflected in the tension between the opening and closing expressions of 30:7, between *hwy* and *wmmnh ywšʿ*. The verse opens with a cry which recalls a funeral lament, one which reflects or at least suggests the presence of death and destruction. Yet this same verse ends on a note of hope. Despite the seemingly hopeless situation in which Jacob finds himself, salvation is coming. Such a note of hope is a surprising change from what precedes, a reversal in two words of the distress which has been developed in three verses. But this concluding remark is important for it introduces and sets the tone for the second stanza.

---

[83] T. Muraoka, *Emphatic Words*, xiii-xiv, notes a similar case in which the addition of *hy'* does not change the basic relationship between subject and predicate but emphasizes the latter.

[84] This, according to S. Böhmer, *Heimkehr*, 58, indicates that these lines were not originally from Jeremiah.

[85] H.-J. Zobel, "*yʿq(w)b*," *TWAT* III, 772-73.

[86] W. Holladay, "Style, Irony and Authenticity in Jeremiah" *JBL* 81 (1962) 53-54; *ibid.*, *Jeremiah: Spokesman Out of Time*, Philadelphia: United Church Press, 1974, 111-12, sees this as a sarcastic question in the original poem but notes that it was included here because of the note of hope which it conveys. According to Rudolph, 190, n. 1, such an admission that in the present context there is clearly an element of hope, belies the validity of an ironic interpretation. Bright, 279; Thompson, 556; Carroll, 574; N. Lohfink, "Der junge Jeremia," 354, n. 18, all mention Holladay's suggestion without further elaboration. W. G. E. Watson, *Classical Hebrew Poetry*, 307, uses this line to illustrate irony in the Hebrew Bible.

3.3.2 Stanza 2 — *Yhwh's Saving Presence* (30:8-11)

The second stanza opens with what many interpret to be one of the prose intrusions into this poetic cycle,[87] yet this line can equally well be seen as heightened prose or near-poetry.[88] The opening line (*whyh bywm hhw'*, 30:8) refers immediately back to the first stanza, to the great day of distress (*hywm hhw'*, 30:7). The extraordinariness of what will occur is here given not a temporal but a personal referent: the powerful God who controls armies and peoples as well as nature and creation (*yhwh ṣb'wt*).[89] His deed, which will be a deed of power, is expressed in a metaphor commonly used and easily understood: *'šbr ʿlw mʿl ṣw'rk wmwsrwtyk 'ntq* (30:8).

Despite the clarity of the concept, 30:8 presents one of the most discussed text-critical problems of Poem I. The difficulties revolve around two issues: first, the referents of the pronomial suffixes of *ʿlw*, *ṣw'rk*, *bw*, and *wmwsrwtyk*; second, what some see as confusion, caused by the presence of both 2 and 3 m.s. suffixes which appear inconsistent with the 3 m. pl. subject of the verb *wʿbdw* in 30:9. The LXX reflects the problem in its consistent use of 3 m. pl. rather than 2 m. s. suffixes and in its elimination of the suffix from *ʿlw*: *ton zugon apo tou traxēlou autōn kai desmous autōn diarrēksō*.[90] Some exegetes opt for 3 m. s. suffixes which have as referent the collective 'Jacob,' understanding *ʿlw* as the yoke of the one who bears the same.[91] Giesebrecht's decision to maintain the MT has found contemporary support from Barthélemy, who accepts the MT reading as the best choice.[92]

From a literary standpoint the MT is perfectly logical as long as one clarifies the referents of the several pronominal suffixes. The 2 m. s. suffix refers to Jacob who is addressed, as becomes explicit in 30:10-11. The 3 m. s. suffix of *ʿlw* refers to the oppressor, while that of *bw* stands for Jacob. The 3 m. pl. suffixes clearly denote the people.

Such a shift between 2nd and 3rd person to refer to the one addressed (30:8-9) is not unusual, but a fairly common phenomenon in

---

[87] Volz, 274; Bright, 270; S. Böhmer, *Heimkehr*, 59; Rudolph, 190; Carroll, 575.

[88] Both Condamin, 216, and Weiser, 260, construe this as poetry. Thompson, 556, presents what he sees as a possible poetic form for these lines.

[89] B. Wambacq, *L'épithète divine Jahvé Ṣᵉba'ôt. Etude philologique, historique et exégétique*, Brugge: Desclée De Brouwer, 1947; O. Eissfeldt, "Jahwe Zebaoth" in R. Sellheim und F. Maass, Hrsg., *Kleine Schriften* 3. Band, Tübingen: J.C.B. Mohr (Paul Siebeck), 1966, 103-23; F.M. Cross, *Canaanite Myth and Hebrew Epic. Essays in the History of the Religion of Israel*, Cambridge: Harvard University Press, 1973, 68-71; A.S. van der Woude, "*ṣb'*," *THAT* II, 503-07.

[90] Volz, 274; Condamin, 216-17; Bright, 270; Thompson, 555; Carroll, 575, all emend the MT to agree with the LXX.

[91] Cornill, 325; Weiser, 260; Rudolph, 190.

[92] Giesebrecht, 162; D. Barthélemy, *Critique textuelle* II, 682-83.

the Hebrew scriptures.[93] Thus 30:8-9 can be interpreted as Yhwh first speaking to Jacob (collective name for the people) with the assurance that their oppression will soon end (30:8a) and then reflecting on the results of such a deed, either to himself or to the prophet (30:8b-9).

ʿlw is 'his yoke,' the yoke of the oppressor, for *ʿl* as a metaphor commonly bespoke servitude, slavery, or subjection to another.[94] Jer alone uses the parallel *šbr ʿl* and *mwsrwt ntq*, and does so three times: 2:20; 5:5; and 30:8. The first two passages refer to the yoke as the religious ordinances of Yhwh which the people broke, while the third features Yhwh as the one who breaks the people's bonds of subservience to a foreign power. The opposition between serving other nations and serving Yhwh, hinted at here by recalling the expressions of 2:20 and 5:5, is made explicit in the following line which opposes the servitude enforced by oppressors to the service required by Yhwh.

Since *ʿbd b* is understood as "to work by means of another, to use another as slave"[95] it reflects the same reality as that of *ʿl*, a servitude which is oppressive. The relationship expressed by the root *ʿbd* does imply a certain level of dependence but, depending on the context, this dependence may be positive (have security in the relationship) or negative (be enslaved). Here in 30:9 the verb is used in both senses. By a 'turn,'[96] the author reverses the content, using the same verb to express two opposite realities. Although the people's state of being *ʿbd* will be changed by Yhwh, it will not be done away with completely. The fact of being *ʿbd* remains. While the grammatical subject of the verb changes from *zrym* (30:8b) to the people of Yhwh (30:9), the logical subject of service is the same (people of Yhwh) and the logical object changes from *zrym* to *yhwh* and *dwd*. The presence of *ʿbd* in its two opposing meanings draws attention to the idea expressed and to

---

[93] G. Ramsey, "Speech-Forms in Hebrew Law and Prophetic Oracles" *JBL* 96 (1977) 43-58, shows an interest in the issue by his seeking a historical explanation for the change from 2nd to 3rd person speech in prophetic judgment speeches.

[94] A.T. Olmstead, *History of Assyria*, Chicago: University of Chicago Press, 1951, 112, 116, 138, 497, 640, places this metaphor in the Assyrian context, while A. Feldman, *The Parables and Similes of the Rabbis, Agricultural and Pastoral*, Cambridge: Cambridge University Press, 1924, places it in a Judaic one. Biblical statements which reflect this concept as servitude under their own king include 1 Kg 12:4-14; 2 Chr 10:4-14; or under the king of Babylon: Is 9:3; 14:25; 47:6; Jer 27:8-12; 28:2-14. C. Westermann, "*ʿbd*," *THAT* II, 190, notes that the yoke is the typical image for slavery and servitude in the OT.

[95] BDB, s.v. "*ʿbd*," vb. 2; C. Lindhagen, *The Servant Motif in the Old Testament. A Preliminary Study to the 'Ebed-Yahweh Problem' in Deutero-Isaiah*, Uppsala: Lundequistska Bokhandeln, 1950, 67; H. Ringgren, *et al.*, "*ʿbd*," *TWAT* V, 985-1012.

[96] W.G.E. Watson, *Classical Hebrew Poetry*, 239.

the fact that Israel lives as *'bd* at all times, either slave of foreign powers and their gods or servant of Yhwh.[97]

The use of *'bdy* addressed to Jacob in 30:10 points back to the repetition of the root *'bd* in 30:9 and reinforces the notion that the totality of existence is lived in relationship to Yhwh.[98] This same relationship of *'bd* is hinted at by the parallel pair *y'qb – yśr'l* (30:10) which recalls the Gn story in which Jacob, as servant of Yhwh, put away foreign gods and went to Bethel where Yhwh appeared to him, changed his name to *yśr'l*, and promised him land and descendants (Gn 35:1-15).

So the salvation hinted at in 30:7 takes the specific shape of serving Yhwh and being dependent on him, a dependence which is freedom.

Yhwh has presented himself as the one who acts in favor of his people both negatively (destroying bonds) and positively (raising up their king). After the opening appellation of *yhwh ṣb'wt* which emphasizes his power, Yhwh is foregrounded in 30:8-9 as the one who creates the future for 'Jacob' since the statement both begins and ends with verbs portraying actions of Yhwh: *'šbr ... 'qym*.

With 30:10 Yhwh begins to address the people who, as Jacob / Israel, are brought into the text as active participants by the double imperative *'l-tyr' ... w'l-tḥt*. Given the situation represented in 30:5-7, the command "Fear not" appears to be a response to the panic and terror already described. Although the origin of the expression may have been cultic,[99] there is no need to posit a cultic context for this particular statement. However, since it is Yhwh's presence which provides the reassurance, the imperative hints at a theophany.[100]

hnny + participle (*mwšy'k*) indicates Yhwh as present and active now rather than in some future moment,[101] although his deed of *yš'* is directed toward both the present (*-k*) and the future (*w't-zr'k*)

---

[97] Although *'bd* is used ten times in Jer to express Israel's serving false gods (5:19; 8:2; 11:10; 13:10; 16:11,13; 22:9; 25:6; 35:15; 44:3), that is not its use here. Despite possible religious content, it is not necessary to link this word with cultic activity, *pace* I. Riesener, *Der Stamm 'bd im Alten Testament. Eine Wortuntersuchung unter Berücksichtigung neuerer sprachwissenschaftlicher Methoden*, BZAW 149, Berlin, New York: Walter de Gruyter, 1979, 183.

[98] C. Westermann, "*'bd*," *THAT* II, 182-200.

[99] J. Begrich, "Das priesterliche Heilsorakel" *ZAW* 52 (1934) 81-92.

[100] H. F. Fuhs, "*yr'*," *TWAT* III, 883-85, notes four basic usages of *'l tyr'* in OT, ranging from comfort for ordinary distress to the introduction of a salvation oracle with its theophanic tenor; J. Becker, *Gottesfurcht im Alten Testament*, AnBib 25, Rome: Biblical Institute Press, 1965, 51-54, accents the theophanic allusion.

[101] Cf. W. A. M. Beuken, "Isaiah LIV: The Multiple Identity of the Person Addressed" in *Language and Meaning. Studies in Hebrew Language and Biblical Exegesis*, OTS 19, Leiden: E. J. Brill, 1974, 34.

generations. The parallel direct objects and prepositional phrases (adverbial) are not repetitive but expansive in value. The second member extends the recipients of Yhwh's deed to include both the present generation and their progeny, and it specifies his action as saving not only from afar but also from the land of oppression which points to the Exile as the context of *mrḥwq*.[102]

Yhwh's saving presence has several effects: *wšb yʿqb wšqṭ wšʾnn wʾyn mḥryd* (30:10). Both the triple repetition of /š/ and the step development, with each succeeding verbal expression having one more syllable than the preceding,[103] effectively focus attention on these words. This line repeats the same major sounds of /ḥ/ and /š/ found in 30:5[104] yet reverses their frequencies, indicating a similar reversal of the situation. In 30:5 /ḥ/-/q/ is found 3 times in expressions of fear/distress, /š/ once in the phrase which negates peace; in 30:10 /š/ is used 3 times to refer to the state of peace or salvation, /ḥ/ once to negate the situation of fear/distress. Thus the promise of peace is reinforced in 30:10, reversing by sound as well as by content the situation described in 30:5.

The distress (*ḥrdh ... wʾyn šlwm*) of 30:5 changes into an end to distress (*wʾyn mḥryd*) in 30:10.[105] *qwl ḥrdh*, *pḥd* and *wʾyn šlwm* (stanza 1) are transformed into *šb*, *šqṭ*, *šʾnn* and *wʾyn mḥryd* (stanza 2). Jacob will return, he will settle and find peace, as the repetition of /š/ emphasizes.

This would appear to be an adequate ending to the poem: distress — reversal of distress — peace and security; yet the poem continues. The final verse of Poem I reiterates the presence of Yhwh not in some general stance but in relation to the people (*ʾtk*) and asserts again that his deed is salvation (*yšʿ*). This time, however, *yšʿ* is not determined or specified vis-à-vis Jacob (*yʿqb*) but vis-à-vis the other nations (*hgwym*, 30:11). Yhwh's deed in favor of his own people is an action against the other nations: *ʿʾśh klh bkl-hgwym ʾšr hpṣwtyk šm*. *ʿśh klh* indicates the destruction and complete annihilation[106] which Yhwh brings on the heads of those who oppress Israel.

---

[102] Cf. Giesebrecht, 162; S. Böhmer, *Heimkehr*, 62; Carroll, 578.

[103] W. H. Irwin, *Isaiah 28-33. Translation and Philological Notes*, BibOr 30, Rome: Biblical Institute Press, 1977, 39, 54, 117, calls this phenomenon, as seen in Is, the "Law of Increasing Members" and notes its use with alliterative pairs or trios.

[104] Cf. above, pp. 34-35.

[105] This same expression is used in Lev 26:6 to describe a state of peace which is Yhwh's blessing for obedience, a state of total security and safe dwelling in the land.

[106] *HAL (AT)*, s.v. "*klh*": "Vernichtung"; BDB, s.v. "*klh*": "complete destruction; annihilation." F. J. Helfmeyer, "*klh*," *TWAT* IV, 168-71.

In 30:11 the repetition of *'šh klh* effectively compares Yhwh's deeds for Israel with his deeds for other peoples (*gwym*). The technique used here is like that used in 30:9 which, by repeating *'bd*, contrasted Israel's relationship to foreigners (*zrym*) with her relationship to her God (*yhwh*). He will destroy the nations which oppressed his people, but he will certainly (*'k*) not do the same to Israel. This is much like the salvific action of the Exodus event when Yhwh saved the Israelites while their enemy, the Egyptians, suffered great losses. The hope which had been raised is not in vain.

Despite the repeated assurance of salvation throughout stanza 2, the poem ends on an unexpected note. The promise of salvation made in 30:8-11a, is now, in 30:11b, replaced by an assurance of punishment. Israel can look forward to a deserved but educative chastisement (*wysrtyk lmšpṭ*).[107]

Besides the contrast and connection achieved by the alternating use of 'you' and 'I/me' throughout 30:10-11, the 'repetition initial' of *ky–ky–ky–'k* unifies these two verses, expressing completeness and reinforcing their structure by dramatic effect.[108] The final line of stanza 2 (which is also the final line of the poem) is indeed climactic. It opens with *'k*, in alliterative repetition of the /k/ already heard 3 times at the beginning of a line, repeats *'tk* which was heard in the second *ky*-clause, and then goes on to negate of Jacob (*l'-'šh klh*) what has been affirmed of the 'nations' (*'šh klh*). This second stanza thus closes by reversing (though not absolutely) that peaceful existence which had been described in 30:8-11b, a change hinted at by the series of reversals which precede the final compound statement.

The promised salvation is qualified. Yhwh acts on behalf of his people, but his action is not entirely positive, as the previous statements might have led one to believe. Yhwh promises not unconditional positive action but salvation tempered by assured punishment (*wysrtyk lmšpṭ wnqh l' 'nqk*, 30:11b). The certainty of punishment is conveyed both in the choice of words and in the choice of forms: the use of the *piel* (intensive) for both *ysr* and *nqh*, as well as the use of the infinitive absolute *nqh* to intensify the verbal idea.

Just as 30:5-7 develops the negative dimension, focusing on pain, anguish, death and destruction, yet ends on a note of hope (*wmmnh ywš'*), 30:8-11 reverses the procedure. It builds up the hope of salvation, defining it and making it ever more precise until the last half-line when suddenly, though hope is not eliminated, the people's joy is attenuated by the assurance of chastisement. 30:5-7 develops the image of a suffering

107 C. Lindhagen, *The Servant Motif in the Old Testament*, 195.
108 W. G. E. Watson, *Classical Hebrew Poetry*, 279.

people yet concludes with the notion that the situation will change. 30:8-11 emphasizes Yhwh's action for his people Israel, accenting his saving presence. It is somewhat surprising then that this stanza (30:8-11) ends on a brief note which changes the notion of Yhwh's action as positive to one which includes some negativity (though unspecified). In the process it implicates the people for they are not guiltless. They will be punished, albeit justly. Their actions play a determining role in their situation, past, present, future.

The introductory Poem I is a study in contrasts. A statement is made and then negated. Destruction is assured, then salvation is promised. Yhwh's action shifts from salvific to punitive. It is not surprising, then, that Poem I ends on a note of uncertainty. The restoration of fortunes, so clearly stated in 30:1-4, is not denied, but questioned. Will Yhwh save or punish?

3.4 POEM II — 30:12-17

12 *ky kh ’mr yhwh*

’nwš lšbrk
nḥlh mktk

13 *’yn-dn dynk lmzwr*
rp’wt tʿlh ’yn lk

14 *kl-m’hbyk škḥwk*
’wtk l’-ydršw

ky mkt ’wyb hkytyk
mwsr ’kzry

ʿl rb ʿwnk
ʿṣmw ḥṭ’tyk

15 *mh-tzʿq ʿl-šbrk*

’nwš mk’bk

ʿl rb ʿwnk
ʿṣmw ḥṭ’tyk

ʿśyty ’lh lk

šbr
ʿlh
rp’
drš

---

16 *lkn kl-’klyk y’klw*
wkl-ṣryk klm bšby ylkw

whyw š’syk lmšsh
wkl-bzzyk ’tn lbz

17 *ky ’ʿlh ’rkh lk*
wmmkwtyk ’rp’k n’m yhwh

ky ndḥh qr’w lk
ṣywn hy’ drš ’yn lh

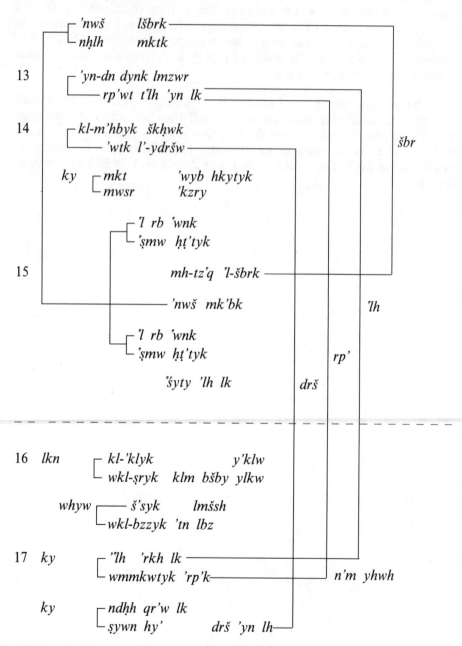

3.4 *Poem II* — HEALING FOR THE INCURABLE WOUND (30:12-17)

Poem II[109] opens on the same note of punishment with which the first poem closed. What is described, however, appears to be more than punishment, for it bodes total destruction. Yet Poem II shifts focus from the first to the second stanza, as did Poem I, though in the opposite direction. Opening with what appears to be hopelessness, 30:12-17 closes with hope renewed.

3.4.1 Stanza 1 — *The Incurable Wound* (30:12-15)

The first stanza of this poem paints a bleak picture: a people sick unto death, wounded beyond healing and responsible for their own plight. Their hopelessness, pictured in the opening line which sets the framework for what follows, is reiterated by parallelism and by the repetition of words, sounds and lines throughout the stanza.

Although the only second person verb of stanza 1 is masculine rather than feminine in form, the repeated use of the 2 f.s. pronominal suffix throughout stanza 1[110] makes it clear that Poem II is addressed to a feminine audience.[111] From the very beginning the feminine audience is brought face to face with its own destruction. To this end, the first line itself uses three literary devices: repetition (here seen in alliteration /š/, /ḥ/-/k/), parallelism (*'nwš lšbrk // nḥlh mktk*) and emphatic construction (emphatic *lamedh* and emphatic position for the adjectives). These three devices are interwoven to form the fabric of the first line (*'nwš lšbrk nḥlh mktk*).

The use of synonymous parallelism (*'nwš lšbrk // nḥlh mktk*) is the most obvious means to reiterate the devastation. The first description uses the substantive *šbr* (a crushing, shattering) whose result is

---

[109] Condamin, 218; Bright, 270-71; Rudolph, 191; Thompson, 557-58; S. Böhmer, *Heimkehr*, 62-63; Carroll, 580-81, consider these six verses to be a single unit, even if some hold 30:12-15 to be authentic and 30:16-17 a later addition. N. Lohfink, "Der junge Jeremia," 354-55, limits his study to 30:12-15 (the authentic words).

[110] It is found twice in the first line and a total of 15 times in the first stanza.

[111] V. 15 contains the only 2nd person verb of the stanza and it is 2 m. rather than 2 f.s. Duhm, 241; Volz, 285, n.s; Rudolph, 192; Carroll, 581, all note the presence of the masculine, and all simply say that it should be read as feminine. There are other instances in the MT where the context requires a 2 f.s. although the 2 m.s. form is found: e.g., Jdg 4:20; Mi 1:13; Zech 13:7. G-K (§§ 47k, 69r, 110k, 144a, 145t) notes that a masculine verb is sometimes used in place of an expected feminine, although this phenomenon is often found after a single feminine verb or a series of feminine verbs. W. L. Holladay notes the same phenomenon in Jer 3:5; cf. *Jeremiah 1. A Commentary on the Book of the Prophet Jeremiah Chapters 1-25*, Hermeneia, Philadelphia: Fortress Press, 1986, 116. (His proposed emendation of Jer 13:27 also presupposes this as an element of Hebrew style; cf. *ibid.*, 417.)

destruction or annihilation.[112] As "evil ... in its strongest form, ... an infringement upon the whole which is peace,"[113] *šbr* is more than debilitating, for it threatens existence itself.[114] Worse still, this shattering is *'nwš*, without healing.

The parallel term *mkh* means 'blow' together with its resultant injury, thus encompassing both cause and effect, though in this poem, the context focuses on the effect or result.[115] And this too is without healing: *nḥlh*.

The twofold use of emphatic construction in these opening words is another means to focus attention on the content. The extremity of the situation is accented by the emphatic first position of the predicate adjectives *'nwš* and *nḥlh*.[116]

Similarly, in such a context where economy of phrase is important, the problematic *lamedh* of *lšbrk* might best be construed as an emphatic *lamedh*.[117] If the predicate adjective is given priority of position, the emphatic *lamedh* serves to point up the importance of the subject-noun as well.

There are no wasted words, no lengthy descriptions, but a terse statement paraphrased immediately by another just as dense and tightly constructed. By the use of emphatic *lamedh*, emphatic word order, verbal economy, synonymous parallelism and assonance, attention is focused immediately on this opening statement in all its negativity.

The second line (30:13) carries along the negative tone set by the opening words, for it opens and closes with the negative particle *'yn*. It does not negate *šlwm*, the state of peace or well-being (as did 30:5), but negates *dn-dynk*, an expression taken from juridical rather than from medical terminology which otherwise dominates this stanza.

---

[112] Cf. J. Muilenburg, "Terminology of Adversity in Jeremiah" in H. T. Frank and W. L. Reed, eds., *Translating and Understanding the Old Testament*, Fs. H. May, New York: Abingdon Press, 1970, 46; and G. Bertram, "*suntribō*," *TDNT* VII, 920. In Jer 48:3,5; 50:22; 51:54; Is 51:19; 59:7, etc., it is used to express the destruction of a people under the power of an enemy.

[113] J. Pedersen, *Israel* I-II, 313.

[114] This is seen clearly in Jer 6:14 and 8:11 which oppose *šlwm* to *šbr*.

[115] Cf. G. Fohrer, "Twofold Aspects of Hebrew Words" in P. Ackroyd and B. Lindars, eds., *Words and Meanings*, Fs. D. W. Thomas, Cambridge: Cambridge University Press, 1968, 103; *HAL (AT)*, s.v. "*mkh*."

[116] T. Muraoka, *Emphatic Words*, 15.

[117] Cf. G-K § 143e; F. Nötscher, "Zum emphatischen Lamed" *VT* 3 (1953) 372-80; Bright, 279; Thompson, 559; Carroll, 580. Among those who take a different view of the subject are: Volz, 281, n.m, who construes the 'unlikely' *lamedh* as an abbreviation for Israel; Rudolph, 190, who emends the text to read *lk šbrk*; and M. Dahood, "Ugaritic-Hebrew Parallel Pairs" in L. Fisher, ed., *Ras Shamra Parallels. The Texts from Ugarit and the Hebrew Bible* Vol. II, AnOr 50, Rome: Biblical Institute Press, 1975, 33, who views this as a dative, a "*l* of agency" and translates it "weakened by your fracture." (Elsewhere, M. Dahood does note the use of an emphatic *lamedh*. Cf. *ibid.*, *Psalms* III, 101-150, AB 17A, Garden City: Doubleday and Company, Inc., 1970, 406.)

Since it is outside the realm of medical imagery, most scholars treat *dn-dynk* as a gloss. Some remove it[118] while others emend the consonantal text.[119] A third group retains the consonantal text but emends the Masoretic accents, reading the verse as three rather than two lines: *'yn-dn dynk / lmzwr rp'wt / t'lh 'yn lk*,[120] despite the presence of the major disjunctive accent, *atnaḥ*, with *lmzwr*. Clearly, the general tendency is to smooth out what is seen to be a logical problem.[121] Yet it is precisely at those points where a 'mathematical' logic is lacking that one must look for a 'poetic' logic and a deeper meaning.[122]

The MT (and the LXX) makes deep poetic sense as it stands, including its accents. *'yn-dn dynk lmzwr* is meaningful not despite the mixed metaphor but, on the contrary, because of it. It is part of the originality and the beauty of poetry that two images, foreign to each other at first glance, can come together to enlarge and enrich the meaning. Furthermore, as oxymoron, the contradictory nature of the images is valuable in its ability to jar consciousness.[123]

Although *dyn* most often includes the idea of justice or that which is owed to or deserved by an individual, there are several instances in which it includes the notion of compassion or salvation (Ps 54:3; 135:14; Dt 32:36; Gn 30:6). While the legal aspects of *dn dnyk* cannot be denied, the expression might well be understood to mean 'There is no one to show you compassion regarding your wounds' or, accepting the sense rejected by Thompson, 'No one pleads the case for your healing.'[124] The legal aspect, however, ought not to be too lightly dismissed, for a 'wound' (especially *mkh*) was often considered a judgment of Yhwh on the sinfulness of the people.[125] Thus what would be needed for healing would be a positive rather than a negative judgment, a reversal of the original decision to punish/wound.

---

118 Volz, 281, n.o; Bright, 271; Weiser, 260; Thompson, 558, n. 1; J. Muilenburg, "The Terminology of Adversity," 47; N. Lohfink, "Der junge Jeremia," 354, n. 17.

119 Rudolph, 190, reads *rkkym* "Linderung" (cf. Is 1:6) for this expression which he considers almost completely out of context.

120 Carroll, 580, proposes this division because: "MT is either a failure to understand the metaphor, or a variant."

121 Y. Avishur, "Pairs of Synonymous Words in the Construct State (and in Appositional Hendiadys) in Biblical Hebrew" *Semitics* 2 (1971) 70, n. 222, is one of the very few who accept the MT reading (as appositional hendiadys), but his translation of this line contradicts his explanation.

122 Cf. C. Brooks, *The Well Wrought Urn*, 9.

123 Cf. above, p. 38.

124 Thompson, 558, n. 1.

125 G. von Rad, *Old Testament Theology* I, 275; L. Köhler, *Der hebräische Mensch*, Tübingen: J. C. B. Mohr (Paul Siebeck), 1953, 41-42; J. Hempel, "Heilung als Symbol und Wirklichkeit im biblischen Schrifttum" *Nachrichten der Akademie der Wissenschaften im Göttingen* 3 (1958) 280-81. The connection also appears in Lev 26:21; Dt 28:21,59,61. A parallel occurs in several Assyrian prayers which use the term *dini din* in conjunction with the healing of disease as shown in L. W. King, *Babylonian Magic and Sorcery being "The Prayers of the Lifting of the Hand"*, London: Luzac and Co., 1896, 12:59-60; 50:11,17-18. Cf. Condamin, 217-18.

The prepositional phrase which modifies *'yn-dn dynk*, *lmzwr*, need not be repointed to include the definite article, for the indefinite form is simply "indeterminateness for the sake of amplification."[126] The very use of *mzwr* is a kind of amplification in itself, since it expands the imagery of woundedness to make it yet more vivid. First called *šbr*, which is destructive yet not always visually perceptible, the wound becomes *mkh* which as 'blow' or 'plague' is readily visible in its consequences, and finally *mzwr* which as 'ulcer' or 'running sore'[127] is open, visually repulsive and possibly malodorous.

The repetition of *'yn* at the opening and closing of 30:13 is yet another indication of the hopelessness conveyed. The negation is absolute.[128] One device after another, both syntactic form and lexeme, focus on the extremity of the situation.

Unlike Jer 8:22, where healing is connected with medical science (balm, physician), healing here depends on an interior, spiritual activity. Thus in the present context, *dn dynk* serves to emphasize the spiritual component of both the situation and its resolution, for all healing and sickness ultimately depend on Yhwh, whose forgiveness is the first step in recovery.[129]

Since the poem is not depicting actual physical malady but using the physical to express a spiritual or moral debility, *rp'wt t'lh 'yn lk*[130] is semantically parallel to *'yn-dn dynk lmzwr*. Both speak of healing on a spiritual level (one using juridical, the other medical, language), but a healing denied to the people.

Implicit in 30:13 is the fact that Yhwh has left Israel to her own devices,[131] an experience which 30:14a makes explicit in its description of

---

[126] G-K § 125c.

[127] The proposed translations include 'ulcer, boil' (*HAL [AT]*), "*mzwr*"); 'festering wound' (P. Wernberg-Møller, "A Note on *zwr* 'to Stink'" *VT* 4 [1954] 325); 'running sore' (M. Dahood, "Philological Notes on Jer 18:14-15" *ZAW* 74 [1962] 208); 'plaies purulentes' (P. Humbert, "Maladie et médecine dans l'Ancien Testament" *RevHPhRel* 44 [1964] 4).

[128] W. Brueggemann, "The 'Uncared For' Now Cared For (Jer 30:12-17): A Methodological Consideration" *JBL* 104 (1985) 420.

[129] Cf. A. Oepke "*iaomai*," *TDNT* III, 200-03; H. W. Wolff, *Anthropology of the Old Testament*, trans. from the German by M. Kohl, London: SCM Press, Ltd; Philadelphia: Fortress Press, 1974, 147-48; K. Seybold and U. B. Mueller, *Sickness and Healing*, trans. from the German by D. W. Scott, Biblical Encounter Series, Nashville: Abingdon Press, 1981, 86-96. Cf. also Ps 32:5b; 107:20; Ex 15:26; Is 33:24.

[130] There is no need to emend the text by suppressing *rp'wt* as a gloss as suggested by Rudolph, 190. The language is consistent and could be construed 'remedy/medicine of healing' (cf. BDB and Jer 46:11). In fact the MT results in a well-balanced line with remarkably balanced assonance between 30:13a and 30:13b:

ê, ā / î, ē / ᵉ, ā, ô // ᵉ, u, ô / ᵉ, ā, ā / ê, ā .

[131] Although the name 'Israel' is masculine, a nation is considered as feminine (cf. Joüon § 134g and G-K § 122i). Thus in this context, a feminine pronoun is acceptable. An example of this usage can be found in H. H. Rowley, *Worship in Ancient Israel. Its Form and Meaning*, London: SPCK, 1967, 56.

Israel as forsaken, without friends or lovers. All who were attached to her by *'hb* have put her out of their minds, an unusual image for the OT. More common is the image of Israel as a harlot pursuing her lovers (*m'hbym*)[132] who are usually foreign nations or their gods. The uniqueness of Jer 30:14 lies in the fact that not Israel but her lovers (*m'hbym*) take the initiative in the relationship.[133] Elsewhere it is Israel who seeks her lovers, who plays the harlot by pursuing them, not vice versa. This expression appears to be a *hapax*.

Most scholars understand *m'hbym* to refer to Judah's political allies, who are only fair-weather friends.[134] No textual element imposes the interpretation of 'foreign nations' on *m'hbyk*, but neither is such an understanding precluded. In itself, *'hb* encompasses a relationship which is deeply personal and all-consuming, one which includes not only an inner disposition but also conscious deeds on behalf of the beloved.[135] Based on this, *m'hbyk* might best be understood in its metaphoric significance, as a reference to those with whom there was a sense of belonging and caring, a sense of community; those or the one toward whom the whole of life was directed,[136] and not merely 'allies.'

Therefore even if these 'lovers' were her political allies,[137] the term *'hb* accents the all-encompassing nature of the relationship. As *m'hbyk* their entire lives and being ought to have been directed toward Israel, a fact indicated by the pronomial adjective 'your' (*-k* here is repeated 3 times in succession). Her 'lovers' have forgotten her (*škḥwk*); they no longer give their attention to her for they no longer seek her (*l' ydršw*). Those on whom she counted have abandoned her. She is completely alone.

---

[132] Of the 16 occurrences of the *piel* part. of *'hb*, 13 refer to Israel's initiative; in one (Ez 23:22) it is not incompatible with the basic sense and one (Zech 13:6) uses it to mean simply 'friends'.

[133] Only in Ps 38:12 and 88:19 does one see *'hb* (*qal* part., m.s.) distancing himself. But in these instances the expression is *'hb wr'*, with emphasis on a relationship of friendship. In no other case is a participle of *'hb* found as the subject of *drš* or any similar verb (one having the same semantic content).

[134] Giesebrecht, 163; Volz, 286; Condamin, 218; Bright, 279; Thompson, 559; W. Brueggemann, "The 'Uncared For' Now Cared For," 421; and E. Jenni, "*'hb*," *THAT* I, 72. G. Wallis, "*'hb*," *TWAT* I, 123, understands this as "Israel goes after lovers"! S. Böhmer, *Heimkehr*, 63, differentiates three possible meanings for *m'hbyk*: leaders of the nation, foreign gods, foreign allies, and says that it is not clear which is the referent of the term in 30:14.

[135] G. Wallis, "*'hb*," *TWAT* I, 110-14.

[136] J. Pedersen, *Israel* I-II, 309: "Love is not a more or less superficial sentiment. It is identical with peace itself, with the unity of wills. To 'speak peace' with one another and to 'speak love' are two manners of expressing the maintenance of the common covenant; it is practiced by those who 'know' each other, because knowing indicates a thorough, mutual feeling."

[137] J.A. Thompson, "Israel's 'Lovers'" *VT* 27 (1977) 480-81.

The repetition of /k/–/ḥ/ (6 times) and /š/ (2 times) in 30:14a recalls the alliteration of distress-salvation noted in Poem I (30:5,10b), where the predominance of the sibilant echoed salvation, the predominance of the palatal/guttural evoked distress.[138] From this viewpoint, the repetition of the second person pronoun (*-k*) accents the distress while at the same time linking it closely with the people addressed in this poem.

30:12-14a simply states the facts. It presents a negative situation in essentially impersonal language ('It is so...'). With 30:14b Yhwh enters the discussion in the first person singular. The importance of his presence is indicated by an emphatic *ky*[139] and by a pivot pattern which connects *hkytyk* to both *mkt 'wyb* and *mwsr 'kzry*. This same pivot pattern also marks a climax,[140] after which the focus moves from sickness to guilt. The balance of the line draws attention to the verbal action, for the verb is framed by two objects (*mkt 'wyb* and *mwsr 'kzry*). Both have the same initial consonant for the object-noun, /m/, and its attribute, /'/, and both have the same grammatical construction: noun in construct followed by an adjectival genitive.

The use of the *hiphil* (*hkytyk*) also foregrounds Yhwh's activity; he acts to *cause* a specific result. In this case the action is presented as threatening to his people, a threat already developed in 30:12-14a under the rubric of *mkh* (introduced in 30:12). Now, the source of this *mkh* is seen to be none other than Yhwh for in 30:14b *nkh* is predicated of him both verbally (*hkytyk*) and nominally (*mkt*), as the result of his action.

Yet it is not merely the deed of *mkh* which is the source of distress but the fact that it is *mkt 'wyb*.[141] The negativity of this image is overwhelming since in Jeremiah the 'enemy' is the one who seeks to destroy the life of the people.[142]

Although the second object (*mwsr*) seems to attenuate the threatened destruction, the modifying noun (*'kzry*) reinforces the extremity of Yhwh's action. While *mwsr* means 'chastisement' or 'correction,' and usually in the sense of education, here the attribution of cruelty (*'kzry*)[143] accents Yhwh's attitude of enmity toward the people. He is responsible not only for *mwsr* but for *mwsr 'kzry*,[144] which is not simply the

---

[138] The same phenomenon is also present in the first line of this poem with /š/ repeated twice and /ḥ/-/k/ four times.

[139] G-K §§ 148d, 159ee. Also, J. Muilenburg, "The Linguistic and Rhetorical Usages of the Particle *ky* in the Old Testament" *HUCA* 32 (1961) 135-60.

[140] W. G. E. Watson, *Classical Hebrew Poetry*, 214-19.

[141] J. Hempel, "Heilung als Symbol und Wirklichkeit," 272, n. 3.

[142] Cf., e.g., Jer 15:9; 19:7; 20:4; 44:30. Elsewhere in the MT Yhwh is explicitly called *'wyb* only in Is 63:10 and Lam 2:5, and in both instances it is because he acts in a way contrary to the people's welfare.

[143] This is based on retaining the MT with *mswr* in the construct state and construing the genitive in an adjectival sense, cf. G-K § 128p.

[144] Bright, 271; Rudolph, 190; Thompson, 558, n. 2, all revocalize *mwsr* to be the absolute rather than the construct form. Carroll, 580, notes the possibility but chooses to follow the MT.

correction expressed at the end of Poem I but rather the chastisement of a 'cruel one.' Yhwh's position is even more striking when one realizes that the incurable wound which he inflicted on the people was considered a treaty curse.[145] The one who had blessed them now 'curses' them.

This characterization of Yhwh as the enemy (*'wyb*) and the cruel one (*'kzry*) appears to be an ironic statement, repeating if not actually quoting what the people thought and how *they* saw their suffering.[146] The irony of the attribution appears in the following line, where the ultimate source of suffering is not the 'enemy' nor the 'cruel one' but rather the people themselves. The reason for the approaching end, for the terminal illness, is none other than their own sinfulness: *'l rb 'wnk 'ṣmw ḥṭ'tyk*.[147] Although the sins and offenses of the people are not specified, the words *'wn* and *ḥṭ't* suggest actions which include the notion of failure, of irregular or 'crooked' action and of infringement upon a psychic totality.[148]

The first stanza comes to a close with a rhetorical question (30:15)[149] which recalls the opening sound-of-distress image of Poem I (*mh-tz'q 'l-šbrk*, 30:5-7) by repeating two words of 30:12a: *šbrk* and *'nwš*. The final line then reiterates the reason for this suffering. With the repetition of 30:14b (*'l rb ... ḥṭ'tyk*) the poem insists upon the guilt of the people and their responsibility for what has befallen them. Yhwh is the one who brings about their distress, but he does so *because* (*'l*) of the greatness of their sin.

The first stanza, framed by the key words *'nwš* and *šbrk* which express its principal theme,[150] repeats the terms *mkt*, *'wnk*, *ḥṭ'tyk*, indicating the importance of repetition in this text.[151] Thus there is good reason for maintaining the MT with its double *'l-rb ... ḥṭ'tyk*,[152] since repetition of a word or phrase is often used in the OT to "center the thought" and to "give continuity."[153] The double use of this statement reiterates the responsibility of the people and achieves a sense of closure.

---

[145] D. Hillers, *Treaty Curses*, 64-66.

[146] S. H. Blank, "Irony by Way of Attribution" *Semitics* 1 (1970) 3-6, notes how, in prophetic literature, an ironic statement is placed in the mouth of one other than the prophet and done without any explicit mention of this.

[147] This self-inflicted distress is noted by Rudolph, 191.

[148] Sin is first a breach of relationship and then comes to mean the consequences of such a breach, with its concomitant need for atonement or punishment. Cf. K. Koch, "*ḥṭ'*," *TWAT* II, 860-61; J. Pedersen, *Israel* I-II, 415.

[149] W. Brueggemann, "Jeremiah's Use of Rhetorical Questions," 358-74, shows the importance of double and triple rhetorical questions in Jeremiah. The single question as found here (30:16) is also to be noted, although Brueggemann does not deal with it.

[150] Cf. W. G. E. Watson, *Classical Hebrew Poetry*, 287-88.

[151] E. Zurro, *Procedimientos iterativos en la poesía ugarítica y hebrea*, BibOr 43, Rome: Biblical Institute Press, 1987, effectively demonstrates the importance of repetition in Hebrew poetry.

[152] Volz, 281; Bright, 271; Rudolph, 190, eliminate this line because it repeats 30:14b.

[153] J. Muilenburg, "A Study in Hebrew Rhetoric: Repetition and Style," 99.

The futility of the people's cry (*tz'q*, 30:15a) is accented, for they are responsible for their own plight.

As the only clause not standing in parallelism with a contiguous member (although it is parallel in meaning to 30:14b), the final statement (*'šyty 'lh lk*) is emphatic.[154] It insists on the fact that Yhwh's punitive action was a response to the people's sin. The salvation promised in the prose conclusion and in Poem I has disappeared from sight.

3.4.2 Stanza 2 — *Promise of Healing* (30:16-17)

The second stanza moves from the hopelessness and distress portrayed in 30:12-15 to a sense of hope: Israel's destroyers and enemies will suffer the same fate they caused Israel to endure; her 'wound-er' will reverse his deed and heal them.

Since the punishment of her enemies is not a logical consequence of Israel's suffering, *lkn*, with its usual meaning of 'therefore,' appears to be out of place as the introductory conjunction of 30:16.[155] Despite this difficulty, *lkn* can be maintained, but with an adversative sense[156] such as Rudolph and Thompson arrive at through text emendation.[157]

It is possible that *lkn* was purposely chosen to serve as an adversative conjunction in 30:16 precisely because it evokes 'therefore.' If the actions against Israel's enemies were seen as Yhwh's response to the cry from the people (30:15), then 'therefore' would fit well. Thus, although *lkn* in 30:16 does not actually denote, it could well connote 'therefore,' implying that Yhwh does not let prayers go unheard and unanswered.

Yhwh's action for his people is expressed indirectly in the first three clauses of 30:16 and becomes explicit only in the fourth. Their oppressors will be destroyed, will suffer the same fate they have imposed on the Israelites. Three times the subject appears in participial form with Israel the object of the participial action. Each time the finite verb presents the subject as suffering the same fate as that for which they were responsible: *kl-'klyk y'klw ... whyw š'syk lmšsh wkl-bzzyk 'tn lbz* (30:16).[158]

---

[154] Cf. A. Berlin, *Dynamics of Biblical Parallelism*, 134-35; R. Alter, *Art of Biblical Poetry*, 7.

[155] For this reason, Volz, 275, considers it a gloss. Bright, 271, calls it 'logically unsuitable.' Carroll, 581, maintains *lkn*, 'therefore,' but sees no logical connection between 30:15 and 30:16 which would justify this conjunction.

[156] Cf. Zorell, s.v. "*kn*": "vel sic, tamen, nihilominus"; E. König, *Wörterbuch*, s.v. "*kn*," I, 3, b: Konzessive konj., ... "trotzdem uä." I. Eitan, "Hebrew and Semitic Particles" (con.) Comparative Studies in Semitic Philology, *AJSL* 45 (1928-29) 200, notes that it is best seen as adversative in several OT texts, based on comparative etymology of a similar Arabic particle.

[157] Rudolph, 192, emends *lkn* to *wkl*, proposing *lk* as dittography, with an adversative *waw*, 'aber.' Thompson, 558, translates it 'yet.'

[158] This correspondence between the deed and its punishment is clearly presented by the repetition of the root *'kl* in two different conjugations. Cf. E. Zurro, *Procedimientos iterativos*, 252.

The second clause alone (30:16a), *wkl-ṣryk klm bšby ylkw*, contains no root repetition, but exhibits a verbal connection (*šby*) with Poem I, stanza 2 (30:10) where Yhwh presents himself as the one who will save the people's progeny *m'rṣ šbym*. The same 'captivity' (*šby*) suffered by Israel in 30:10 (Poem I) will be experienced by her oppressors (*ṣryk*) according to 30:16 (Poem II). Thus 30:16aβ, though different in structure from the other three clauses, which all repeat the root/deed as falling on the heads of those who perpetrated it, does make the same kind of statement but with a more distant link. The fate to be suffered by Israel's enemies refers back to a deed stated not in the subject of this clause but to one found in 30:10.

Although the content of these lines is a promised end to Israel's suffering, both the mode of expression and repetition draw attention to a situation of destruction. The participles which describe the enemy in negative terms all have 2 f.s. pronominal object suffixes referring to Israel (*kl-'klyk, wkl-ṣryk, š'syk, wkl-bzzyk*) which highlights the extremity of her present situation. The overwhelming repetition of /k/ and /l/ in 30:16a serves to focus on two concepts: totality (*kl*) and destruction (*'kl*): *lkn kl-'klyk y'klw wkl-ṣryk klm bšby ylkw*.[159] There is continued use of these two consonants throughout the stanza but with consistently reduced occurrence as if to move away from total destruction on the level of sound as well as imagery.[160] But a sense of destruction always remains if only in the background.

With such emphasis on totality and destruction, the presence of *klm* in 30:16b makes textual sense as the intensification of the idea. There is no need to delete it as "sachl. und metr. überflüssig"[161] or to emend it to follow the LXX,[162] for the MT as it stands has real poetic value. It reiterates both the totality and the destruction which underlie these lines.

Finally, 30:17 makes Yhwh's positive deed for the people explicit. Introduced by an emphatic *ky*, 30:17a predicates two actions of Yhwh. Unlike his two actions of 30:12-15 (*hkytyk, 'śyty*, the latter recalling *''śh* of 30:11) which were negative and directed against his people, his two interventions in 30:17 are favorable: *''lh, 'rp'k*. The vocabulary of

159 Cf. W.G.E. Watson, *Classical Hebrew Poetry*, 228; L. Alonso Schökel, *Estudios*, 115.

160 30:16a — /k/ - 9x; /l/ - 7x
30:16b — /k/ - 3x; /l/ - 3x
30:17a — /k/ - 6x; /l/ - 2x
30:17b — /k/ - 2x; /l/ - 2x

161 Giesebrecht, 163; so also Bright, 271. Carroll, 580-81, retains the MT.

162 Cf. Cornill, 327; Volz, 275. Similarly, M. Dahood, "The Word Pair *'ākal // kālāh* in Jer 30:16" *VT* 27 (1977) 482, proposes repointing to follow the LXX based on the word pair found also in Ugaritic, an argument developed in *ibid.*, "Ugaritic-Hebrew Parallel Pairs" in L. Fischer, ed., *Ras Shamra Parallels*, II, 34, basing the argument on play on roots containing consonants /k/, /l/, plus a weak radical: *hlk – klh – 'kl.*

wounding has been reversed to become the vocabulary of healing. The people no longer experience *mkh* (30:12 and 30:14) but instead receive healing 'of their wounds' (*mmkwtyk*, 30:17). Despite the earlier emphasis on the incurableness of the wound, now the reverse is assured with forcefulness by the use of an emphatic *ky*. Earlier the people were told that their sin was the cause of their suffering; now they are assured of unconditional healing.

The healing which was denied in 30:13 (*t'lh 'yn lk*) is affirmed in 30:17 (*'lh 'rkh lk*); the wound which was incurable in 30:12 (*nḥlh mktk*) is promised healing in 30:17 (*mmkwtyk 'rp'k*); and both promises are stamped by Yhwh's assurance: *n'm yhwh*.[163] Although Yhwh is the one who strikes with wounds or disease, he is also the one who heals.[164] By repetition of vocabulary and roots as well as by the reversal of imagery, this line unifies the two stanzas.

Just as 30:14b,15b give the reason for the wound (*'l rb*...) so also 30:17b provides the reason for the healing (*ky*...). Yhwh's change of heart is linked not to the cry of the people but to the derogatory remarks of her enemy, the taunt that she is forsaken (*ndḥh ... ṣywn hy' drš 'yn lh*, 30:17b). Like 30:6, the closing line of this poem (30:17) has Yhwh quoting others, but unlike 30:6, here Yhwh cites the words of the enemy rather than those of the people themselves. What is predicated of Sion is really an accusation against Yhwh himself since he is the cause of her being *ndḥh*.[165] Thus this taunt of *ndḥh* and *drš 'yn lh* (forsaken, with none who seek her) touches the ears and heart of Yhwh who responds in defense of his people.[166]

The last line (30:17b) finally names the referent of *-k*. By repeating the *drš* of 30:14 in 30:17,[167] the poem identifies the one addressed in the 2 f.s. throughout stanza 1 as Sion. The words of her detractors in 30:17 (*drš 'yn lh*) are the same as those of Yhwh in 30:14a (*'wtk l' ydršw*).

Even if *ṣywn* is a later addition,[168] the MT reading still makes sense.

---

[163] G. Rinaldi, "Alcuni Termini," 272-73.

[164] P. Humbert, "Maladie et médecine," 8,16; J. Muilenburg, "Terminology of Adversity," 61.

[165] Of 18 occurrences in Jeremiah (13 *hiphil*, 5 *niphal*), *ndḥh* has Yhwh as explicit source of the action 15 times. Of the 3 remaining instances, 2 imply that it is the foreign nations who are the cause but Yhwh is still the ultimate or implicit source of the action (Jer 40:12; 43:5).

[166] W. Brueggemann, "A Shape for Old Testament Theology II: Embrace of Pain" *CBQ* 47 (1985) 413; *ibid.*, "The 'Uncared For' Now Cared For," 419-28.

[167] W. Brueggemann, "The 'Uncared For' Now Cared For," 422, notes the importance of this repetition for the poem.

[168] *ṣywn* in this verse is often seen as redactional, based to a great extent on the presupposition that this poem was originally addressed to the Northern Kingdom, and thus could not include references to Judah or Jerusalem. Another indication of possible redactional activity is the LXX rendering 'she is your quarry' (*thereuma humōn* [G]; *ṣydnw*

Since the addressee of the poem has not been identified in any way, nor has any person or place been named, it is fitting that there be some type of identification (which is found in every other poem or prose section of this cycle). This identification is given in 30:17 by the presence of *ṣywn*,[169] who is addressed in her distress and sinfulness. Since, however, only people can sin or suffer, and since the appellation of 'banished' or 'expelled' is given her, the referent of *ṣywn* must be people rather than place or city. The one addressed is indeed *ṣywn*, not as a geographical locus or the dwelling place of Yhwh, but rather as a symbol of the community.[170]

"Sion" is alone. First Yhwh noted this fact (30:14) and then it was used as a taunt against her (30:17). Finally Yhwh responds to the taunt of the nations. He no longer inflicts wounds but now heals them.

The major image of this poem, woundedness turned to healing, is sustained formally by alliteration and repeated parallelism. This image clearly constitutes a metaphor for sinfulness and forgiveness, for relationship broken and reestablished. As a metaphor it makes its point vividly and repeats it without accusation. It is certainly not because the people are deserving that they have experienced Yhwh's healing, but because he chose to favor them with this caring deed.[171] Yhwh shows his care but does so only when the people are reduced to their lowest.

This second poem has a single well-developed image as its focal point, yet it does not fail to surprise the careful reader. After tracing the lines of the bleakest picture imaginable, it presents a glimmer of light. Healing is possible and is coming. Perhaps the most startling aspect, however, is the reason for Yhwh's 'change of heart,' for his turning from punishment to healing – Israel is now totally alone, with no one to support her. Even her enemies repudiate her. But Yhwh will not let her suffer derision at the hands of others. He can punish her, but other nations must respect her. Yhwh shows that he truly cares for his people.

[H]). Cf. Cornill, 327; Weiser, 273, n. 1; Rudolph, 192; S. Böhmer, *Heimkehr*, 63 and n. 63; H. L. Ellison, "The Prophecy of Jeremiah" (con.) *EvQ* 36 (1964) 94-95.

[169] Bright, 271, and Thompson, 558, both retain the MT. Carroll, 582, justifies the MT's *ṣywn* as an explanation of the feminine forms used throughout the poem.

[170] S.v. "Zion," *EncJud* 16, 1030 (ed. staff); G. Fohrer, *et al.*, "*Sion*," *TDNT* VII, 308-09; W. Beyerlin, "*Wir Sind wie Träumende.*" *Studien zur 126. Psalm*, SBS 89, Stuttgart: Verlag Katholisches Bibelwerk GmbH, 1978, 44-45.

[171] The two *ky* statements with which this poem closes make this emphatic. Cf. J. Muilenburg, "The Particle *ky*," 142, 148-49.

3.5 POEM III — 30:18-31:1

18 *kh* *’mr yhwh*

hnny — *šb šbwt*

’hly yʿqwb

wmškntyw

’rḥm

wnbnth

ʿyr

w’rmwn

ʿl-tlh

ʿl-mšpṭw

yšb

19 *wyṣ’ mhm*

twdh

wqwl mśḥqym

whrbtym

wl’ ymʿṭw

whkbdtym

wl’ yṣʿrw

20 *whyw*

bnyw kqdm

wʿdtw lpny

tkwn

wpqdty ʿl kl-lḥṣyw

21 *whyh*

’dyrw mmnw

wmšlw mqrbw

yṣ’

whqrbtyw

wngš ’ly

ky *my hw’-zh ʿrb ’t-lbw*

lgšt ’ly *n’m yhwh*

22 { *whyytm ly lʿm*
{ *w’nky ’hyh lkm l’lhym*

- -

23 *hnh*

sʿrt yhwh

ḥmh *yṣ’h*

sʿr mtgwrr

ʿl r’š ršʿym yḥwl

24 *l’ yšwb ḥrwn ’p-yhwh*

ʿd-ʿśtw

wʿd-hqymw mzmwt lbw

b’ḥryt hymym ttbwnnw bh

1 *bʿt hhy’* *n’m yhwh*

{ *’hyh l’lhym lkl mšpḥwt yśr’l*
{ *whmh yhyw -ly lʿm*

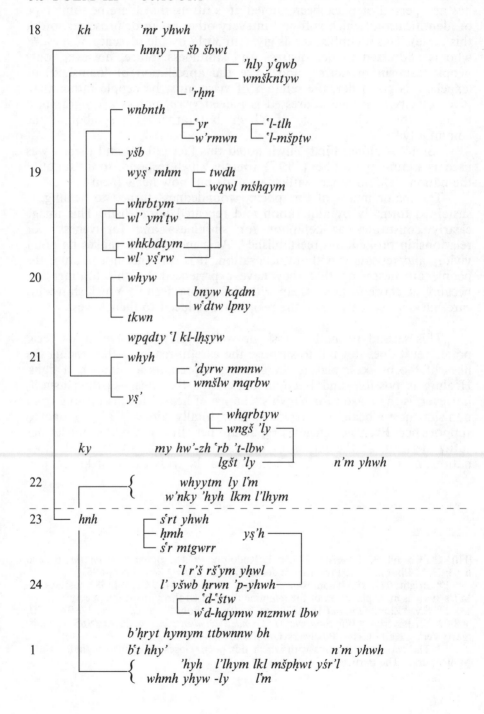

3.5 *Poem III* — YHWH'S CARING AND CHASTISING PRESENCE (30:18-31:1)

Poem III can be divided into two stanzas: 30:18-22 and 30:23-31:1. Each opens with the demonstrative *hnh* and each closes with the covenant formula. Although the image of Yhwh presented in the first stanza is positive while that of the second stanza is negative, there are general thematic links between the two. The negativity of stanza 2 is hinted at toward the end of stanza 1 while the overriding positive imagery of stanza 1 is alluded to in the final line of stanza 2.

3.5.1 Stanza 1 — *Yhwh's Caring Presence* (30:18-22)

The first stanza of the third poem (30:18-22)[172] opens with a self-presentation of Yhwh (*hnny*)[173] in the role first mentioned in the prose introduction, that of one who acts to restore fortunes: *šwb šbwt*.[174] The opening line is structured, as are most of the following lines, by semantic parallelism and syntactic chiasm:

hnny - šb šbwt (a) ╲╱ (b) *ʾhly yʿqwb*
wmškntyw (b′) ╱╲ (a′) *ʾrḥm*

This strict semantic parallelism in chiastic syntactical form serves to focus on the deeds of *šwb šbwt* and *rḥm*. Attention is drawn to Yhwh's deeds not only by the conjunction of these two literary devices but also by *hnny* which, with its demonstrative value, introduces the line. Metonymy[175] also adds to the total effect since, in referring to things rather than persons,[176] it moves attention away from the recipients of Yhwh's deed to focus it on the action itself.

---

[172] S. Böhmer, *Heimkehr*, 63, and N. Lohfink, "Der junge Jeremia," 360, both consider 30:18-21 to be a unit and authentic.

[173] This is placed not in an unspecified future moment but in the present or immediate future, by the introductory *hnny*. Cf. above, p. 42.

[174] Cf. above, p. 30 (and notes) for discussion of the meaning of *šwb šbwt* and the choice of 'restore fortunes' as its translation.

[175] J. T. Shipley, *Dictionary of World Literary Terms, ad loc.*

[176] The deed of Yhwh is directed toward *ʾhly yʿqwb*, a term which is used metonymically to designate the progeny of Jacob. Though it speaks of 'tent' dwellers, the reference is not so much to tents *per se* as to the people's dwelling places even after settlement, even in a city. (Cf. P. A. H. de Boer, *Fatherhood and Motherhood in Israelite and Judean Piety*, Leiden: E. J. Brill, 1974, 8.) Similarly, *miškn* refers to human dwelling places in general, be they the temporary shelters of nomads or permanent city dwellings (D. Kellermann, "*miškn*," *TWAT* V, 64-65).

The first verb (*šwb šbwt*) with its range of meanings is applicable to groups, nations, or cities, while the second (*rḥm*) bears a more personal and even emotional tone[177]: compassion can be shown only to a living being and true compassion only to a human being. Thus the deeply personal aspect of what follows is already hinted at in the second poetic line.

Despite the presence of this personal aspect, the impersonal dominates the opening lines through repeated reference to things, beginning with restoration of a city (*wnbnth ʿyr ʿl-tlh*, 30:18), which will be built on its mound of ruins, i.e., rebuilt.[178] From mention of the general *ʿyr* (city), the poem moves to a specific edifice within it: *ʾrmwn* (citadel, palace).[179] The fortification will rest *ʿl-mšpṭw*, a simple statement that uses a polysemantic pun playing on the fact that the city's future is based on both a physical and a spiritual reality. *mšpṭ* of 30:18 is normally translated 'in its former or proper place,'[180] though in general the meaning of *mšpṭ* is 'that which one can expect, that to which one has the right,' including right relationship (between human beings or objects). This more usual meaning is extended to include the sense given by most exegetes to *mšpṭ* in this verse.[181]

Since *ʿl-mšpṭw* is parallel with *ʿl-tlh*, the translation 'in its former place' responds to the demands of parallelism; yet since the text is poetry rather than prose, the careful reader is led to consider a possible wordplay. This phrase may well have two levels of meaning, the one very obvious and fitting, the other, less obvious but more suggestive and having a more profound significance.[182]

The basic meaning of *ʿl* is 'upon,' including a more specific sense 'on the foundation of' as used in the expression *ʿl-tlh*.[183] If one accepts the possibility of parallelism of meaning as well as parallelism of form for the prepositional phrase, *ʾrmwn ʿl-mšpṭw yšb* would read "And the citadel will rest on the foundation of *mšpṭw*."

---

[177] H. J. Stoebe, "*rḥm*," *THAT* II, 761-68; P. Trible, "The Journey of a Metaphor" in *God and the Rhetoric of Sexuality*. Overtures to Biblical Theology, Philadelphia: Fortress Press, 1978, 31-59.

[178] The implication is that it has been totally destroyed if all that is left is *tlh*. This indicates the exilic provenance of this text.

[179] Such motion from a larger to a smaller geographical space is a typical device of biblical poetic parallelism. Cf. R. Alter, *Art of Biblical Poetry*, 19.

[180] Cornill, 328; Giesebrecht, 163; Volz, 275; Condamin, 219; Weiser, 261; Rudolph, 192; Carroll, 583. Thompson, 561, n. 4, says "MT reads 'according to its rights.' The sense is not clear." BDB, s.v. "*mšpṭ*" (*špṭ*), understands it to mean 'plan' here as well as in Ex 26:30 and 1 Kg 6:38.

[181] G. Liedke, "*špṭ*," *THAT* II, 1005; B. Johnson, "*mšpṭ*," *TWAT* V, 105-06. Cf. also Ex 26:30; 1 Kg 6:38.

[182] Cf. W. G. E. Watson, *Classical Hebrew Poetry*, 241-46.

[183] G-K § 119aa-dd.

The primary meaning of *mšpṭ* is 'right and duty,' or, to expand the idea, "all the daily actions maintaining ... the true relation between beings"[184] including the "capacity to make a basic and actual distinction between good and evil."[185] If *mšpṭ* retains its primary sense of rectitude or right action, this line would read: "And the citadel will rest on the foundation of its rectitude." Since the citadel is the means of protection and safety for the people of the city, the line would mean that the hope and guarantee of a safe existence lies in the rectitude or the right conduct of Jacob / Israel.[186] The people's protection is to be found not in a physical bulwark but in their life lived in conformity to their obligations to Yhwh, yet another indication of the 'personal' quality of what Yhwh expects.

After the promise of rebuilding, 30:19 offers a vision of its results, for Yhwh's deeds evoke the people's response. The voices which were raised in cries of distress in Poems I and II (*qwl ḥrdh*, 30:5, and *mh-tzʿq ʾl-šbrk*, 30:15) are now lifted up in joy and merry-making (*twdh wqwl mśḥqym*, 30:19), a possibility only when there is hope and promise for the future.

twdh expresses praise and thanks to Yhwh, be it in word or in deed, a way of recognizing his sovereignty and saving action.[187] The parallelism moves from the particular (*twdh*), praise of Yhwh, to a more general notion (*qwl mśḥqym*), the sound or voice of those who are making music with instruments or by song.[188] Thus the praise of Yhwh is linked to a joy which permeates the whole of the people's existence and not merely the cultic expression of this praise.

The following line (30:19b) describes the people as recipients of Yhwh's effective action, by the use of two *hiphil* verbs (*whrbtym ... whkbdtym*). The centrality of Yhwh and his deeds is reiterated by the literary figure of litotes which makes a positive statement by negating its opposite.[189] In this case, 'they,' the people, are the subject of the negative verbs (*wlʾ ymʿṭw ... wlʾ yṣʿrw*), while Yhwh is the subject of the positive verbs (*hrbh* and *hkbd*). Thus 'he will make them many and they will not be few.'

---

[184] J. Pedersen, *Israel* I-II, 350. B. Johnson, "*mšpṭ*," *TWAT* V, 95-96, distinguishes the several meanings, disagreeing with the attempts to derive them from a common idea, the opposite stance from, e.g., J. van der Ploeg, "Studies in Hebrew Law" *CBQ* 12 (1950) 248-50.

[185] V. Herntrich & Büschel, F., "*krinō*," *TDNT* III, 924-28.

[186] Cf. Jer 22:13.

[187] C. Westermann, "*ydh*," *THAT* I, 675; G. Mayer, "*ydh*," *TWAT* III, 462; D. Bach, "Rites et paroles dans l'Ancien Testament. Nouveaux éléments apportés par l'étude de *Todah*" *VT* 28 (1978) 10-19.

[188] BDB, s.v. "*śḥq*."

[189] J. T. Shipley, *Dictionary of World Literary Terms*, s.v. "litotes." *Pace* G. B. Caird, *The Language and Imagery of the Bible*, London: Duckworth, 1980, 134.

Furthermore, two unusual expressions draw attention to these lines. Both *kbd* (*hi.*), used in the sense of 'cause to be honored,' and the verb *ṣʿr* are each found only three times in the MT.[190]

Everything works together to focus on the blessing of Yhwh. *rbh* with its meaning of 'become many, become great' recalls the patriarchal promises of progeny made to Abraham and to Jacob / Israel.[191] *kbd* accents not so much the blessing itself but its resultant honor — they will not be insignificant (*ṣʿr*). It is not that the people will be set above others, but that their position within society will be recognized.[192]

The importance of these lines is signaled not only by the vocabulary, literary devices and their central position in the stanza[193] but also by their literary structure. While the surrounding statements use semantic parallelism together with syntactic chiasm, this statement alone displays both syntactic and semantic parallelism:

whrbtym *wl' ymʿṭw*
whkbdtym *wl' yṣʿrw.*

The remarkable parallelism (every statement with a contiguous one) which opens this stanza continues in the next line: *whyw bnyw kqdm* // *wʿdtw lpny tkwn* (30:20). This is the first clear reference to the past (*kqdm*) and implies that the former status of the people was one of greatness. 30:20 is also the first time in Poem III that the people are mentioned in their relationship to Yhwh: *wʿdtw lpny tkwn*.

Although the *ʿdh* of 30:20 is before Yhwh (*lpny*), it does not necessarily have a specific cultic context,[194] for the term *ʿdh* denotes community assembled for cultic *or* for political purposes.[195] Thus the expression alludes to their unity rather than their multiplicity, to the fact that they form a single body, firmly established (*tkwn*) in relationship to

---

190 BDB, *ad loc.* and Mandelkern.

191 Cf. Gn 13:16; 28:14; Dt 30:5 and also Dt 7:7-8 where the people were chosen by Yhwh not because they were many, for in fact they were few. His choice is based on his love and from this they grow in numbers. H.-J. Zobel, "*mʿṭ*," *TWAT* IV, 1033-34.

192 C. Westermann, "*kbd*," *THAT* I, 798. In human society, this often means recognition by another, according to P. Stenmans, "*kbd*," *TWAT* IV, 19-21, although he interprets the use in 30:19 to mean "zahlreich und reich, d.h. glücklich."

193 Cf. schema, p. 58.

194 So, Bright, 280; Thompson, 562. S. Böhmer, *Heimkehr*, 64, sees the hand of P here. Rudolph, 193, limits the group to a political assembly, while Weiser, 273, and Carroll, 583, consider it a sacred congregation.

195 R. Gordis, "Democratic Origins in Ancient Israel — the Biblical *ʿedah*" in S. Lieberman, ed., *Alexander Marx Jubilee Volume*, New York: The Jewish Theological Assembly of America, 1950, 380-84, considers it a people's assembly. Cf. also, Levy and J. Milgrom, "*ʿdh*," *TWAT* V, 1087-88.

Yhwh rather than in relationship to other nations or some other reality.[196] While the previous line spoke of the respect given by other nations or other persons (*hkbd*), in this line Israel stands united before Yhwh (*ʿdh lpny*) with some stability (*tkwn*).

The statement which follows (*wpqdty ʿl kl-lḥṣyw*, 30:20) appears unconnected to its immediate context. It is the only line not in parallel construction with another line and the only one which makes reference not to the people but to their oppressors. Although it repeats no word or root from the previous poems, it is linked with them in recalling Yhwh's promise to destroy the enemies of the people, a theme developed at greater length in Poems I (30:11) and II (30:16). The fact that Yhwh will 'punish all their oppressors' assures the people that power rests not in the hands of their enemies but in the hands of their God. Since it predicates a negative deed of Yhwh, it sets the stage within Poem III for the way he is presented in the second stanza which portrays the destructive potential of his presence.

Gradually, the promise becomes more particularized: the focal point of the promise is no longer the rather amorphous *'hly-yʿqwb*, *mšknt* or *ʿyr* (30:18), nor the group of individuals expressed by *bnyw* or *ʿdh* (30:20), but now the leaders *'dyrw ... wmšlw* (30:21). The glorious or noble one[197] will not be chosen from among foreigners but *mmnw*[198] ('from him'), i.e., from 'Jacob' and his progeny. The next line (*wmšlw mqrbw yṣ'*) makes the image still more specific by referring to the 'noble one' as *mšl*, a person of authority and lordship, whose rank is close to that of a *mlk*.[199] He goes out from their midst (*mqrbw yṣ'*) as one who is in some sense set apart from the people, and yet still belongs and is intimately connected with their reality (*mqrbw*).

The outward motion is paralleled by another, an inward one, and the two are linked by means of a 'turn,' a wordplay in which the root is repeated but given a different nuance.[200] The leader moves from intimacy with the people (*mqrbw*) to intimacy with Yhwh (*hqrbtyw*) and the use of the *hiphil* (*hqrbtyw*, 30:21) makes it clear that this latter action is Yhwh's doing.

---

196 BDB, s.v. "*kwn*," *ni.*: "be firm, be established, be fixed."

197 *'dyr* is a prince, one who has not only power and might but one who is noble, glorious, without any particular reference to his social position. Cf. E. Jenni, "*'dyr*," *THAT* I, 39; and G. W. Ahlström, "*'dyr*," *TWAT* I, 79.

198 Rudolph, 192, proposes the emendation of *'dyrw mmnw* to *'dyr mhm* on the basis that it is "identisch mit dem Folgenden." Hebrew poetry, however, is known for its use of repetition, which is seldom pure synonymity, for language by its very nature tends to introduce "small wedges of difference between closely akin terms." (R. Alter, *The Art of Biblical Poetry*, 10).

199 H. Gross, "*mšl*" II, *TWAT* V, 74.

200 W. G. E. Watson, *Classical Hebrew Poetry*, 239.

Such double motion reflects and recalls the earlier statements which spoke of the people being given respect by the human community (30:19) and then being established in relationship to Yhwh (30:20):

hkbdtym (30:19)	—	*wʿdtw lpny tkwn*	(30:20)
mqrbw yṣʾ	—	*whqrbtyw*	(30:21)

Referring both to the people and to their leader, the text considers the relationship first on the human then on the human-divine plane.

Yhwh will draw this leader close to himself with the result that the leader will draw near: *wngš ʾly*. The leader's approach in response to Yhwh's action emphasizes that Yhwh's deed requires the reciprocity of human cooperation.[201]

Most major commentators understand *ngš* to refer to the leader or king in a priestly role.[202] Volz alone denies him such a priestly function and prefers to connect *ngš* to a religio-social reality much like that of *bn* in 2 Sm 7:14 or the attitude of Josiah who was present before Yhwh to conclude a covenant in the name of the people (2 Kg 23:3).[203]

Suddenly, in 31:21b, the poem virtually stops its inexorable forward motion which had been developing with every succeeding line. The *ky*, which is both an explanatory and an emphatic particle ("For/Indeed, just who is the one who...?"), plus the clustering of interrogative and demonstrative pronouns[204] together halt the flow of the poem and focus on the impossibility of the stated situation. Could one indeed find an individual who would risk his life (*ʿrb ʾt-lbw*)[205] to draw near to

---

[201] In 30:19 the voice of joy and praise implies a response to Yhwh's deeds, though not one which is directed specifically toward him. It is rather an expression of life renewed.

[202] Condamin, 220; Bright, 280; S. Böhmer, *Heimkehr*, 65; Rudolph, 193; Thompson, 562; Carroll, 583, though Carroll considers this personage to be a leader who is a cultic figure *rather* than a king.

[203] Cf. Volz, 287. Despite the fact that many understand *ngš* and *qrb* in a cultic sense (which is the case for P), the verbs of themselves do not have this aspect as an essential part of their content. Moses in his role of intercessor draws near to Yhwh (*ngš* Ex 20:21; 24:2) much as the people draw near to him to receive his message (Ex 34:32); yet Moses' role is not specifically priestly or cultic.

[204] These three pronouns are found together only two other times in the MT: Ps 24:10 and Est 7:5. In Ps 24:10 it is a rhetorical question which expresses a sense of awe, of wonder, of majesty. Est 7:5 shows utter incredulity at the previous statement. Cf. G-K § 136c concerning this as emphatic. Volz, 275, speaks of the heightening of the intensive particles.

[205] For *lb* as life, cf. Condamin, 220, and H.W. Wolff, *Anthropology of the Old Testament*, 54.

Yhwh?[206] Although the perfect verb: "Who is the one who has...?" suggests that there was no one in the past, it also implies that there will be no one in the future.

Yet here the threat is centered not in actual contact but rather in the fact that any human person would dare take the initiative in such a relationship, for if Yhwh does so (*whqrbtyw wngš 'ly*), it does not appear to carry the same danger. The repetition of *ngš 'ly* contrasts these two statements,[207] highlighting the initiator of the action, since the action remains the same.

The *ky* statement is foregrounded[208] not only by the emphatic particle and the almost prosaic presentation but also by the fact that it begins differently from every other line of this stanza. This is the only line (except for the opening one) which does not begin with alliterative repetition of *waw*. This together with the introductory *ky* and the concluding *n'm yhwh*[209] draw attention to the line and thus to the impossibility of the action *'rb 't-lbw lgšt 'ly* (30:21).

Thus the text finally focuses on the activity of Yhwh as intrinsic not only to the restoration of fortunes but also to the restoration of relationship. This has already been hinted at by the subjects of the verbs in this stanza: of the thirteen verbs, six have Yhwh as subject; three have a personal subject other than Yhwh; and four are either passive, impersonal or simply predication of fact. The final rhetorical question, which halts the ongoing development and expresses incredulity[210] at the possibility or the thought of a human person approaching Yhwh, accents the essential importance of Yhwh's deed. Stanza 1 draws to a close by emphasizing the distance between an individual (even an important one) and Yhwh, a distance unbridgeable by any human action yet bridgeable by the action and initiative of Yhwh alone.

The 'covenant formula'[211] of 30:22 expresses the relationship which will flow from Yhwh's deed. 30:22 reiterates the initiative on Yhwh's

---

[206] It had long been believed that nearness to Yhwh (physical nearness) was dangerous to life. The threat to existence itself was well-known and well-developed (cf. e.g., Ex 19:12; 24:2; 33:20; Num 8:19; Jdg 6:22).

[207] Cf. J. Muilenburg, "A Study in Hebrew Rhetoric," 99.

[208] W. G. E. Watson, *Classical Hebrew Poetry*, 265, n. 52.

[209] This is the sole appearance of *n'm yhwh* in this stanza. A formulaic expression, it calls attention to itself and to the immediately surrounding statements as word of God.

[210] As a rhetorical question it is an emphatic negation. Cf. W. G. E. Watson, *Classical Hebrew Poetry*, 341.

[211] This expression is used to signify that means of defining the relationship between Yhwh and his people as seen in Dt 26:16-19 and other OT texts (cf. K. Baltzer, *The Covenant Formulary in the Old Testament. Jewish and Early Christian Writings*, trans. from German by D. E. Green, Philadelphia: Fortress Press, 1971, 37 and n. 90). Despite the recent discussion concerning the correctness of attributing the term 'covenant' to Israel's

part, which was the focus of what precedes, not only by the position of the subject pronoun *'nky* but by its very presence.[212] The change from third person address in 30:18-21 to second person address in 30:22[213] is not uncommon[214] and here serves to stress the relational quality of Yhwh's actions. The statement itself sums up the goal of the promises.[215] Thus stanza 1 ends on a note that admits reciprocity but accents Yhwh's primacy in relationship.

This stanza moves from the people presented metonymically by reference first, to their dwelling places (*'hly y'qwb, mškntyw, 'yr, 'rmwn*), then to their existence as a collectivity (*bnyw, 'dtw*) and finally to their incorporation in the person of a single individual, their leader (*'dyrw, mšlw*). They are presented with increasing specificity,[216] in ever more personal terms, and thus in a way which expresses more and more the possibility of relationship.

A series of parallelisms, both semantic and syntactic, structures the stanza to move toward an ever more relational situation. Ideas are both contrasted and equated with seeming redundancy which, in fact, is often polysemy.[217] In a way that constantly sustains interest, stanza 1 moves from Yhwh (*hnny*, 30:18) to Yhwh (*'nky*, 30:22) whose action draws the people gradually into a closer and closer contact with himself.

---

formal relationship with Yhwh (cf. E. Kutsch, "Gottes Zuspruch und Anspruch. *b^e^rît* in der alttestamentlichen Theologie" in C. Brekelmans, ed., *Questions disputées d'Ancien Testament. Méthode et Théologie*, BEThL 33, Gembloux: Editions J. Duculot/Leuven: Leuven University Press, 1974, 71-90), still the fact of the relationship remains, as well as the fact that it was often expressed by the somewhat formulaic 'I/you will be your/our God; you/we will be my/your people' (17 times in the prophets, of which 14 are in Jer and Ez). Such a formula does reflect ANE legal formulae used in declarations of marriage and adoption (cf. P. Kalluveettil, *Declaration and Covenant. A Comprehensive Review of Covenant Formulae from the Old Testament and the Ancient Near East*, AnBib 88, Rome: Biblical Institute Press, 1982, 108-11). Thus for the sake of convenience the term 'covenant formula' will be retained to refer to this particular expression of the relationship.

[212] T. Muraoka, *Emphatic Words*, 51-56.

[213] Due to the shift in person, both Volz, 275, and Condamin, 220, consider 30:22 a gloss; Bright, 277, an editorial addition; and Carroll, 584, an indication of the secondary nature of the statement.

[214] Weiser, 274, and above, p. 41, n. 93.

[215] Thompson, 563; Carroll, 584.

[216] This is an important device of biblical poetic parallelism. Cf. R. Alter, *The Art of Biblical Poetry*, 20.

[217] Cf. A. Berlin, *Dynamics of Biblical Parallelism*, 99.

3.5.2 Stanza 2 — *Yhwh's Chastising Presence* (30:23-31:1)

The second stanza, like the first, begins with *hnh* and ends with the 'covenant formula.' However, unlike 30:19, the *hnh* in 30:23 introduces not Yhwh's saving deeds but his destructive or punitive power in the form of *s'rt yhwh*.[218] The 'storm-wind' is further specified in its destructive potential as *ḥmh*, the "wrath" of Yhwh. Despite the discussion concerning the presence of *ḥmh*,[219] for rhythm and parallelism *ḥmh* would be better retained:

s'rt yhwh	(3+2)	subject
ḥmh yṣ'h	(2+3)	noun in apposition + verb
s'r mtgwrr	(2+3)	subject repeated

mtgwrr poses a more trying text-critical problem than does *ḥmh* and is often emended to the more common *mtḥwll* following 23:19.[220] Although *mtgwrr* is not frequently found,[221] there is little data, apart from Jer 23:19, to support textual emendation.[222] Its two other occurrences (in 1 Kg and the Damascus Document) give evidence, which, while hardly conclusive, can justify retaining the MT and construing *mtgwrr* as 'abiding, remaining' with a sense of semipermanence, that of sojourning.[223] This would imply that the storm of the wrath of Yhwh abides for some, albeit a limited, time, leaving open the possibility of change.

---

[218] *s'rt* is a storm-wind or tempest (BDB, *ad loc.*), most often expressing Yhwh's deeds of power either positive or negative. (Zech 9:14-16 reflects this double-edged power.)

[219] *ḥmh* is omitted by many commentators including Weiser, 261; Rudolph, 192; Bright, 272. Carroll, 459, omits it because it turns one statement into two (a poetic device according to A. Berlin, *Dynamics of Biblical Parallelism*, 13, in her analysis of Jdg 5:25). G. R. Driver, "Hebrew Roots and Words," *Die Welt des Orients* 1 (1950) 413, finds *ḥmh* "grammatically difficult to explain," though in fact it seems to be a noun in apposition to *s'rt yhwh* specifying its content as negative rather than positive.

[220] Volz, 276, considers *mtgwrr* untranslatable; Bright, 272, its "meaning uncertain." Weiser, 262, and Rudolph, 192, follow BHK. E. Zurro, *Procedimientos iterativos*, 279, considers *mtḥwll* an example of root repetition using two different conjugations: *Hithpolel* and *Qal*, thus supporting BHK.

[221] It is attested twice in the MT, once in the Damascus Document.

[222] In fact, Kennicott (*ad loc.*) gives Ms evidence for *mtgwrr* (Cod. 4, 116, 249) over *mtḥwll* (Cod. 201).

[223] The word *mtgwrr* is attested in 1 Kg 17:20 where it is used by the prophet Elijah when, in a prayer to Yhwh, he refers to himself as *mtgwrr 'mh* ('the one sojourning with her,' i.e., with the widow). The text is not disputed and the context makes the meaning clear. Similarly in the Damascus Document, the expression *šny mtgwrrm* is interpreted as "the years of their sojourning" (L. Rost, *Die Damaskusschrift*. Kleine Texte für Vorlesungen und Übungen, 167, Berlin: Walter de Gruyter & Co., 1933, 12; S. Schechter, trans. and ed., *Documents of Jewish Sectaries I: Fragments of a Zadokite Work*, New York: KTAV Publishing House, 1970, 67.)

In contrast to the verb *mtgwrr*, which conveys a sense of stability and semipermanence, the verb *yḥwl* denotes frenetic activity which will catch up in itself the one so touched.[224]

This statement, appearing after the hope-filled, salvation-oriented first stanza, is so startling, that many authors consider these two verses (30:23-24) a secondary addition drawn from 23:19-20.[225] The scholars who accept its insertion here usually understand it as a threat against Jacob's oppressors, since the general context of this poem is salvation sayings.[226] Yet there is nothing here to indicate that *ršʿym* are the enemies or oppressors of Israel. In fact, in Jer 23:19-20 this same statement refers to evildoers among the Israelites (with specific reference to the prophets).[227]

An interpretation which considers *ršʿym* as referring to the people of Israel[228] (or part of them) would be consistent with the poetic cycle as it has been developing up to this point. In Poem I and Poem II both distress and salvation were directed to Israel:

Poem I:	Stanza 1 —	distress (death)
	Stanza 2 —	salvation
Poem II:	Stanza 1 —	distress (wounds)
	Stanza 2 —	salvation

In both instances, the intensity of the distress overrides the image of salvation. It is not surprising, then, to find a similar pattern here:

Poem III:	Stanza 1 —	salvation
	Stanza 2 —	possible distress (wrath for the wicked)

In its presentation of the saving power and saving deeds of Yhwh, Poem III emphasizes that his salvation, though gratuitous, is not unconditional. Evildoers will not receive his promises, but will rather

---

224 *ḥwl*: 'dance, writhe, whirl about' (BDB, *ad loc.*).

225 Volz, 276; Condamin, 221; Bright, 280; Weiser, 274; Rudolph, 193; S. Böhmer, *Heimkehr*, 65. Carroll, 585, is undecided as to which context is better.

226 Volz, 276, admits that the godless could be those internal or external enemies of Sion; Bright, 280, sees them as "nations of the world, generally." Rudolph, 193, who says that this is needed here since a general word of punishment against the gentiles is lacking, is supported by S. Böhmer, *Heimkehr*, 65; Thompson, 563; Carroll, 585.

227 Carroll, 585, notes that the 'wicked' of 23:19-20 are the prophets but here identifies the 'wicked' with the oppressors of Israel, because the context indicates such an interpretation.

228 So, Condamin, 221.

experience his punitive or destructive power in a deed which will endure: *l' yšwb ḥrwn 'p-yhwh* (30:24).[229]

Yhwh's anger, expressed in 30:24 as in 30:23 with imagery taken from nature (*ḥrwn* in 30:24, *s'r* in 30:23), has a single goal: to accomplish and establish his innermost intentions. For all the negativity inherent in this image, its end is positive: the certitude that Yhwh's designs will be accomplished. And this is made yet more emphatic by the repetition of *'d ... w'd*.

Then follows (30:24b), in a stage whisper, a kind of 'aside': 'You will understand this, if not yet, after it all occurs' (*b'ḥryt hymym*). *b'ḥryt hymym* can be understood simply as a temporal idiom referring to a future moment.[230] In this context where it points to a coming time when Yhwh's designs will be accomplished, it may be considered 'eschatological' in the broad sense of the term.[231] After the time of distress will come understanding, and with this undertaking (*b't hhy'*), the renewed relationship: *'hyh l'lhym lkl mšpḥwt yśr'l whmh yhyw-ly l'm* (31:1). The temporal reference *b't hhy'* links the covenant formula of 31:1 with the previous verse (30:24), indicating that the relationship conveyed by the statement is connected to a rational acceptance by the human partners. Once they reach understanding, the relationship can succeed.

The first clause of the closing 'covenant formula' is unusual[232] in the specificity it gives to the indirect object (*lkl mšpḥwt yśr'l*). Those who are in a covenant relationship with Yhwh are not some amorphous 'they' but a very specific *kl mšpḥwt yśr'l*. This inclusive statement embraces the whole of the people, both Northern and Southern Kingdoms.[233]

Although 31:1 is often considered to be the introduction to 31:1-22 rather than the conclusion to 30:18-31:1,[234] it is connected to the preceding statements (to a greater or lesser extent).[235]

---

[229] The deletion of *ḥrwn* because it is lacking in 23:20 is suggested by the apparatus of BHS, and also by Bright, 272; Weiser, 261; Rudolph, 192. Carroll, 585, maintains *ḥrwn* with an adjectival sense. In fact this same expression is found elsewhere in the MT, e.g., Num 25:4; 32:14.

[230] G.W. Buchanan, "Eschatology and the 'End of Days'" *JNES* 20 (1961) 190-91.

[231] Cf. above, p. 29, n. 32. Th. Vriezen, "Prophecy and Eschatology," 202, n. 2: In Jer 30:24 "The eschatological meaning cannot be denied."

[232] N. Lohfink, "Der junge Jeremia," 355, n. 21, considers it atypical.

[233] Rudolph, 193. J. Pedersen, *Israel* I-II, 48, says the *mšpḥh* indicates a group who have a common character, a common flesh and blood. Thus the whole people of Israel form a single *mšpḥh* vis-à-vis the other peoples of the earth.

[234] Bright, 280; Weiser, 274; Rudolph, 193; Carroll, 586-87.

[235] S. Böhmer, *Heimkehr*, 66, notes a loose temporal connection with the preceding as does Carroll, 587. Thompson, 563, considers the verse to have a 'double function': conclusion of 30:1-24 and introduction for 31:1-40.

Indeed, because the general structure of stanza 2 is parallel to that of stanza 1, 31:1 is a very fitting conclusion to the second stanza of Poem III:

St. 1:	*hnny*	(30:18)	—	'covenant formula' (30:22)
St. 2:	*hnh*	(30:23)	—	'covenant formula' (31:1)

It also forms a semantic inclusion with the opening line of the poem by a reference to the people identified in both instances with an ancestor:

30:18	*'hly y'qwb ... wmšknty w*
31:1	*mšpḥwt yśr'l*

Beyond this, the opening clause of the poem, 'I am restoring the fortunes of the tents of Jacob' (*hnny-šb šbwt 'hly y'qwb*, 30:18), finds its fulfillment in the final clause: 'They will be my people' (*whmh yhyw-ly l'm*, 31:1).

In sum, the whole of Poem III is structured with the use of parallelism, root-repetition and chiasm to focus on the importance of relationship with Yhwh, giving particular emphasis to the fact that he is the one who initiates this relationship and gives it gratuitously.

3.6 POEM IV — 31:2-6

2 *kh ’mr yhwh*

mṣ’ ḥn bmdbr *ʿm śrydy ḥrb*
hlwk lhrgyʿw *yśr’l*

3 *mrḥwq yhwh nr’h ly*

w’hbt ʿwlm
’hbtyk
ʿl-kn *mšktyk*
ḥsd

---

4 *ʿwd* *’bnk*
wnbnyt btwlt yśr’l

ʿwd *tʿdy tpyk*
wyṣ’t bmḥwl mśḥqym

5 *ʿwd* *tṭʿy krmym* *bhry šmrwn*

nṭʿw nṭʿym
wḥllw

6 *ky yš-ywm qr’w nṣrym* *bhr ’prym*

qwmw
wnʿlh
ṣywn
’l-yhwh ’lhynw

3.6 *Poem IV* — ONCE ...; AGAIN ... (31:2-6)

The fourth poem is the shortest of this cycle and, like the poems considered thus far, may be divided into two stanzas: 31:2-3 and 31:4-6. Stanza 1 (31:2-3) is delimited by its reference to the past and the inclusio formed by *ḥn* ... *ḥsd.* Stanza 2 (31:4-6), on the other hand, speaks of the future (though in relation to the past). Structured by a triple *ʿwd,* it concludes with an explanatory *ky* statement which expresses a motion toward Yhwh.

3.6.1 Stanza 1 — '*Once* ...' (31:2-3)

The introductory words, *mṣ' ḥn bmdbr* (31:2), point to the Exodus as the literary background of the stanza. Since it is predominantly in Ex that *mṣ' ḥn* is found with Yhwh as subject,[236] 31:2 is an implicit reference to Ex 33:1,12-17[237] or, in the terminology of Watson, is an 'inner biblical allusion.'[238] The acknowledgment of the Exodus allusion has two implications. First, it points to accepting the traditional understanding of *ḥn* as 'favor'[239] in this verse. Second, the Ex presentation qualifies *mṣ' ḥn* by *bʿyny,* indicating the importance of the giver, while Jer 31:2 does not qualify the expression and thus emphasizes the recipient.[240]

Since *mṣ' ḥn bmdbr* (31:2) directs attention to the Exodus, then this same context appears to be the literary referent of the other clauses and phrases of Jer 31:2b-3a as well. In this case *ʿm śrydy ḥrb* (31:2) would refer to those who escaped the threat of death under Pharaoh, which is presented as a threat of the sword in Ex 5:21; 15:9; 18:4.[241] This may also refer to a second, less obvious, threat of the sword which was part of the Exodus experience. After the incident of the golden calf those who were on Yhwh's side put on their swords and slew their neighbors and their brothers. In his conversation with Yhwh (Ex 33:12-16) Moses represented a people who had escaped both the sword of Pharaoh (Ex 18:4) and the sword of their fellow Israelites (Ex 32:25-29). The true people of Yhwh had twice survived the sword.

---

236 This expression is found 6 times in Ex, twice in Gn and once in 2 Sm.

237 Cf. A. Gelin, "Le sens du mot 'Israël' en Jer 30/31" in *Memorial J. Chaine*, Bibliothèque de la Faculté Catholique de Théologie de Lyon 5, Lyon: Facultés Catholiques, 1950, 167.

238 W. G. E. Watson, *Classical Hebrew Poetry*, 299-303.

239 *Pace* J. Reider, "Etymological Studies in Biblical Hebrew" *VT* 4 (1954) 277, who proposes interpreting it as 'a resting place.'

240 H. J. Stoebe, "*ḥnn*," *THAT* I, 591.

241 S. Böhmer, *Heimkehr*, 54. For an opposing opinion cf. Weiser, 275, who understands the 'sword' to be the destruction of war experienced by the exiles.

The Exodus allusion of *hlwk lhrgyʿw yśr'l* (31:2) is uncontested despite its grammatical ambiguity. Grammatically, the subject of *hlwk* (31:2b) could be either Israel or Yhwh.[242] In fact, the infinitive absolute which begins this colon could be linked with either the noun which precedes (*ʿm*) or the one which follows (*yśr'l* or *yhwh*). As an infinitive absolute, it can either continue the action of the preceding verb or replace a finite verb at the beginning of a section.[243] The infinitive absolute is here continued by an infinitive construct whose suffix can grammatically be either its object or its subject.[244] Since *yśr'l* is clearly in apposition to the pronominal suffix, the question becomes whether Israel is the subject or the object of *lhrgyʿw*. The presence of the *hiphil* form of the infinitive construct does not offer a solution to the problem, for the *hiphil* of *rgʿ* can mean 'cause oneself to rest' and thus 'Israel sought its rest,' or 'cause another to rest' and thus 'he gave rest to Israel.'[245]

The Exodus context would seem to favor the interpretation 'he (Yhwh) gave rest to Israel' since Ex 33:14 states clearly that Yhwh shows his favor (*mṣ' ḥn*) to Moses by 'going to give' him rest (*pny ylkw whnḥty lk*). Although Ex 33 uses *nwḥ* and Jer 31 *rgʿ*, the content of the terms is the same: Israel knows Yhwh's favor by his going with them to give them rest. This would indicate that, similarly, in Jer 31:2, it is Yhwh who gives rest to Israel though the subject of the verb appears only in the next clause, an instance of delayed identification.[246]

Despite this evidence, the inherent ambiguity or polysemy of the subject must be respected for the ambiguity itself hints at a reciprocity of action. Even if Yhwh is the one who takes the initiative and gives rest, the fact that Israel can also be the subject of *rgʿ* indicates that her role is also an active one.

For the exilic generation,[247] the Exodus reference is a metaphor for their own experience and gives insight into their own situation by

---

[242] Those who construe it to be Israel are in the majority: Volz, 282; Condamin, 220; Bright, 280; Rudolph, 192; Weiser, 261; S. Böhmer, *Heimkehr*, 53; Carroll, 586. L. Delekat, "Zum hebräischen Wörterbuch" *VT* 14 (1964) 60, notes the ambiguity. Aquila, Symmachus, Targum Jonathan understand the subject to be Yhwh.

[243] G-K § 113aa.

[244] G-K § 115.

[245] BDB, s.v. "*rgʿ*" II.

[246] W. G. E. Watson, *Classical Hebrew Poetry*, 336-38, considers this a device used to achieve suspense.

[247] Commentators are divided as to whether the reference is to the Exodus or the Exile. Among those who opt for the Exile are: Condamin, 221; Bright, 280; Rudolph, 193; S. Böhmer, *Heimkehr*, 53. Volz, 287; Thompson, 566, both choose to read an Exodus reference. Weiser, 275, understands this as a promise to those who have survived the 'sword' of war, i.e., to the exiles, but using as a backdrop the Exodus event.

explicitly mentioning another, alluding to the similarity in two dissimilars.[248]

Continuing with Exodus allusions, in 31:3 the text specifies the content of *mṣ' ḥn*. The 'favor' (*ḥn*) received was Yhwh's presence from afar: *hlwk lhrgy'w yśr'l mrḥwq yhwh nr'h ly* (31:2b-3a).

The meaning of *mrḥwq* as applied to Yhwh's appearance is somewhat problematic. Some interpret it to signify his 'appearance from afar' to those in Exile, those at a distance from Jerusalem and Sion where he dwelt.[249]

Although *rḥq*/*mrḥwq* is used most often to express distance between persons or lands, it is also found in several texts to describe the relationship between Yhwh and a human person (or the lack thereof).[250] In these latter instances it usually refers either to that awe which requires a healthy distance from Yhwh, for to approach him is dangerous to life,[251] or to that distance which means Yhwh's non-presence to a person, resulting in suffering, oppression by enemies, illness, and threat of death.[252] Yhwh at a distance means punishment, suffering, disaster, curse; his being near at hand, however, betokens salvation.

Within the larger context of the poetic cycle, *mrḥwq* (31:3) contrasts with *qrb* (30:21) of the previous poem. In 30:21 (Poem III) the leader is presented as one who will be near to (and therefore have access to the counsel of) Yhwh. Poem IV, however, presents Yhwh at a distance, establishing contact *mrḥwq* (31:3).

Since 23:19-24 uses similar imagery in a similar context, these lines may shed some light on the meaning of *mrḥwq* in 31:3. Jer 23:19-20 is addressed to the prophets and accuses them of not listening to the word of the Lord. This is followed in 23:23 by three rhetorical questions which discuss the relationship of Yhwh and the people, the first being whether Yhwh is *'lhy mqrb ... wl' 'lhy mrḥq*, an expression which in its context could well indicate the distinction between a saving God and a punishing one.[253]

---

[248] P. Wheelwright, *Metaphor and Reality*, Ch. 4: "Two Ways of Metaphor" and Ch. 5: "From Metaphor to Symbol." As he clearly states (p. 92), the metaphor becomes a symbol when it is considered capable of being used many times over (which is true of the Exodus).

[249] Thompson, 566, mentions this as a possibility yet prefers to interpret it as 'long ago' and thus as a reference to the Sinai theophany. Weiser, 276, similarly sees it as a theophanic presentation whose roots are in the Sinai tradition. Rudolph, 193, considers *mrḥwq* a reference to the situation of Exile. In his short study of precisely this problem, A. Feuillet, "Note sur la traduction de Jer xxxi, 3c" *VT* 12 (1962) 122, translates it as "... 'de loin', c'est à dire de Sion, et lui annonce qu'il va délivrer de l'exile ..."

[250] Cf. J. Kühlewein, "*rḥq*," *THAT* II, 769-71, re: theological use of the term.

[251] Cf., e.g., Ex 20:18,21 where the people remained at a distance while Yhwh appeared to Moses.

[252] Cf., e.g., Ps 22:12,20; 35:22; 38:22; 71:12, all of which are cries to Yhwh not to remain at a distance but to come near with his salvation.

[253] This is a very likely interpretation of Jer 23:23 according to Carroll, 467.

It is possible that the use of *mrḥwq* in 31:3 is, like that of 23:23, a reference to a punishing God, to a God who is no longer present to his people. For Yhwh to appear *mrḥwq*, then, could mean that even in his seeming absence, when Israel experienced distress (e.g., *bmdbr*), Yhwh was in fact present, though in a way not clearly seen or understood — i.e., in a hidden way. In the context of the whole poetic cycle such an interpretation would make sense, for it alludes to the distress or judgment already portrayed in Poems I, II, III.

The appearance is *ly* ('to him'). Although most commentators prefer to emend the text to read *lw*[254] (an understandable choice given the easy confusion between *yodh* and *waw* in Mss[255]), still Hebrew Ms evidence favors *ly*[256] which is widely attested in the MT with the sense 'to/for him,' i.e., *-y* as a 3 m.s. rather than a 1 s. pronominal suffix.[257]

The favor (*ḥn*) which was also an appearance (*nr'h ly*) becomes realized in *'hbh* and *ḥsd* (31:3). *'hbh*, unlike *ḥsd*, does not presuppose an existing relationship, even though, like *ḥsd*, *'hbh* does express itself in concrete actions for the beloved.[258] It is clear that the love expressed in *'hbh* precedes the established relationship of Yhwh with Israel, for it precedes his choice of her.[259] *'hbh* may be closely linked to *ḥsd*, but the two are not to be identified. If anything, *'hbh* appears to be the precondition for *ḥsd* since *'hbh* is a clearly gratuitous act which can be neither expected nor demanded, whereas *ḥsd* may be required on the basis of an established relationship.

---

[254] Condamin, 222; Bright, 273; Weiser, 261; Rudolph, 194; Thompson, 565; Carroll, 586-87. Volz, 276, and D. Barthélemy, *Critique textuelle* II, 683-84, however, opt to retain the MT and interpret the suffix of *ly* as 1 s.

[255] Cf. F. M. Cross, "The Development of the Jewish Scripts" in G. E. Wright, ed., *The Bible and the Ancient Near East*, Fs. W. F. Albright, Garden City, N. Y.: Doubleday and Co., Inc., 1961, 170. He notes confusion between *yodh* and *waw* especially in the Mss of the Hasmonian period.

[256] A. Sperber, ed., *The Prophets according to Codex Reuchlinianus*, Leiden: E. J. Brill, 1969, 234; and H. L. Strack, ed., *The Hebrew Bible. The Latter Prophets*, The Babylonian Codex of Petrograd, New York: KTAV Publishing House, Inc., 1971, 886. Kennicott shows no Ms evidence to the contrary.

[257] M. Dahood, *Psalms* III, 375-76, in "The Grammar of the Psalter" lists 51 examples of this. *Ibid.*, "Northwest Semitic Texts and Textual Criticism of the Hebrew Bible" in C. Brekelmans, ed., *Questions disputées d'Ancien Testament. Méthode et Théologie*, BEThL 33, Leuven: Leuven University Press, 1974, 16-17, upholds this interpretation of *-y* and notes fifteen other scholars who concur. Z. Zevit, "The Linguistic and Contextual Arguments in Support of a Hebrew 3 ms Suffix *-y*" *UF* 9 (1977) 315-28, questions Dahood's conclusion that *-y* was a common alternative to *-w* or *-yw* without, however, denying that the MT does have *-y* for 3 m.s. suffix in more than one instance.

[258] G. Wallis, "*'hb*," *TWAT* I, 115-16; H.-J. Zobel, "*ḥsd*," *TWAT* III, 56-58.

[259] Cf., e.g., Dt 4:37; 7:8; 10:15.

The poem, focusing attention on *'hbh* by *waw emphaticum*[260] and root-repetition,[261] stresses the free, gratuitous nature of Yhwh's relationship with Israel.

It is for this reason (*'l-kn*) that he has acted *mšktyk ḥsd.* This relatively clear expression has been the subject of debate concerning whether the pronominal suffix *-k* should be construed as a dative and *ḥsd* as direct object[262] or *ḥsd* as an adverb and the pronominal suffix *-k* as direct object.[263] The problem does not lie with accepting the pronominal suffix as a dative.[264] It is, rather, the near redundancy together with the explanatory *'l-kn* which leads one to question such an interpretation and thus indicates the need for a closer look at the content of *mšktyk ḥsd.* Although *mšk* could be construed as 'draw towards,'[265] this poem does not include such an aspect of the divine-human relationship. On the other hand, *mšktyk ḥsd* as 'extend *ḥsd* to' another, is in synonymous parallelism with *w'hbt 'wlm 'hbtyk*. But synonymity is not tautology.[266] Since parallelism constantly balances between redundancy and polysemy,[267] *ḥsd*, though like *'hbh*, is contrasted with it in this statement.

ḥsd, usually rendered 'loving kindness' or 'covenant love,' is certainly 'responsibility-in-relationship,'[268] since every act of *ḥsd* is a responsible act based on a personal (and often intimate) relationship. The presence of *ḥsd*, then, extends the relationship of 'love / loving kindness' to include reciprocity.

31:3, with its context of *'hbh*, addresses the people with a 2 f.s. pronoun suffix, a striking change from the immediately preceding 3 m.s. references. Besides setting the stage for 31:4 with its addressee *btwlt yśr'l*, the feminine pronoun also evokes a relationship which is one of unearned devotion and love, similar to the image of Israel portrayed in Hosea 2:16-25 and Ez 16:6-14. Israel's expected response to such an initiative of

---

260 The *waw* of *w'hbt* seems best construed as a *waw emphaticum*, since it is otherwise inexplicable. Cf., M. Pope, "'Pleonastic' *Waw* before Nouns in Ugaritic and Hebrew" *JAOS* 73 (1953) 98; P. Wernberg-Møller, "'Pleonastic' *Waw* in Classical Hebrew" *JSS* 3 (1958) 321-26; M. Dahood, *Psalms* III, "The Grammar of the Psalter," notes 43 uses in the psalms.

261 *'hb* is present in both nominal and verbal form.

262 M. Dahood, "Ugaritic Studies and the Bible" *Greg* 43 (1962) 67; Volz, 282; Weiser, 261; Rudolph, 194; K. D. Sakenfeld, *The Meaning of Ḥesed in the Hebrew Bible. A New Inquiry*, HSM 17, Missoula: Scholars Press, 1978, 194.

263 Bright, 280; Carroll, 587; A. Feuillet, "Note sur la traduction," 122.

264 This has long been accepted; cf. G-K § 117x; Joüon § 125b and n. 2. This understanding has been given support more recently by Dahood's Ugaritic research. Cf. M. Dahood, "Ugaritic Studies and the Bible," 67.

265 *HAL (AT), ad loc.*: "ziehen, hinziehen, lang bewahren."

266 *Pace* A. Feuillet, "Note sur la traduction," 122.

267 A. Berlin, *The Dynamics of Biblical Parallelism*, 98-99.

268 K. D. Sakenfeld, *The Meaning of Ḥesed*, 213.

Yhwh is alluded to by the use of *ḥsd* which recalls an ideal moment in her past when she did show him *ḥsd* and *'hbh bmdbr* (Jer 2:2).

Stanza 1 then moves from *ḥn*, which is without tie or claim[269] and which is focused in this instance on the recipient, to *'hbt 'wlm*, that gratuitous love which a superior extends to an inferior, and finally to *ḥsd* with its implied reciprocity. The ambiguity of subject in *hlwk lhrgy'w yśr'l* (31:2) similarly hints at reciprocity.

Root-repetition, parallelism, inner biblical allusion are used in these few lines to convey the message that Yhwh is present to his people even in their distress. And by balancing on the edge of redundancy, the poem also hints at reciprocity in relationship. Through metaphor it reassures the people that the experience they had of Yhwh's power in the Exodus is still valid and can give hope in their present circumstances.

3.6.2 Stanza 2 — "*Again* ..." (31:4-6)

Stanza 2 of Poem IV (31:4-6) has a more obvious poetic structure than does stanza 1. It is formed of three *'wd* statements (31:4-5) which hold out hope for the future but always in relationship to the past. And it concludes with an explanatory and emphatic *ky* statement (31:6), which foresees a day when the people will reciprocate Yhwh's deeds.

Each of the three *'wd* statements gives specific content to *'hbt 'wlm* and *ḥsd* of stanza 1 (31:3). Each is an act of God's love, and each is gratuitous. The three statements shift attention from the action of Yhwh for Israel (*'bnk*, 31:4) to Israel's own activity (*tṭ'y krmym*, 31:5); from a private, almost intimate act with enduring consequences (*'bnk*, 31:4) to one which is public but temporary in nature (*t'dy tpyk*, 31:4), and finally to a public action with lasting results (*tṭ'y krmym*, 31:5).

The repetition of *'wd* focuses and refocuses attention on the link between the past and the future, the reliving in the future of past experiences. The fact that this post-positive particle[270] is the first word of each statement adds still more emphasis to the continuity between past and future.

The first *'wd* statement, addressed to *btwlt yśr'l*, uses the metaphor *bnh* to describe Yhwh's action. It refers not to the construction of a physical dwelling place but to the 'building up' of those who will fill the house, i.e., the progeny.[271] When applied to a childless woman,[272] it refers to her being given children.

---

[269] W. F. Lofthouse, "Ḥen and Ḥesed in the Old Testament" *ZAW* 51 (1933) 30, 33.
[270] G-K § 142g.
[271] Cf., e.g., Dt 25:9; 1 Sm 2:35; 2 Sm 7:27; 1 Kg 11:38.
[272] In Gn 16:2 and 30:3 it is used to refer to Sarah and Rachel (respectively).

Thus if *btwlt yśr'l* is to be built (*bnh, niph.*) by Yhwh (31:4), the implication is that he will bless her with children, a theme already introduced in 30:19-20 (*whrbtym wl' ymʿṭw ... whyw bnyw kqdm*). Such a promise could be directed to the capital city[273] but is really made to the people as a whole. The promise is made to *btwlt yśr'l*, accenting the effective activity of Yhwh (the male) in such a deed. Both the root repetition and the *qal-niphal* sequence which expresses action-result serve to focus attention on the deed and its source (Yhwh).[274]

The second *ʿwd* statement expresses the joy the people will experience when such a deed will be accomplished. *tʿdy tpyk wyṣ't bmḥwl mśḥqym* (31:4b) recalls other instances in the OT when women went out with timbrels in dance,[275] celebrating victory over the enemy. In each case the external threat had been overcome by the power of Yhwh. Now, too, the same is promised. Israel sees a peaceful future which women will celebrate with a dance of joy.[276]

31:5, the third *ʿwd* statement, develops the idea of permanency, for *ʿwd tṭʿy krmym bhry šmrwn*. The root repetition in *nṭʿw nṭʿym wḥllw*, recalls the earlier *tṭʿy* and highlights the planting of vines with its resultant *wḥllw*.[277] The meaning of *ḥll* is 'to profane'[278] which, in this context, takes on the significance 'to enjoy the fruit.'

A look at Dt clarifies the meaning of *ḥllw*. Dt 20:6 (*nṭʿ krm wl' ḥllw*) and Dt 28:30 (*krm tṭʿ wl' tḥllnw*), together with Jer 31:5, are the only occurrences in the MT of *ḥll* meaning 'to enjoy the fruit.' Both the Targum Onkelos and Rashi's commentary[279] explain Dt 20:6 and 28:30

---

[273] "Capital de Israel," according to L. Alonso Schökel and J. L. Sicré Diaz, *Profetas* I, 555, 560, is a cipher for the people.

[274] M. Held, "The Action-Result (Factitive-Passive) Sequence of Identical Verbs in Biblical Hebrew and Ugaritic" *JBL* 84 (1965) 272-82.

[275] Jdg 11:34 (Jephthah's daughter); 1 Sm 18:6 (women who welcomed David); Ex 15:20f. (Miriam and the women going out in a dance of joy (*wbmḥlt*) with their timbrels (*btpym*) to celebrate their salvation from the Egyptians).

[276] W. O. E. Oesterley, *The Sacred Dance. A Study in Comparative Folklore*, Cambridge: The University Press, 1923, 159-63 and 173-74, does not include Jer 31 in this dance of victory. Cf. also J. Pedersen, *Israel* III-IV, 21. A. Caquot, "Les danses sacrées en Israël et à l'entour" in *Les danses sacrées*, Sources Orientales 6, Paris: Editions du Seuil, 1963, 125, places this dance in the context of an autumn festival.

[277] There is a variety of interpretations given this line. It is eliminated as a prosaic gloss by Volz, 282; Rudolph, 194; repointed following BHK/S by Cornill, 333; Bright, 281; Weiser, 262; kept according to the MT by Carroll, 586-87.

[278] *HAL (AT)*, s.v. "*ḥll*" I, *Pi.* 1. 'entweihen'; 2. 'in Gebrauch nehmen.' Thompson, 566, notes two possible interpretations: (a) put to secular use; (b) defile in the sense of Baʿal worship, as seen in Hos 2. Cf. Is 55:21-22 and Am 5:11 for a similar concept.

[279] I. Dragin, *Targum Onkelos to Deuteronomy. An English Translation of the Text with Analysis and Commentaries*, (New York): KTAV Publishing House, Inc., 1982, 192-93, 242; and M. Rosenbaum and A. M. Silberman, trans., *Pentateuch with Targum Onkelos, Haphtaroth and Rashi's Commentary. Deuteronomy*, New York: Hebrew Publishing Company, s.d., 102, 136.

to mean that the fruit of a vine was to remain uneaten until the fourth year. Then the owner would redeem his vine by either eating of its fruit in Jerusalem or paying a redemption fee for it. Once redeemed, the vine was considered 'profane(d),' that is, ready for common use (cf. Lev 19:23-25). Thus *ḥll* does mean 'to profane,' but in a positive sense. And since those who plant will certainly[280] enjoy the fruit of the vine, but only after they have made it 'profane' (only after four years), *ḥll* also indicates a certain stability or permanence in the land.

Although mention of *bhry šmrwn* may indicate that the original audience was the exiles from the Northern Kingdom, a wider poetic interpretation of the expression is also possible. Since the Israelites were a people at home only in the hill-country and to leave the hills would be to become strangers in a strange land,[281] the explicit mention of 'hills' emphasizes that the people were indeed in *their* land.

The final statement, introduced by *ky*, is an emphatic conclusion to what precedes. It announces a day when *qr'w nṣrym ... qwmw wn'lh ṣywn*. All are called to proceed toward Sion, toward Yhwh's dwelling place.

nṣrym, understood in its usual sense of 'watchers / watchmen,'[282] fits this context[283] because from their vantage point watchmen would be the first to espy and to announce the saving deeds of Yhwh — the land is now planted, the people are many and they live in peace and joy.

This is restoration indeed; this is indeed *šwb šbwt*. The people once again will have the opportunity to join in pilgrimage to Sion, the high point of life for an Israelite.[284]

The poem progresses from *bmdbr* (desert and Exodus) through *tṭ'y krmym* (settlement in the land) to *ṣywn* (not only presence in the land but presence with Yhwh). Addressed to an exilic audience, it re-presents a moment of their history (the Exodus, 31:2-3) and then considers the future, a future always interpreted in light of the past when the people were many (*'wd 'bnk*) and were victorious over their enemies (*'wd t'dy tpyk*) and thus were assured peace in the land (*'wd tṭ'y krmym*). With this vision in mind, the poem announces with certainty[285] a pilgrimage to

---

280 The *qatal* is used to express an assured future. Cf. G-K § 106.

281 D. Baly, *The Geography of the Bible*, New York, London: Harper and Row Publishers, 1974, 86-87.

282 *HAL (AT)*, *ad loc.*

283 C. Rabin, "*noṣerim*" *Textus* 5 (1966) 46-47, proposes translating this as 'joyous throng' which also makes sense in the context. N. Lohfink, "Der junge Jeremia," 356, n. 22, follows Rabin.

284 H. J. Kraus, *Worship in Israel. A Cultic History of the Old Testament*, trans. fr. German by G. Buswell, Oxford: Basil Blackwell, 1966, 209. For a discussion of the cult festival at Jerusalem cf. *ibid.*, 208-18.

285 *qr'w* is a *perfectum confidentiae*, cf. G-K § 106n.

Sion and thereby keeps alive in the hearts of the exiles the hope that this would be part of their future, too.

Thus the pattern which emerged in Poems I-III appears again here:

I:	distress = definitive destruction	— salvation promised then attenuated
II:	distress = lasting suffering	— salvation for the people = destruction of enemies
III:	salvation = numbers, leader, hope	— distress = wrath for the wicked
IV:	distress = time of hope/promise	— salvation = peace in the land

Poem I moves from definitive, life-threatening distress to a promise of salvation attenuated by an assurance of punishment. Poem II focuses first on the incurable wounds of the people, before it presents a promise of salvation, articulated not in a positive deed for the people but in destruction of their enemies. In a more positive vein, Poem III develops at length the blessings which Yhwh will bestow and moves slowly toward relationship with him; however, in the second stanza it assures them that his wrath will remain over the wicked. And now the same positive-negative tension is found in Poem IV, with the added nuance that the positive element becomes more specific and the negative more muted — a feature already encountered in Poems I-III. Poem IV opens with a reminder that Yhwh was always present, even in the people's past distress and then portrays a bright future by evoking a past joyful experience. Israel will again be at peace and will be able to go in pilgrimage to Sion.

3.7 POEM V — 31:7-14

7 *ky-kh 'mr yhwh*
rnw ly'qb śmḥh
wṣhlw br'š hgwym
hšmy'w
hllw
w'mrw *hwš' yhwh* *'t-'mk*
't š'ryt yśr'l

8 *hnny* *mby' 'wtm* *m'rṣ ṣpwn*
wqbṣtym *myrkty-'rṣ*
bm
'wr
wpsḥ
hrh
wyldt *yḥdw*
qhl gdwl
yšwbw hnh

9 *bbky* *yb'w*
wbtḥnwnym *'wbylm*
'wlykm *'l-nḥly mym*
bdrk yšr
l' ykšlw *bh*
ky - hyyty *lyśr'l l'b* *'m*
w'prym bkry hw' *(yhwh)* *śmḥ*

---

10 *šm'w dbr-yhwh gwym*
whgydw b'yym mmrḥq
w'mrw *mzrh yśr'l* *yqbṣnw*
wšmrw kr'h 'drw

11 *ky - pdh yhwh 't-y'qb*
wg'lw *myd ḥzq mmnw*

12 *wb'w*
wrnnw *bmrwm-ṣywn*
wnhrw *'l-ṭwb yhwh*
'l-dgn
w'l-tyrš
w'l-yṣhr
w'l-bny-ṣ'n wbqr
whyth npšm kgn-rwh
wl'-ywsypw ld'bh 'wd

13 *'z tśmḥ* *btwlh* *bmḥwl*
wbḥrym
wzqnym *yḥdw*
whpkty *'blm lśśwn*
wnḥmtym
wśmḥtym *mygwnm*

14 *wrwyty* *npš hkhnym dšn*
w'my *'t-ṭwby* *yśb'w*
n'm-yhwh

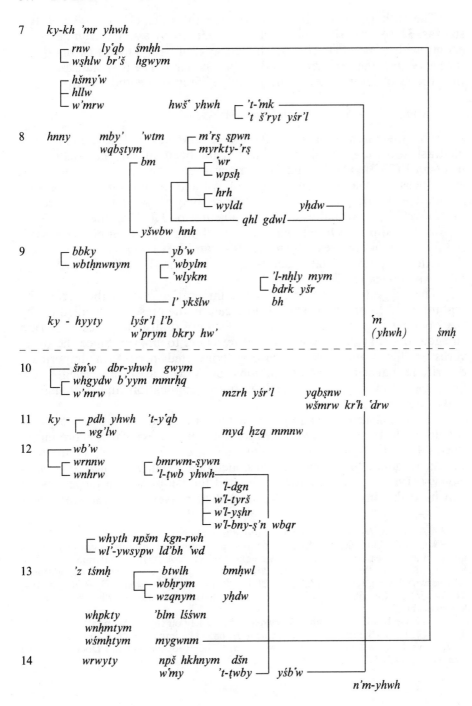

3.7 *Poem V* — YHWH'S GREAT ASSEMBLY (31:7-14)

The fifth poem of this cycle is, like the others, composed of two stanzas: 31:7-9 and 31:10-14. Each is introduced by a series of imperatives ending with *w'mrw* (31:7,10). Both stanzas deal with Yhwh's caring deeds for his people, their return to, and joy in, the land. The first stanza accents the process of return; the second portrays life in peace and security.

3.7.1 Stanza 1 — *Return from Afar* (31:7-9)

The first stanza opens with shouts and cries of joy, in striking contrast to the cries of distress heard at the beginning of the poetic cycle in Poem I (30:5). The five parallel imperatives are similar in content, yet each focuses on a different aspect of what is to be done.[285] The first imperative of 31:7 (*rnw ... śmḥh*) sets a tone of great joy; the second (*wṣhlw br'š hgwym*) makes clear the position of Jacob as the first of the nations; the third (*hšmy'w*) places responsibility on the people addressed; the fourth (*hllw*) praises Yhwh; the fifth and last (*w'mrw*) simply orders the action: "speak!" That which is to be announced follows immediately: *hwš' yhwh 't-'mk* (31:7).

The suggested emendation of the imperative *hwš'* to the perfect by repointing,[286] in order to express more clearly the present joy called for by the opening imperatives, is a *lectio facilior*. It also requires a second emendation, that of the consonantal text (*'mk* to *'mw*).[287] Since the other verbs in the stanza are all future (converted perfect or imperfect), describing particular salvific actions of Yhwh as future events, the presence of an imperative which is both supplication and acclamation makes textual sense.[288]

As supplication, the imperative indicates that all is not yet as it should be. In this way it continues the tone of distress which is present in Poems I-IV, though to an ever-diminishing degree. This cry is, in some way, a response to the call which concluded Poem IV: *wn'lh ... 'l-yhwh 'lhynw* (31:6). In Poem IV the cry invited the people's pilgrimage toward Yhwh; in this instance (Poem V, 31:7) their prayer is that he may come

---

[285] A. Berlin, *Dynamics of Biblical Parallelism*, 88-99.

[286] Cornill, 335; Giesebrecht, 167 (because as a liturgical formula, a cry of praise is not so much a petition as an announcement of joy); Volz, 276; Condamin, 221, 223; Weiser, 262, n. 1, "der Ausdruck *hôschi'a* ist der geprägte terminus für die göttliche Heilsverwirklichung (cf. Ps 118:25; Mt 21:9)"; S. Böhmer, *Heimkehr*, 67; Rudolph, 194; Thompson, 58; Carroll, 590. Bright, 273, admits that the imperative "while possible, fits less smoothly."

[287] This is based not on any Ms evidence but solely on the LXX and T.

[288] Cf. D. Barthélemy, *Critique textuelle* II, 685. The imperative is maintained by the NIV, *Nova Vulgata* (1986) and E. W. Heaton, "The Root *š'r* and the Doctrine of the Remnant" *JThSt* NS 3 (1952) 30.

toward them, that he recognize them as his people (*ʿmk*) and treat them as such.

The people (*ʿmk*) who seek salvation are *š'ryt yśr'l*, the small group who escaped destruction and who rely on Yhwh's presence and promises for the future.[289] The term itself alludes to the Exile and the fact that the population has been decimated, making of this imperative a cry of confidence in both the power of Yhwh and his faithfulness to his promise.[290] Therefore *š'ryt yśr'l* ought not to be considered a gloss[291] but seen in its importance as an explanation of *ʿmk*.

In response to the prayer for salvation, 31:8 presents the words of Yhwh: *hnny mby' 'wtm m'rṣ ṣpwn*. Poetically this line draws attention to itself by the repetition of the final consonant of each word as the first consonant of the following one:

mby'
'wtm
m'rṣ
ṣpwn

In a very effective manner this simple step-pattern, which requires a brief pause between the words, slows down the reader. Thus attention is focused on the content, on the present activity of Yhwh which effects return: *mby' 'wtm m'rṣ ṣpwn*.[292] *hnny mby' 'wtm* (31:8) specifies the content of *hwšʿ* found in the previous verse. Yhwh saves by bringing the people back, immediately repeated in strict semantic and near-syntactic parallelism: *wqbṣtym myrkty-'rṣ* (31:8aβ).

The first clause of 31:8 (*mby' 'wtm m'rṣ ṣpwn*) refers to the simple act of bringing from a single place, while the second (*wqbṣtym myrkty-'rṣ*) presupposes a people scattered over a wide area, a notion highlighted by *myrkty-'rṣ*. Assuming that the final redaction for this text was exilic, the referent could be those who had gone down to Egypt as well as those taken to Babylon. Or it could be hyperbole, serving to emphasize the greatness of Yhwh's salvific deeds.[293]

---

289 F. Dreyfus, "Reste d'Israël," *DBS* X, 415, 418, 420.

290 E. W. Heaton, "The Root *š'r*," 39.

291 *Pace* Cornill, 335; BHS.

292 The presence of *m'rṣ ṣpwn* alludes to the Exile as the context. Cf. S. Böhmer, *Heimkehr*, 67.

293 This is true even if the historical referent of the original poem was the people of the N. Kingdom taken to Assyria. Cf. Thompson, 569.

More surprising than the return or the gathering from far and wide is the group to be brought back:

bm		a
	ʿwr wpsḥ	b
	hrh wyldt	b′
yḥdw		a′

The devices of chiasmus (abb′a′),[294] gender-matched parallelism (m-m // f-f),[295] and merismus[296] are all brought together here with dramatic effect to express the totality as well as the extremes which are included in the *qhl gdwl* (31:8b). It is not the normal *qhl* composed of priests, leaders, warriors,[297] but one of weak individuals, both male and female. The males are *ʿwr wpsḥ*, those who are excluded from public worship (in the temple)[298] or those of priestly family excluded from service of the altar (Lev 21:18). They represent those whose access to Yhwh is limited. The females are *hrh wyldt* (31:8), women who are pregnant, in labor or have just given birth. Through gender-matched parallelism[299] an extraordinary future is announced: *qhl gdwl*.[300] The returnees include the weak and the unclean.[301] No one will be left behind.[302] The contrast between the males who cannot touch Yhwh (and thus bear the mark of death) and the females who are the sign of life and hope is astounding.[303] Both groups exhibit weakness and thus need to rely on Yhwh as well as on the assurance that it is he (and not they) who is responsible for the return. A great assembly will return *hnh*.[304]

---

294 A. Ceresko, "The Function of Chiasmus in Hebrew Poetry" *CBQ* 40 (1978) 1-9.

295 W. G. E. Watson, *Classical Hebrew Poetry*, 123-27.

296 J. Krašovec, "Merism – Polar Expressions in Biblical Hebrew" *Bib* 64 (1983) 232. W. G. E. Watson, *Classical Hebrew Poetry*, 324.

297 S. Böhmer, *Heimkehr*, 67.

298 This follows certain interpretations of 2 Sm 5:8. Cf. P. K. McCarter, *II Samuel*, AB 9, Garden City, N. Y.: Doubleday and Co., Inc, 1984, 140.

299 W. G. E. Watson, *Classical Hebrew Poetry*, 127.

300 K. L. Schmidt, "*ekklēsia*," *TDNT* III, 529, n. 90, recognizes that *qhl* can be (and often is) a cultic assembly but also means an assembly summoned on any given special occasion.

301 In other texts the saving presence of Yhwh is indicated by the healing of the blind and the lame (Is 29:18; 35:5-6; 42:16,18; Ez 34:16); here there is no mention of healing or wonder working.

302 Cf. Volz, 289; Weiser, 277.

303 Carroll, 591.

304 Most commentators follow BHS in emending the adverb *hnh* to the interjection and joining it to 31:9. Cf. Volz, 282; Bright, 274; Weiser, 262; Rudolph, 194-95; Thompson, 568; Carroll, 568. Both Giesebrecht, 167, and Condamin, 221, repoint it but leave it at the end of v. 8. It is, however, poetically better to maintain the MT, with the adverb *hnh* as the concluding word of 31:8, (cf. Carroll, 590; Gesenius, *Wörterbuch*, s.v. "*hnh*" II; BDB, *ad loc.*)

The MT exhibits a strong opening and closing rhyme pattern: *hnny* with *bbky* and *hnh* with *bh*, as well as root-repetition (*bw'* as the first verb in each case), and remarkable parallelism in the macrostructure:

31:8 — *hnny mby'* ...	place from which	... *yšwbw hnh*
31:9 — *bbky yb'w* ...	place to which	... *l' ykšlw bh*

The homophony noticeable between the beginning and the ending of each line (*hnny* - *hnh*; *bbky* - *bh*), while hardly of the emphatic nature noted by Saydon,[305] does accent this parallelism. The *qhl gdwl* will return *hnh*, understanding it to mean 'hither' which includes the sense of movement[306] pervading this stanza.

The people will come weeping (*bbky yb'w*, 31:9). The parallel line *wbtḥnwnym 'wbylm* ('I will bring them with supplications') repeats a content that is much the same as that of the first, yet expresses it in terms which have proved to be problematic. Although *wbtḥnwnym* and *'wbylm* are connected by Masoretic accents, *wbtḥnwnym* has been considered unsuitable as an adverbial modifier of *'wbylm* since it is difficult to explain how the deed of bringing the people back could be done 'with supplications.' Those who do accept the Masoretic accents generally emend the consonantal text to read *btnḥwmym* ('with consolations'),[307] while those who maintain both the consonantal text and the vocalization most often disregard the accents and join *wbtḥnwnym* with *bbky yb'w* and *'wbylm* with *'wlykm*.[308]

The first clause (*bbky yb'w*, 31:9) is simple and easily understood: "With tears they shall return." If tears express the person's dependence on Yhwh, his inadequacy before God and his acknowledgement of God,[309] then both tears and supplications (*btḥnwnym*) could be connected with the seeking of Yhwh,[310] and *'wbylm btḥnwnym* could well mean that Yhwh brings the people back once they have turned to him, or more precisely still, *in* their turning to him. Through parallelism the seemingly

---

305 P. Saydon, "Assonance in Hebrew as a Means of Expressing Emphasis" *Bib* 36 (1955) 36-50, 287-304.

306 *HAL (AT)*, *ad loc.*; Joüon § 102h; G-K § 100f.

307 Cf. BHS; also Cornill, 335; Volz, 282; Bright, 274; Weiser, 262; Rudolph, 194-95; Thompson, 569; Carroll, 590.

308 Giesebrecht, 167; Condamin, 223. Y. Avishur, "Pairs of Synonymous Words," 46, maintains the MT including the accents.

309 F.F. Hvidberg, *Weeping and Laughter in the Old Testament. A Study of Canaanite-Israelite Religion*, Leiden: E.J. Brill, 1962, 143; K.H. Rengstorf, "*klaiō*," *TDNT* III, 723; V. Hamp, "*bkh*," *TWAT* I, 641.

310 In Hos 12:5 the two words are connected to the story of Jacob's struggle with the angel, which in Gn 32:27 appears to refer to his asking for a blessing, thus a turning to Yhwh, through his messenger.

incongruous union of this adverbial expression with the verb *'wbylm* points to relationship, for Yhwh's deed of 'bringing back' is concurrent with the people's supplication, a cry which bespeaks conversion.[311] The verb of the following clause (*'wlykm*) is remarkably similar to the previous one (*'wbylm*). Both are *hiphil*, both have 3 m.pl. suffix and they differ by only a single consonant (although their *qal* forms exhibit little similarity). This is a good example of the poetic technique of paranomasia[312] (i.e., of synonyms of different stems which are almost homophonous[313]), which serves to unify the two lines and to emphasize the promise of return.[314]

The goal of *'wlykm* is *'l-nḥly mym* (31:9). This promise holds out the hope of life offered in the gift of water (cf., e.g., Is 43:19-21), which alone can give the people some measure of security,[315] while mention of the smooth or pleasant path (*bdrk yšr l' ykšlw bh*) articulates the ease of the return. The four verbs of 31:9a are connected to one another by sonoric repetition:

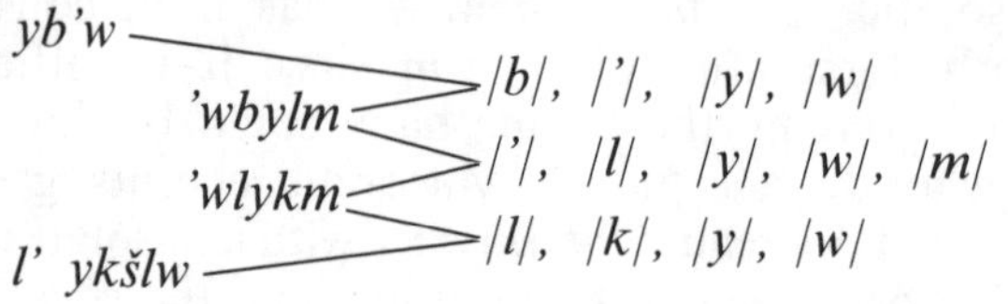

They move from a description of the returnees themselves (*ʿwr wpsḥ hrh wyldt*, 31:8), to a description of how they come (*bbky*, *wbtḥnwnym*, 31:9a), and end with a description of where they are going (*'l-nḥly mym*, *bdrk yšr*, 31:9a). Just as the description of the returnees (*ʿwr wpsḥ* and *hrh wyldt*) alludes to the contrast between death and life, so the description of how and whither they return (*bbky ... wbtḥnwnym* and *'l-nḥly mym bdrk yšr*) contrasts sorrow and need with peace and security.

The last line of stanza 1 (*ky-hyyty lyśr'l l'b w'prym bkry hw'*) assures the promise of relationship expressed in terms which are enduring: father/first-born. The mention of Ephraim indicates not only intimacy but also a choice. The aspect of chosenness forms an inclusio for this stanza. Israel, the youngest of nations, was chosen over the others,[316] as

---

311 D. Barthélemy, *Critique textuelle* II, 686.

312 W. G. E. Watson, *Classical Hebrew Poetry*, 242-43.

313 P. Saydon, "Assonance in Hebrew," 43-44, considers this emphatic though he maintains the consonantal text but not the accents and joins the two verbs as does Condamin, 221, 223.

314 Cf. A. Berlin, *Dynamics of Biblical Parallelism*, 111-12.

315 P. Reymond, *L'eau, sa vie, et sa signification dans l'Ancien Testament*, SVT 6, Leiden: E. J. Brill, 1958, 1-8.

316 M. Tsevat, "*bkwr*," *TWAT* I, 650.

rwš hgwym (31:7) states. Ephraim, the younger son, was chosen over his brother and given the rights of first-born: *'prym bkry* (31:9). The use of Ephraim as the term of comparison between Yhwh and the people highlights both the choice of them as his people and the gratuitousness of his gifts for them.[317]

Through a series of developing images, as well as through the poetic techniques of assonance, homophony, parallelism and inclusio, the caring and saving presence of Yhwh is made explicit not only in specific deeds but in an underlying attitude which gathers the weakest, responds to tears and supplications, keeps their feet from stumbling, and chooses them as *bkry*.

3.7.2 Stanza 2 — *Filled to Satiety* (31:10-14)

Like stanza 1, this stanza also opens with a series of imperatives, the first two having object-complements, the third (like the last of 31:7) being a simple *w'mrw*. The opening phrase *šm'w dbr-yhwh gwym* refers back to the imperatives of the first stanza (which include the verb *hšmy'w*) and also to the prose introduction with its insistence on *dbr-yhwh* (30:1-4). Those who are commanded to listen are not Israel but *gwym*, the other nations. They, too, must pay heed to the words and then announce the message to the distant lands.

The one who scattered Israel (*mzrh yśr'l*)[318] will now gather her, for he is *r'h* (shepherd). The threefold repetition of *-rô-* in as many words (*wšmrw kr'h 'drw*) focuses attention on the image of shepherd (*r'h*)[319] by making it the dominant image for the entire stanza. The essential deeds of Yhwh for his people, those aspects of his care which are pictured in the following verses, reflect the activities of a shepherd.[320]

Yhwh will assure their existence through his deeds of *pdh* and *g'l* (31:11). *pdh* is best construed as 'ransom,' understood as the act of rescuing one from a fate which would lead to slavery or destruction.[321] In itself the deed of *pdh* bespeaks no personal bond; it neither presupposes nor creates a relationship, but accents the deed itself rather than the

---

[317] The identification of the nation with Ephraim reinforces the notion of choice, since Ephraim was 'first-born' by choice rather than by right. Jacob adopted his two grandsons Ephraim and Manasseh and blessed Ephraim, the younger, as firstborn, even after having been reminded of Manasseh's priority by birth. Cf. Gn 48.

[318] This role implicitly bears the negativity already explicitly stated in Poems I-III.

[319] W. G. E. Watson, *Classical Hebrew Poetry*, 228.

[320] A shepherd cares for his flock by leading them to food and water, assuring their survival, caring for the weak and keeping them together as a single group. Cf. P. de Robert, *Le berger d'Israël*, Cahiers Théologiques 57, Neuchâtel: Delachaux et Niestlé, 1968, 27, 95-96.

[321] D. Daube, *Studies in Biblical Law*, Cambridge: University Press, 1947, 39. Cf. Dt 7:8; 9:26; 13:6; 15:15; 21:8; 24:18, where it refers to the ransoming from slavery.

person rescued.[322] The personal element is introduced in 31:11 by naming both subject and object: *yhwh* and *y'qb*.

While *pdh* emphasizes rescue from doom, *g'l* focuses on the relationship which is the foundation for the deed. As one who performs *g'l*, Yhwh is linked to Israel by kinship, which is a familial relationship based on blood ties, adoption or, as in this case, election.[323] He rescues them from their oppressors (*myd ḥzq mmnw*) because he has an obligation to them.[324]

The promised rescue and redemption are given specific content in the following line. The link between the saving deed and its results is achieved poetically by the repetition of /û/ which closes 31:11 and also opens 31:12a, where it is repeated four more times: *wb'w wrnnw ... wnhrw 'l-ṭwb* .... This assonance carries the poetic line along[325] to the final important phrase: *wnhrw 'l-ṭwb yhwh* (31:12). The accent moves from oppression to the blessings of Yhwh: *myd ḥzq mmnw ... 'l-ṭwb yhwh*. Yet in this change the people are the actors; they are the subject of the verbs *wb'w wrnnw ... wnhrw*. That which they were called to do earlier (*rnw*, 31:7) now forms part of their assured future (*wrnnw*, 31:12).

The people will come (*wb'w*), they will cry out on Sion (*wrnnw*) and *nhrw 'l* the good things of the Lord (31:12). The ambiguity of *nhr* in this statement is noteworthy. In a context which develops the sense of movement and in which water plays an important role (*gn rwh* of 31:12), *nhr* could well be construed as meaning 'to stream.'[326] Yet the following lines list the many gifts which lead to satiety and would make the people 'radiant,' as many commentators interpret *nhr*.[327] Because it is a poetic word, it seems best understood as an instance of wordplay and polysemy.[328] Both meanings fit the context and together give semantic fullness to the line. It is in their 'streaming' that the people become radiant; their action and Yhwh's come together for a single effect.

The list which constitutes *ṭwb-yhwh* is, of its nature, prosaic, yet the simple repetition of *'l- ... w'l- ... w'l- ... w'l-* ... adds rhythm and music[329] which is strengthened by the fact that *dgn*, *tyrš* and *yṣhr* consist of two syllables each. The list ends with *w'l-bny-ṣ'n wbqr*, which, since it is longer

---

[322] J. J. Stamm, "*pdh*," *THAT* II, 397.

[323] D. Daube, *Studies in Biblical Law*, 39; O. Procksch and F. Büchsel, "*luō*," *TDNT* IV, 330; J. J. Stamm, "*g'l*," *THAT* I, 386-87.

[324] Even if it be one which he established, as alluded to in 31:9 with its reference to *'prym* as *bkry*.

[325] W. G. E. Watson, *Classical Hebrew Poetry*, 224.

[326] Giesebrecht, 167; Condamin, 222; Weiser, 262; also BDB and Zorell, *ad loc.*

[327] Cornill, 335; Volz, 276; Bright, 274; Rudolph, 194-95; Thompson, 568; Carroll, 593; as is also true for *HAL (AT)*, *ad loc.*

[328] W. G. E. Watson, *Classical Hebrew Poetry*, 237.

[329] W. G. E. Watson, *Classical Hebrew Poetry*, 228, 351.

than the other phrases, stops the forward moving repetition and brings the line to a close.[330]

It is just such repetition and rhythm which focus attention on this list and recall Dt with its blessings and curses based on these items. These are the staples of life and refer to established existence in the land.[331] Since they are the very elements which constitute Yhwh's blessing,[332] as well as the basic necessities whose removal is punishment,[333] they bespeak his presence.[334]

This line whose poetic value is based solely on rhythm and musicality is followed by one where metaphor is the dominant poetic device: *whyth npšm kgn-rwh* (31:12). The metaphor (a well-watered garden) speaks of fertility, abundance, security and hope to the Israelites, a people constantly struggling to find water sufficient for survival.[335]

Litotes[336] reinforces this pregnant metaphor and emphasizes the sense of fullness by saying that the people will no longer experience want. Their future situation will differ from their present experience, as indicated by *l' ... 'wd* (31:12). They are given the promise of blessings, not in some eschatological future, but in their human, earthly existence.[337]

The entire community responds with joy to such an announcement. The fact that all are involved is expressed by merismus and gender-matched parallelism[338]: young, marriageable women; young, strong men; and old, wise men, the extremes of youth and old age. One (*bḥwr*, young men) gives hope for the future, while another (*zqn*, old men) conveys a sense of fulfillment; one (*btwlt*, virgin) is ready to begin a family, while another (*zqn*, old, wise man) represents the family established and ordered.[339] Totality is also accented by *yḥdw* which, like the usage in 31:8, is best construed as 'together,' according to the MT.[340]

---

330 R. Alter, *The Art of Biblical Poetry*, 7.

331 Their presence is linked to possession of the land, for the Israelites were people of the hill country where these three agricultural products could be grown together. (Cf. D. Baly, *Geography*, 86-87).

332 Dt 7:14; 11:14.

333 Dt 12:17; 14:23.

334 H. Ringgren, "*yṣhr*," *TWAT* III, 825.

335 P. Reymond, *L'eau, sa vie*, 113.

336 Cf. p. 61, n. 189.

337 This is indicated by the use of *npš* to refer to their life. Cf. D. Lys, *Nèpèsh. Histoire de l'âme dans la révélation d'Israël au sein des religions proches-orientales*, Etudes d'Histoire et de Philosophie Religieuses 50, Paris: Presses Universitaires de France, 1958, 197-202.

338 J. Krašovec, *Der Merismus*, 84, 87; W. G. E. Watson, *Classical Hebrew Poetry*, 125.

339 J. Conrad, "*zqn*," *TWAT* II, 642-43.

340 If parallelism is seen as virtual repetition of an idea, then repointing *yḥdw* to concur with the LXX and be synonymous with *tśmḥ* would be called for, as done by Cornill, 336; Weiser, 262; Rudolph, 194-95. Giesebrecht, 168; Volz, 277; Condamin, 223;

Like its counterpart in 31:8, *yḥdw* of 31:12 indicates the totality of the people, both male and female, as returnees in the first stanza and as present in the land in the second.

Such rejoicing is made possible by Yhwh's deed, expressed in three parallel verbs, each accentuating a different aspect of what he will do. The first action predicated of him is *whpkty 'blm lśśwn*, which, by the use of *hpk*, contrasts the 'change' spoken of here with that of Poem I (30:6). In the first poem the change was to deathliness, while here it is the opposite. That sadness which accompanies death or disaster, here articulated by *'blm*,[341] will be transformed to joy. Such a change is not wrought by an impersonal act but is undergirt by empathy as made explicit in the use of *nḥm (pi.)*.[342]

In the final phrase (*wśmḥtym mygwnm*) the change becomes yet more remarkable. Yhwh will remove *ygwn*, suffering which bears the threat of death or destruction[343] and in the face of which the only possible response is resigned acceptance.[344] Yet *śmḥtym* is more than a simple removal of the threat. Yhwh will turn the seeming hopelessness of the people into a spontaneous, boundless joy which springs forth and permeates their existence.[345]

Such joy which penetrates every aspect of life would seem a fitting conclusion to the poem, yet there is another closing remark: *wrwyty npš hkhnym dšn w'my 't-ṭwby yśb'w* (31:14). This last line forms a type of inclusio with *wšmrw kr'h 'drw* (31:10) by repeating the essence of shepherding: giving food to the sheep. But 31:14 speaks not merely of the ordinary food (as was the case in 31:12), for it accents the abundance of *gn-rwh*. First the priests are assured satiety (31:14), not of grain and wine and oil, but of *dšn* (fat-things, fat-food). Although *dšn* does denote that part of the sacrificial animal which was set aside for Yhwh, it also represents a richness and a superfluity far exceeding mere need or

---

Bright, 274; Thompson, 569, all maintain the MT, though this last says that the LXX suits the context as well. D. Barthélemy, *Critique textuelle* II, 686-87, maintains the MT, considering the two groups of men to be united by *yḥdw*, and understanding the verb to be repeated in the second clause.

[341] *'bl* expresses the extreme rite of mourning which follows a death, during which normal duties and functions are restricted. J. Morgenstern, *Rites of Birth, Marriage, Death and Kindred Occasions Among the Semites*, Cincinnati: Hebrew Union College Press and Chicago: Quadrangle Books, 1966, 164. Cf. also, F. Stolz, "*'bl*," *THAT* I, 29-30.

[342] The meaning is simply 'console' or 'comfort,' yet the verb includes the aspect of sharing the pain or suffering of the other and acting concretely to lighten that burden. H. Simian-Yofre, "*nḥm*," *THAT* V, 379; H. Van Dyke Parunak, "A Semantic Study of NḤM" *Bib* 56 (1975) 516-17.

[343] S. Wagner, "*ygh*," *TWAT* III, 407.

[344] J. Scharbert, *Der Schmerz im Alten Testament*, 35-36.

[345] E. Ruprecht, "*śmḥ*," *THAT* II, 829-30.

expectation.[346] This poem closes, however, with an assurance which reaches far beyond the priests, to all the people: *wʿmy ʾt-ṭwby yśbʿw*. They, too, will be satisfied with the blessings of Yhwh. And all this is emphatically his doing as is made clear by the assonance of /î/ in 31:13b-14.[347]

Poem V concludes on a note which accentuates the presence and activity of Yhwh for all his people and describes the resultant unbounded joy, satiety, and end to distress. His deeds of *pdh* and *gʾl* have a very specific content. What Yhwh offers his people is life in the land with all its gifts: life far beyond mere survival, life which is overabundance of food and joy.

Poem I promised 'Jacob' peace and security in the land; Poem II safety from enemies. Poem III sees city and government reestablished; Poem IV envisages sufficient stability that agriculture can be undertaken and enjoyed. Poem V is a promise of fullness of life, of overabundance of food and of joy.

---

346 A. Negoiță and H. Ringgren, "*dšn*," *TWAT* II, 332-33.

347 Of twelve occurrences in these two lines, six occurrences of /î/ refer directly to Yhwh, four as 1 s. verbal suffixes having Yhwh as understood subject, two as 1 s. pronominal suffixes whose referent is Yhwh. The other six uses merely reiterate the sound and the content. Cf. W. G. E. Watson, *Classical Hebrew Poetry*, 223-24.

3.8 POEM VI — 31:15-22

15 *kh 'mr yhwh*
qwl brmh nšmʿ
nhy
bky tmrwrym
rḥl mbkh *ʿl-bnyh*
mʾnh lhnḥm *ʿl-bnyh ky 'ynnw*

16 *kh 'mr yhwh*
mnʿy *qwlk mbky*
wʿynyk mdmʿh
ky *yš śkr lpʿltk* *n'm yhwh*
wšbw m'rṣ 'wyb
17 *wyš-tqwh l'ḥrytk* *n'm yhwh*
wšbw bnym lgbwlm

---

18 *šmwʿ šmʿty 'prym mtnwdd*
ysrtny
w'wsr
kʿgl l' lmd
hšybny
w'šwbh
ky 'th yhwh 'lhy

19 *ky* *'ḥry šwby* *nḥmty*
w *'ḥry hwdʿy* *spqty ʿl-yrk*
bšty
wgm-nklmty
ky nś'ty ḥrpt nʿwry

20 *hbn yqyr ly 'prym*
'm yld šʿšʿym
ky - *mdy dbry bw*
zkr 'zkrnw ʿwd
ʿl-kn *hmw mʿy lw*
rḥm 'rḥmnw *n'm-yhwh*

---

21 *hṣyby* *lk ṣynym*
śmy *lk tmrwrym*
šty lbk *lmslh*
drk hlkty
šwby *btwlt yśr'l*
šby 'l-ʿryk 'lh

22 *ʿd-mty ttḥmqyn hbt hšwbbh*
ky - br' yhwh *ḥdšh b'rṣ*
nqbh tswbb gbr

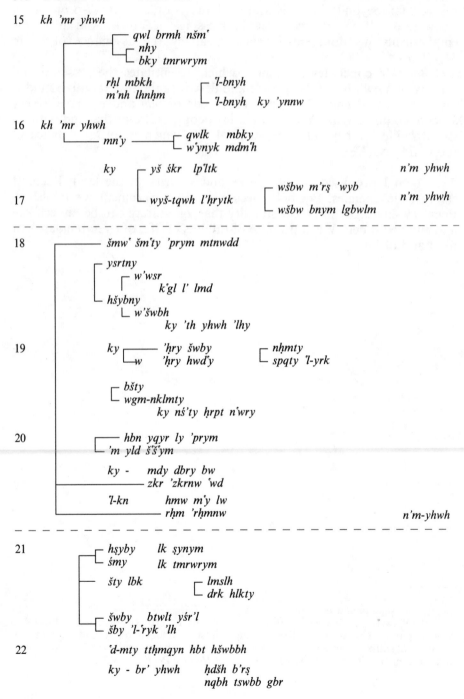

3.8 *Poem VI* — HOPE RENEWED (31:15-22)

The last poem of this cycle is composed of three stanzas which are distinguished from one another by the change of person who constitutes the subject and/or addressee of each. The first stanza (31:15-17) speaks of and to Rachel, the second (31:18-20) is addressed to and contains the words of Ephraim, while the third (31:21-22) is addressed to 'virgin Israel.' The tone of Poem VI is strikingly different from that of the preceding one. While 31:7-14 depicts a scene of joy, satiety, salvation and the presence of Yhwh, 31:15-22 is a picture of sorrow, weeping, shame and distance from the Lord, although he is still present as consoler.

3.8.1 Stanza 1 — *Inconsolable Rachel* (31:15-17)

The final poem of this cycle (31:15-22) opens, like the first (30:5-11), with *qwl ... šmʿ* (30:5 and 31:15), an aural image of suffering and pain. Like 30:5-11, 31:15-17 begins with a description which bodes destruction yet it ends on a note of hope.

A sense of hopelessness fills these opening lines, for what is heard is *nhy*, an expression which has strong funerary overtones.[348] The reference to destruction contained in *nhy* (lament) is reinforced by *bky tmrwrym* which accents the depth of the sorrow and the bitterness of the one who is weeping.[349] The intensity of emotion is emphasized through repetition which is sonoric as well as semantic,[350] since *nhy* and *bky* repeat the same vowel pattern: ᵉ, î / ᵉ, î.

In the second line the picture becomes more explicit. It is not just any funeral lament but that of a single woman, Rachel. And yet attention is immediately focused on her sons by the use of inverted staircase parallelism[351] which repeats *ʿl-bnyh*

rḥl	*mbkh*	*ʿl-bnyh*
mʾnh	*lhnḥm*	*ʿl-bnyh.*

[348] Found seven times in the MT with five of these in Jeremiah, *nhy* in Jer 9 (four occurrences, in vv. 9, 17, 18, 19) is used to describe the action of those trained in funeral laments who are to wail over the destruction and death of the people and the land. H.-J. Krause, "*hôj* als profetische Leichenklage über das eigene Volk im 8. Jahrhundert" *ZAW* 85 (1973) 22, describes the funerary content of this term.

[349] *bky* is used to refer to the three days after death and interment, days given to violent weeping, according to J. Morgenstern, *Rites of Birth, Marriage, Death*, 164 and n. 235. The intensity of the sorrow is also indicated by the form *tmrwrym* which is found only in the plural intensive. (Cf. BDB, *ad loc.*).

[350] P. Saydon, "Assonance in Hebrew," 45, notes the emphatic nature of this repetition.

[351] W. G. E. Watson, *Classical Hebrew Poetry*, 150-56, 358-59.

Rachel is there as a foil, as a means of expressing the extremity and desperation felt in this circumstance. Only after the vivid portrayal of the depth of her distress is the situation of her sons made explicit: *'ynnw* ("They are not!").[352]

Although Rabbinic interpretation (and some modern commentators) have understood *brmh* as the geographical location of Rachel's tomb,[353] lack of the definite article[354] as well as the absence of any other reference to a burial place indicates 'on a height' as the preferred reading.[355] Yet whatever the geographical or actual referent of *brmh*, Rachel,[356] as a metaphor for Israel, weeps disconsolately over the destruction of her sons.

The presence of Rachel, even in her distress, softens an otherwise bleak picture. Although she was a person who suffered lack of favor (according to Jewish standards) inasmuch as she was barren,[357] she was also favored[358] and, even more, became the mother of the nation. To recall Rachel in her emptiness-become-fullness is to offer hope that the nation Israel will enjoy the same experience. Rachel was 'given sons' (Gn 30:1-24) who were important ancestors of the nation (Joseph and Benjamin) and, moreover, one of her grandsons, Ephraim, was the beloved of Yhwh (Jer 31:19). Thus, she is a symbol of Yhwh's working for his people in a continuous way despite overwhelming negative odds from a human point of view.

---

[352] These final words of 31:15, while considered by some earlier exegetes as metrically superfluous and thus to be eliminated (cf. Giesebrecht, 168. Cornill, 337, omits only the repetitive *'l-bnyh*, as does Condamin, 226), are important to the poetry of these lines. Their repetitiveness emphasizes the fact that attention is to be given not to Rachel but to *bnyh*, since repetition serves to focus the thought and indicate the stress of the poem or line. (Cf. J. Muilenburg, "Hebrew Rhetoric: Repetition and Style," 99.)

[353] S. R. Driver, s.v. "Rachel," *Hastings Dictionary* IV, 193; Condamin, 266; Bright, 282; GenR 82,10. Rudolph, 197, takes an opposing position.

[354] For the place name, Ramah, the definite article is present except in Neh 11:33 and here (if this is a place name). Cf. BDB, s.v. "*rwm*"; Joüon § 137b.

[355] M. Tsevat, "Rachel's Tomb," *IDBS*, 724-25. This interpretation is given added weight by the connection of this text with Jer 3:21.

[356] Rachel has been considered a personification of the nation by Thompson, 573, and H. Freedman, trans., *Midrash Rabbah: Genesis* II, London: The Soncino Press, 1939, 760, n. 7.

[357] C. Breyfolge, "The Social Status of Woman in the Old Testament" *The Biblical World* 35 (1910) 108-10; J. Pedersen, *Israel* I-II, 231; P. Trible, "Images of Woman in the Old Testament" in R. Reuther, ed., *Religion and Sexism, Images of Woman in the Jewish and Christian Traditions*, New York: Simon and Schuster, 1974, 51.

[358] Rachel was the well-beloved wife of her husband, the wife who was loved gratuitously for her beauty (Gn 29:30-31), not because she had done something (like bearing sons) to deserve his love.

The consolation denied to Rachel in stanza 1 is predicated of her grandson in stanza 2: *m'nh lhnḥm* of Rachel (31:15) becomes *nḥmty* for Ephraim (31:19). The same change of circumstance is also highlighted in Yhwh's words to her. The cause of her sorrow, *'l-bnyh ky 'ynnw* (31:15), is emphatically negated by the twice-repeated affirmation *yš* ... *wšbw* (31:16-17).

This emptiness-become-fullness of the historical Rachel appears in 31:15-17 as hopelessness-turned-to-hope for the metaphorical Rachel. Immediately after the description of her inconsolable sorrow, she is addressed by Yhwh with the imperative *mn'y qwlk mbky w'ynyk mdm'h* (31:16).[359] Her voice is to cease from mourning, her eyes are to cease from weeping (literally, 'from tears'), two acts which are similar but not synonymous. The near-redundancy gives depth to the text.[360] While mourning accentuates the internal aspect, weeping is the physical manifestation of this emotion.

This command already hints at the hope which will be articulated in the final two lines. Rachel is told that her cries have not been in vain:

ky yš śkr	*lp'ltk*	*n'm yhwh*	*wšbw m'rṣ 'wyb*
wyš-tqwh	*l'ḥrytk*	*n'm yhwh*	*wšbw bnym lgbwlm*

Her efforts have borne fruit, much as did her cries to Jacob which Yhwh answered with sons (Gn 30:6,22). This time it is not the birth of sons[361] which is her reward but the return of her children from enemy land.[362] The almost perfect syntactic parallelism of these two lines, especially in the first clauses of 31:16b-17, and their extremely close semantic parallelism, both draw attention to them and bring closure to this stanza.[363]

The close parallelism of these lines also aids in the interpretation of the stanza. Rachel's tears may be understood as prayer.[364] Her labor

---

[359] The presence of *kh 'mr yhwh* here is an assurance that the one who responds is not Jacob, her historical husband, nor the prophet, but Yhwh himself. As such, there is authority in the command and an assurance that the promise will be fulfilled.

[360] A. Berlin, *Dynamics of Biblical Parallelism*, 99.

[361] This is true despite the interpretation of *p'lh* as the labor of childbirth, proposed by Volz, 290, and Rudolph, 197, and implied by Weiser, 280, n. 1.

[362] Cornill, 337-38; Giesebrecht, 168; Thompson, 574.

[363] Cornill, 338, deletes the whole of 31:17 as a doublet of 31:16b. Volz, 277; Weiser, 263; and Rudolph, 194-95, delete the double *n'm yhwh*. Condamin, 224, and Carroll, 595-96, delete the *n'm yhwh* of 31:16. Bright, 275, and Thompson, 572, retain both occurrences here, a choice with which D. Barthélemy, *Critique textuelle* II, 644-45, concurs. In fact, the presence of *n'm yhwh* in both lines accents the parallelism and insists upon the fact that the hope is based not in some anonymous deed but in the presence of Yhwh.

[364] P. R. Ackroyd, "Hosea and Jacob" *VT* 13 (1963) 250-51, offers an interpretation of weeping as prayer, though specifically in the context of Hos 12:5.

(weeping), in fact, is rewarded by their return from enemy land (*wšbw m'rṣ 'wyb* and *wšbw bnym lgbwlm*, 31:16-17). Thus the accent moves from the past and the present toward a hopeful future. They will return to their own 'boundaries,' which may refer to territories or to cities.[365]

As the stanza progresses, it shifts from an image of death and hopelessness to a promise of hope. She who wept because her sons were not (*'l-bnyh ky 'ynnw*, 31:15) is told that they will return (*wšbw bnym*, 31:17). Her future is not the destruction echoed by *nhy* ... *bky* but the hope of *'ḥrytk*: *bnym* who will return from the land of exile to their own territory.

3.8.2 Stanza 2 — *Ephraim Consoled* (31:18-20)

The second stanza opens, like the first, with an aural image, *šmʿ*, a repetition which might raise expectations that the sound of mourning in 31:15 would be echoed in 31:18.

The voice is that of Ephraim and his state of being is *mtnwdd*.[366] There is evident word-play in the choice of this vocable since the single word *mtnwdd* includes, besides the dominant meaning of lamenting or bemoaning (one's distance — from Yhwh? from the land?),[367] the sense of consolation,[368] present or imminent. While it might seem contradictory to posit both 'console' and 'bemoan' as meanings, polysemy indicates the conjunction of the two attitudes in the person of Ephraim. As presented in this stanza, Ephraim is consoled in the recognition of his plight.

First Ephraim recalls a moment of his past, *ysrtny w'wsr kʿgl l' lmd*, a time of his youth when Yhwh's discipline (*ysr*) was effective. It was a time when he was naive and malleable as depicted by the image of an untrained calf (*ʿgl*).[369]

With this reference to his past, Ephraim calls on Yhwh to act again: *hšbny w'šwbh* (31:18), a plea that he be brought back to the land and/or

---

[365] *gbwl* means a territory which is defined, bounded or enclosed (as is a city). Cf. *HAL (AT)*, *ad loc.*

[366] *mtnwdd*, which conveys a shaking or rocking motion in the *qal*, includes such diverse meanings as shake one's head (in horror or sympathy) and be without a homeland, go into exile (wander back and forth); cf. *HAL(AT)*, s.v. "*nwd.*"

[367] Cornill, 338; Giesebrecht, 169; Volz, 277, 282, *Hithp.* intensive: ever-increasing distress; Condamin, 224; Bright, 275; Weiser, 263; Rudolph, 194; Thompson, 572; Carroll, 595.

[368] M.I. Gruber, *Aspects of Non-Verbal Communication in the Ancient Near East*, Studia Pohl 12, Rome: Biblical Institute Press, 1980, 406-407, n. 3.

[369] *ysr* often refers to the training given to children or animals, which is effective for acceptable behavior. Cf. R.D. Branson, "*ysr*," *TWAT* III, 690-91, 697. A similar image is found in Hos 10:11, also in reference to Ephraim.

back to Yhwh.[370] Both the *ky-* clause (*ky 'th yhwh 'lhy*), which identifies Yhwh as 'my God,' and the action-result (factitive-passive) sequence,[371] express confidence in Yhwh's effective deeds. The triple root-repetition (*šmwʿ šmʿty*, *ysrtny w'wsr*, *hšybny w'šwbh*) and the near alliteration of the root consonant /š/, /s/, indicate the interdependence of these phrases, thus linking the prayer for the future (*šwb*) with past experience (*ysr*).

Introduced by an emphatic *ky*,[372] the syntactically and semantically parallel first lines of 31:19 intensify the interdependence of past and future by temporal ambiguity[373]:

'ḥry šwby nḥmty
w'ḥry hwdʿy spqty ʿl-yrk

They can be construed as pluperfect-perfect ('after I had done ... I did') or future perfect-future ('after I will have done ... I will').[374]

Temporal ambiguity is matched by semantic ambiguity in the first line: *'ḥry šwby nḥmty* (31:18). In this context, *šwb* can mean 'turn back,' 'return'[375] or 'turn away.'[376] Similarly, *nḥm* can mean 'be consoled'[377] or 'be sorry.'[378]

Polysemy suggests that the line can be read on two levels, with both meanings intended: in the past, after turning away from Yhwh, Ephraim experienced sorrow and regret; but in his turning back, he received consolation. This would be an equally valid interpretation even if *šwb*

---

370 The ambiguity has been noted by several contemporary scholars, e.g., Weiser, 281; Rudolph, 197. W. Holladay, *The Root ŠÛBH*, 56, 58, considers it to be an example of 'discontinuous ambiguity,' i.e., an expression that has two possible interpretations both of which fit the context, yet having no prepositional or adverbial phrase, no subject or object, which makes the sense explicit.

371 Cf. M. Held, "The Action-Result (Factitive-Passive) Sequence," 274-75; U. Cassuto, *The Goddess Anath*, trans. from Hebrew by I. Abrahams, Jerusalem: Magnes Press, 1971, 47; A. Berlin, *Dynamics of Biblical Parallelism*, 36-40.

372 Here it maintains its original deictic value. Cf. J. Muilenburg, "The Particle *ky*," 136-37, 160.

373 As already noted, this poem, like the entire cycle, identifies certain past experiences with present ones, through the use of several devices, including ambiguity of verbal tense.

374 *'ḥry* + infinitive construct relates the so-described action temporally to the following verb, placing the finite verb in a position temporally posterior to the infinitive. For an understanding of the perfect as *futurum exactum*, cf. G-K § 106o.

375 Cornill, 338; Giesebrecht, 169.

376 Volz, 277; Condamin, 224; Bright, 275; Weiser, 263; Rudolph, 194; Thompson, 572; Carroll, 595.

377 H. Simian-Yofre, "*nḥm*," *TWAT* V, 378; *HAL (AT)*, *ad loc.*

378 H. J. Stoebe, "*nḥm*," *THAT* II, 63-64; H. Van Dyke Parunak, "A Semantic Study of NḤM" *Bib* 56 (1975) 519.

means 'return to the land,' since the latter is a metaphor which expresses the 'turning back' of the heart.[379]

The following line minimizes the ambiguity without, however, eliminating it. *spqty ʿl-yrk*, consequent upon *ydʿ*, is as ambiguous in content as is *nḥm*. Both can have a positive sense (consolation or joy) or a negative one (regret or sorrow). In its only other biblical occurrence (Ez 21:17) *spq ʿl-yrk* is an action of lament parallel to 'cry' and 'wail' found in a description of the people's destruction. It has a broader meaning in Near Eastern literature where it signifies a deep emotion, be it of joy[380] or of annoyance or derision.[381] Homer uses the image of slapping the thigh as an expression of anger, of sorrow or of the depth of emotion which moves one to action.[382] So although *spq ʿl-yrk* is a concrete, physical action, as an expression of emotion it is semantically parallel to *nḥmty*.[383]

Ephraim's words open with a recognition of Yhwh's effective deeds for his training, and close with an admission of his own guilt. His final words are clearly negative: *bšty wgm-nklmty* ('I am ashamed, indeed (*gm*)[384] I am humiliated for I bear the reproach of my youth').[385] He accepts the blame[386] for his past deeds by admitting his guilt.[387]

The whole is a recognition of how essential Yhwh's action is in his life, both past and present. Yhwh is the one who educated him, who turned (and turns) him around, who caused (and causes) him to know or understand.

> Turn me back and I shall turn back, for you are the Lord my God.
> Certainly after I (will) have turned back I will be sorry / take comfort.
> And after I (will) have understood I will slap my thigh (in sorrow or in joy).
> I have been ashamed and felt humiliated for I have borne the reproach of my youth.

---

[379] B. W. Anderson, "'The Lord Has Created,'" 375.

[380] Cf. "Gilgamesh" Tablet VII (iv) 1.3; *ANET*, 86.

[381] Cf. "Descent of Ishtar" (reverse) 1.21; *ANET*, 108.

[382] Cf. Homer, *Iliad* XII, 162; XV, 113, 397; XVI, 125; *Odyssey* XIII, 198.

[383] Such parallelism does not limit the meaning of the preceding *nḥm* to a physical expression, *pace* J. Scharbert, *Der Schmerz im Alten Testament*, 64, who maintains that *nḥm* "hier konkret an das Seufzen vor Reueschmerz gedact ist" since "ein Konkret steht mit einem Konkretum parallel."

[384] For *gm* as emphatic cf. BDB, s.v. "*gmm*"; C. J. Labuschagne, "The Emphasizing Particle *gam* and Its Connotations" in W. C. van Unnik and A. S. van der Woude, eds., *Studia Biblica et Semantica*, Fs. T. C. Vriezen, Wageningen: H. Veenman & Zonen, 1966, 193-203; and T. Muraoka, *Emphatic Words*, 143-46.

[385] Cf. G-K § 106g for the use of the perfect to express an action or condition whose effects remain in the present.

[386] E. Kutsch, "*ḥrp*" II, *TWAT* III, 227.

[387] D. N. Freedman and B. E. Willoughby, "*nśʾ*," *TWAT* V, 633.

Yhwh's response to Ephraim's prayer begins with a rhetorical question, a device used in Jer to refute a counter theme.[388] Here it refutes the fact of distance and shame. It gives assurance for the future yet without specific details or description, for it presents not deeds but an attitude, the attitude of Yhwh toward Ephraim.

The rhetorical question is, actually, a double one. It is introduced by *h- ... 'm*, which, in this case differs from its usual disjunctive meaning and thus adds emphasis to the interrogative statement.[389] The question is striking in its simplicity and profundity, as well as in its reiteration of a single idea in two parallel phrases: *bn yqyr ... yld šʿšʿym* (31:20). Ephraim is related to Yhwh as *bn* and *yld*, son and child. He is called *bn yqyr*, an expression which uses an adjective often predicated of gold or other highly-valued materials not essential for building. Superfluous but beautiful, they add a dimension of pleasure to the object.[390]

Ephraim is not only *bn yqyr*, but also *yld šʿšʿym*: child of delight. The attribute 'delight' is much more subjective than 'precious.' Delight does not reside in the person of whom it is predicated but in the other, who stands in relation to him/her. Hence, by being called child of delight, Ephraim is presented as one who has value above all in the eyes of Yhwh.

The result of the relationship is expressed in the following *ky*-clause (*ky-mdy dbry bw zkr 'zkrnw ʿwd*) which conveys a sense of duration by the words which frame it: *mdy ... ʿwd* ('as often as' ... 'still/besides'). The dual verbal action (*dbr*, *zkr*) is concentrated in *zkr* through root repetition with the use of the (emphatic) infinitive absolute. A positive deed, *zkr*[391] follows upon Yhwh's act of *dbr*, understood either negatively (speak against, punish his sins, specifically in the Exile)[392] or positively (speak of him, extend care to him, bring him back to the land).[393]

The ambiguity which has been noted throughout this stanza appears again in the expression *dbr b-*. This ambiguity brings together the positive and negative deeds of Yhwh for the people in much the same way as the first three poems counterpointed suffering and salvation (the negative and positive experience of the people).

---

388 W. Brueggemann, "Jeremiah's Use of Rhetorical Questions," 366-67.

389 G-K § 150h.

390 Although not frequently predicated of people, the adjective *yqr* is used in Lam 4:2 to describe the value of the 'sons of Sion,' the terms of comparison being gold and pottery. In Is 43:4 it is also used in a value judgment, comparing Israel with Egypt, Ethiopia, Saba. Cf. S. Wagner, "*yqr*," *TWAT* III, 863-64.

391 Cf. H. Eising, "*zkr*," *TWAT* II, 578-81.

392 The negative interpretation is held by Giesebrecht, 169; Condamin, 224; Rudolph, 196-97; Carroll, 595. B.W. Anderson, "'The Lord Has Created,'" 375, n. 23, says: "In the context of Yhwh's discipline of his son 'against' is appropriate."

393 Bright, 282; Weiser, 281; Thompson, 575.

The stanza ends as it began, with the words of Yhwh which use an anthropomorphic figure to describe the depth of his attachment to Ephraim. By this technique, the conclusion repeats the content of *yqyr* and *šʿšʿym* from a different perspective. The imagery of 31:20 is totally visceral as seen in the use of *mʿh* and *rḥm*, internal organs which are the seat of emotions.[394] The first term (*mʿy*) expresses a love which is so strong it is disturbing in its coming to physical expression; the second (*rḥm*) denotes that deep compassion which is often linked to maternal love[395] and expresses an intensity of emotion more frequently predicated of woman than of man. Root repetition makes this second act emphatic. The depth of loss presented in 31:15-16 is transformed to depth of attachment in 31:19-20.

Two formal features signal the end of stanza 2. The root repetition, here found in consecutive lines both at the beginning (*šmʿ*, *ysr*, *šwb* in 31:18) and at the end (*zkr*, *rḥm* in 31:20) of this stanza, forms a syntactic inclusio.[396] Besides this, the simultaneously semantic and syntactic parallelism of *zkr ʾzkrnw* and *rḥm ʾrḥmnw* brings closure to this stanza by repeating the structure of the opening lines.

31:18-20 contains a wealth of ambiguous terms which reflect the interplay between shame and joy, between motion toward and motion away from Yhwh. This second stanza repeats the sorrowful tone of 31:15 yet also develops the note of hope introduced in 31:16-17. Through ambiguity concerning the temporal aspect of given deeds, the past is effectively connected with the present and the future.

3.8.3 Stanza 3 — *A New Creation* (31:21-22)

The third stanza of Poem VI is a bit of a conundrum. While it quite clearly fits the whole with its repetition of *šwb* and its 2 f.s. address, and despite its unproblematic vocabulary, it is nevertheless difficult to understand.

Its opening line gives the impression of simple repetition, adding nothing to the development of thought because of the semantic and syntactic synonymity:

hṣyby	*lk*	*ṣynym*
śmy	*lk*	*tmrwrym*

---

[394] Cf. J. Pedersen, *Israel* I-II, 173-74; A. R. Johnson, *The Vitality of the Individual in the Thought of Ancient Israel*, Cardiff: University of Wales Press, 1949, 74-76.

[395] P. Trible, *God and the Rhetoric of Sexuality*, 45-46. J. Pedersen, *Israel* I-II, 309, considers *rḥm* as the fountain of family feeling.

[396] Inclusio is most often recognized on the semantic level. M. Kessler, "Inclusio in the Hebrew Bible" *Semitics* 6 (1978) 48, also suggests that it can be found in formal textual elements.

Yet there is a clear connection with stanza 1, seen in the feminine address and the repetition of *tmrwrym*. Although *tmrwrym* (marker, post) of stanza 3 is simply another term for *ṣywn* (a stone marker used as a way-mark or a grave-mark),[397] its use points back to stanza 1 where *tmrwrym* has its more usual meaning ('bitter') and is an attribute of Rachel's weeping. This word link alludes to stanza 3 as a continuation or result of stanza 1. *bky tmrwrym* (31:15) finds a response in *śmy lk tmrwrym* (31:21); weeping ends with effective deeds for return and bitterness turns to hope.[398]

The indicated return is expressed in concrete images: road-marks and guideposts are to be set up. But even in this seemingly concrete expression, the ambiguity encountered in stanza 2 is met again. *šty lbk lmslh drk hlkty* can indicate either the return from actual physical exile to the land or turning back from a spiritual separation from Yhwh. The interpretation is based on one's understanding of *lb* which may be an instance of synecdoche.[399] *lb* may represent the person(s) who must return from the Exile; or it may refer to the seat of understanding and decision[400] which must be directed to Yhwh.

Similarly *mslh*,[401] to which virgin Israel is to direct her heart, her steps, and her decisions, can be construed as a physical or a metaphorical reality. As a raised way, *mslh* would be easily seen and easily followed, and in this instance, also known since it is identified with *drk hlkty* (the road previously taken). Yet the metaphorical interpretation appears more convincing since there is no 'geographical' logic in telling one to set up waymarks and also follow a highway whose very existence presupposes that the roadmarks are already in place. But metaphorical waymarks are important[402] since her *lb* (heart) must follow the sure way and return without wavering. She must make sure that she does not wander from the road which leads back to Yhwh.

---

397 Jer 31:21 is the only occurrence of *tmrwrym* used to mean 'guidepost' but the context requires this interpretation. Cf. BDB, *ad loc.*

398 B. W. Anderson, "'The Lord Has Created,'" 58.

399 J. Shipley, *Dictionary of World Literary Terms*, 328.

400 Cf. H. W. Wolff, *Anthropology of the Old Testament*, 44-45.

401 *mslh* is a road constructed for a specific and temporary purpose or for a permanent use. Cf. G. A. Smith, *The Historical Geography of the Holy Land* (25th ed., revised throughout), London: Hodder & Stoughton, 1931, 697. Such a road does not have cultic overtones, *pace* N. Tidwell, "A Road and a Way. A Contribution to the Study of Word-Pairs" *Semitics* 7 (1980) 61-62.

402 A metaphorical interpretation of *ṣynym* is found in the Targums. Cf. C. T. R. Hayward, *The Targum of Jeremiah*, The Aramaic Bible 12, Edinburgh: T. & T. Clark Ltd., 1987, 132 and 133, n. 19.

The commands to prepare the way cede to the final imperatives with their call to return. Using the device of step parallelism[403] which repeats the imperative, this line insists on the importance of *šwb* as an action which Israel can (and must) accomplish:

šwby btwlt yśr'l
šby 'l-ʿryk 'lh

In the first line, the people are addressed as *btwlt yśr'l*, and in the second, the goal of *šwb* is identified: *'l-ʿryk 'lh.*

Despite the fact that *btwlt yśr'l* is generally considered to refer to the capital city (in this case Samaria, if directed to the Northern Kingdom),[404] here its referent appears to be the people.[405] Since *btwlt yśr'l* is told to return to her cities, it is unlikely that the one addressed is the city Jerusalem. Yet another indication that the people are the addressees is the fact that the term 'virgin' is applied to the people of Israel in Jer 18:13,15, to Egypt in Jer 46:1, and to the house of Israel in Am 5:2.

This call to return to 'her cities' could well mean a coming back from Exile to the actual geographical cities of the land — a literal interpretation which fits the line at first glance.[406] Yet the word *šwb* here appears to include a sense of interior motion (as did *lbk* in the previous line). In Jer the two aspects of *šwb* cannot be separated; the return to Yhwh is the basis for return to the land. The nation cannot have the land if she does not have Yhwh.[407] In this context what is essential then is the turning to Yhwh, the recognition of her situation and an awareness that she can return.

The poem closes not with an imperative but with a question: 'How long will you wander?' This appears to be a rhetorical question since the motive clause which follows indicates that the question should not even be asked.

---

[403] W. G. E. Watson, *Classical Hebrew Poetry*, 150-56.

[404] A. F. Fitzgerald, "*BTWLT* and *BT* as Titles for Capital Cities" *CBQ* 37 (1975) 167-77; J. Schmitt, "The Motherhood of God and Zion as Mother" *RB* 92 (1985) 557-69; E. Follis, "The Holy City as Daughter" in E. Follis, ed., *Directions in Biblical Hebrew Poetry*, JSOTS 40, Sheffield: JSOT Press, 173-84.

[405] Carroll, 603, understands the 'woman' as the people in Exile. Such an expression is considered by Joüon to be "génitif du nom propre" being, effectively, a form of apposition (Joüon § 129f). Cf., also, W. F. Stinespring, "Zion, Daughter of," *IDBS*, 985. A. F. Fitzgerald, "*BTWLT* and *BT*," 178-79, recognizes the expression *btwlt yśr'l* of Jer 31:4,21 as a reference to the exiles of the N. Kingdom, i.e., the people in their existence as a political organization.

[406] W. Holladay, *The Root ŠÛBH*, 59, 62, places them under the definition of "physical motion back to the point of departure" and specifically "return from exile."

[407] P. Diepold, *Israels Land*, 138-39.

'd-mty ttḥmqyn hbt hšwbbh
ky- br' yhwh ḥdšh b'rṣ
nqbh tswbb gbr

The meaning of the text, clear in its literal sense, has eluded the best efforts of generations of exegetes. Like the conclusion to stanza 1, the *ky* clause here first makes a general statement recounting an action of Yhwh (*br' yhwh ḥdšh b'rṣ*), which is then specified. But the specification seems a riddle: *nqbh tswbb gbr*.

The general statement that Yhwh is creating something new accents the marvelous, miraculous and perhaps even messianic quality of what is described.[408] In Is 42:19 (the only time apart from Jer 31:22 where *ḥdš* is used as a substantive to describe the deeds of Yhwh) the newness consists in his making a road in the wilderness and streams in the desert. This image which describes nature is spectacular. What Yhwh does, according to Is 42:19, is unexpected, unknown, even impossible from a natural viewpoint. Yet here in Jer 31:22 the newness (*ḥdšh*) consists in *nqbh tswbb gbr*.

Despite the many proposals for interpreting this last statement (*nqbh tswbb gbr*), most exegetes consider these words enigmatic. The interpretations are varied and wide-ranging: the woman will turn into a man[409]; the woman will protect the man since there will be such peace that women will be able to protect the city (metaphor for complete peace)[410]; the woman will court the man, the wife will take the initiative with her husband (metaphor for Israel taking the initiative in her relationship with Yhwh)[411]; the woman will surround or embrace the man in the sense that there will once again be procreation in the land.[412] The various attitudes taken toward 31:22b reflect how serious a problem it presents. Volz considers it a gloss, added by some reader[413]; Bright translates it literally but says that it might be better to leave the colon

---

[408] *ḥdš* is either the modifier of the object or the object of a verb whose subject is Yhwh only in Is 43:19; 65:17; 66:22; Ez 11:19; 36:26 and Jer 31:22, all in eschatological contexts.

[409] Cornill, 342; W. Holladay, "Jeremiah 31:22b Reconsidered: The Woman Encompasses the Man" *VT* 16 (1966) 236-39, considers it in these terms but as a reversal of the treaty curse portrayed in 30:6.

[410] Giesebrecht, 170.

[411] Condamin, 225, 228; E. Jacob, "Féminisme ou Messianisme? A propos de Jérémie 31:22" in H. Donner, *et al.*, eds., *Beiträge zur alttestamentlichen Theologie*, Fs. W. Zimmerli, Göttingen: Vandenhoeck und Ruprecht, 1977, 182-84.

[412] Weiser, 282; L. Alonso Schökel and J.L. Sicré Diaz, *Profetas* I, 563; B.W. Anderson, "'The Lord Has Created,'" 378-80.

[413] Volz, 283.

blank since the meaning is totally obscure[414]; and Rudolph suggests emending the text to read 'the cursed one becomes a lady.'[415]

Both *br' yhwh* and *nqbh* point back to Gn, thus suggesting a new creation,[416] while the close relation between *gbr* and the female (*yldh* in 30:6; *nqbh* in 31:22) indicates a link with Jer 30:5-6. In Poem I (30:5-6) role reversal is seen as a curse; here (31:22) it is an indication of blessing.

Several proposed interpretations of 31:22 do, in fact, reverse the imagery of 30:5-6: women turning into men[417] or taking the initiative either in sexual matters or as protectresses.[418] It is quite clear, however, that 31:22 contains a blessing which reverses a curse, and it could very well be the curse of Gn 3:16 which states that the woman will be subservient to her husband.[419] If this is the case, the blessing of 31:22 would indicate a return to the original state of equality: the woman becomes like the man (equal to him) or takes the initiative in relationship. And as a renewal of the original blessing, it would include the multiplication of progeny, the fact that children would be born in the land.[420]

31:22 may be a proverb whose original meaning eludes present generations. Yet because it is enigmatic it leaves open many interpretive possibilities, not all of which are mutually exclusive. What remains clear is that the initiative for change rests in the hands of Yhwh. He created once and can now re-create. He can turn curse into blessing and restore relationship to its pristine condition.

---

[414] Bright, 282. This also appears to be the (implicit) conclusion of B. Lindars, "'Rachel Weeping,'" 55-62.

[415] Rudolph, 196; BHS. C. Schedl, "'Femina circumdabit virum' oder 'Via Salutis'? Textkritische Untersuchung zu Jer 31,22" *ZKTh* 83 (1961) 435-39, emends 31:22b to read: "Erschaffen ist Neues im Land; / ein Durchbruchspfad gebahnt!"

[416] This is so because *nqbh* is used with *br'* only in Gn 1:27. The other uses are all in the Pentateuch and point to sexual differentiation, the female in opposition to the male. Both Weiser, 282, and L. Alonso Schökel and J. L. Sicré Diaz, *Profetas* I, 563, note a connection with the Gn account.

[417] Cornill, 342.

[418] Giesebrecht, 170; Condamin, 225, 228.

[419] Rabbinic sources and commentaries on Gn 3:16 indicate an understanding of the original situation as one of equality. Ramban (Nachmanides), *Commentary on the Torah: Genesis*, 84, states that the woman's punishment consists in the fact "that she should no longer command him, but instead he should command her entirely at his will." Rashi comments that the conjugal initiative being with the male is part of woman's curse. Hirsch remarks that only with equality of male and female (achieved through obedience to the Torah) is the wife restored to her role as 'crown of the husband,' 'pearl of his life' (Prov 12:4; 31:10). Cf. M. Zlotowitz, *BEREISHIS. Genesis: A New Translation with a Commentary Anthologized from Talmudic, Midrashic and Rabbinic Sources*, New York: Mesorah Publications, 1977, 131.

[420] This is a reversal of the curse of Jer 16.

With its repeated (8 times) and varied use of *šwb*, Poem VI is fitting as the concluding poem for this cycle. Through the device of ambiguity both the physical/geographical (return to the land) and the spiritual/intellectual content (turn away from Yhwh, return to Yhwh) of *šwb* are brought together in the same expression. The return to the land is continually linked to return to Yhwh.

Poem VI gives priority to the feminine figure as the active one. It is *her* deeds which effect a change (Rachel's weeping brings a response in stanza 1). *She* is the one who has the power to turn away or turn back (*btwlt yśr'l* of stanza 3). The turning of the masculine figure Ephraim (stanza 2), on the other hand, is due not to his own activity but to Yhwh's training and chastisement. Yet all three stanzas have a common focus: the interaction between the people and Yhwh. This interaction is presented through the image of familial relationships: the father-child relationship with its obligation and responsibility (Ephraim is the 'son,' Israel the 'daughter' of Yhwh); the mother-child relationship with its care and love (Rachel and her sons). Yhwh indeed acts in favor of his people (Ephraim) but they (virgin Israel) must respond, for he has given them the possibility to begin anew (*br' yhwh ḥdšh b'rṣ*).

3.9 PROSE CONCLUSION — 31:23-40

23 *kh-’mr* *yhwh ṣb’wt*
’lhy yśr’l

ʿwd y’mrw ’t-hdbr hzh

b’rṣ yhwdh
wbʿryw

bšwby ’t-šbwtm

ybrk *k* *yhwh*
nwh-ṣdq
hr hqdš

24 *wyšbw bh*
yhwdh
wkl-ʿryw yḥdw *’krym*
wnsʿw bʿdr

25 *ky* *hrwyty*
npš ʿyph
wkl *npš d’bh*
ml’ty

26 *ʿl-z’t hqyṣty*
w’r’h
wšnty ʿrbh ly

27 *hnh ymym b'ym n'm-yhwh*

wzr'ty ┌ *'t-byt yśr'l*
└ *w't-byt yhwdh*
┌ *zr' 'dm*
└ *wzr' bhmh*

28 *whyh k'šr* ┌ *šqdty 'lyhm* ┌ *lntwš*
├ *wlntwṣ*
├ *wlhrs*
├ *wlh'byd*
└ *wlhr'*

kn └ *'šqd 'lyhm* ┌ *lbnwt*
└ *wlnṭw'*

n'm-yhwh

29 *bymym hhm*

l' - y'mrw 'wd

┌ { *'bwt 'klw bsr*
wšny bnym tqhynh

30 └ { *ky 'm-'yš b'wnw ymwt*
kl-h'dm h'kl hbsr tqhynh šnyw

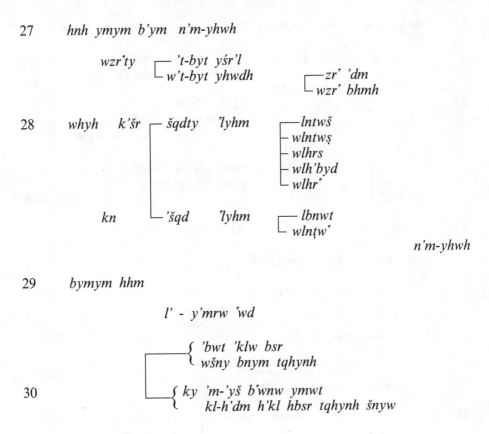

31 *hnh ymym b'ym n'm-yhwh*

wkrty ┌ *'t-byt yśr'l*
└ *w't-byt yhwdh*

bryt ḥdšh

32 ┌ *l' kbryt* ┌ *'šr krty 't-'bwtm*
bywm hḥzyqy bydm
lhwṣy'm m'rṣ mṣrym

├ *'šr - hmh hprw 't-bryty*
w'nky b'lty bm
n'm-yhwh

33 *ky* └ *z't hbryt* └ *'šr 'krt 't-byt yśr'l*

'ḥry hymym hhm n'm-yhwh

┌ *ntty 't-twrty*
┌ *bqrbm*
└ *w'l-lbm*
└ *'ktbnh*

whmh ┌ *whyyty lhm l'lhym*
└ *yhyw - ly l'm*

34 *wl' ylmdw 'wd* ┌ *'yš 't-r'hw*
└ *w'yš 't-'ḥyw l'mr*
d'w 't-yhwh

ky- kwlm yd'w 'wty ┌ *lmqṭnm*
└ *w'd-gdwlm* *n'm-yhwh*

ky ┌ *'slḥ*
┌ *l'wnm*
└ *wlḥṭ'tm*
└ *l' 'zkr-'wd*

– –
– –

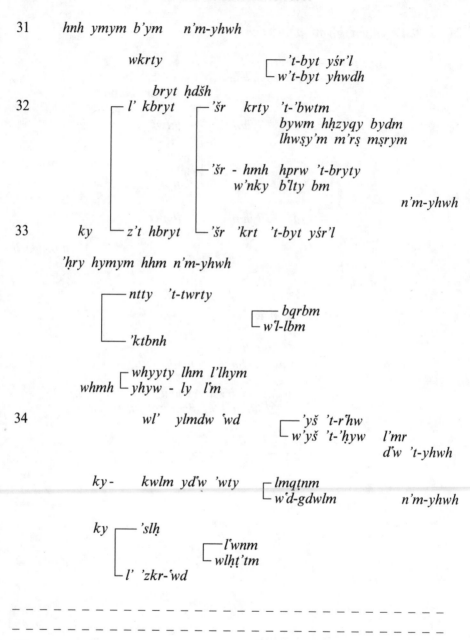

35 *kh 'mr yhwh*

ntn šmš l'wr ywmm
ḥqt yrḥ
wkwkbym l'wr lylh

rgʿ hym wyhmw glyw

yhwh ṣb'wt šmw

36 *'m-ymšw hḥqym h'lh mlpny n'm-yhwh*
gm zrʿ yśr'l yšbtw mhywt gwy lpny
kl-hymym

37 *kh 'mr yhwh*

'm-ymdw šmym mlmʿlh
wyḥqrw mwsdy-'rṣ lmṭh
gm-'ny 'm's bkl-zrʿ yśr'l
ʿl-kl-'šr ʿśw n'm-yhwh

---

38 *hnh ymym (b'ym) n'm-yhwh*

wnbnth hʿyr lyhwh
mmgdl ḥnn'l
šʿr hpnh

39 *wyṣ' ʿwd qwh hmdh ngdw*
ʿl-gbʿt grb
wnsb gʿth

40 *wkl-hʿmq hpgrym*
whdšn
wkl-hšrmwt ʿd-nḥl qdrwn
ʿd-pnt šʿr hswsym mzrḥh

qdš lyhwh

l' - yntš
wl' - yhrs ʿwd
lʿwlm

3.9 *Prose Conclusion* — TOTAL NEWNESS (31:23-40)

Jeremiah 30-31 closes with a lengthy section (18 verses) which is strikingly different not only from the immediately preceding unit (31:15-22) but also from the rest of the Little Book of Consolation. Its uniqueness lies in its obvious prose style, distinguished by longer sentences, many relative and/or explanatory clauses, heavy use of conjunctions, direct-object markers, pronouns, etc. It also lacks that clipped parallel construction so clearly poetic and so much used in the previous lines. In addition, 31:23-40 uses many more expressions which explicitly point to the future[421] and is more consistently in first person-third person style than is true of 30:1-31:22.[422]

These stylistic changes, together with the formulaic introduction *kh 'mr yhwh*, indicate the beginning of a new section whose unity is not weakened by either the internal divisions or the internal use of *kh 'mr yhwh* (in 31:35,37). Thematic unity is found in a consistent presentation of Yhwh as the one who acts in favor of his people to forgive them despite their sinful deeds (31:25-26,28,31-32,34,37,38-40). Formally, the conclusion manifests a better-developed parallelism and a more complex structure than that observed in some of the preceding poetic portions.

This unit is divided into two major sections, both of which can be subdivided. The major divisions are indicated by *kh 'mr yhwh* (31:23,35)[423] with sub-sections introduced by *hnh ymym b'ym n'm yhwh* (31:27,31,38). *l' ... 'wd*, which closes both larger sections (31:34,40), is a lexical and semantic means to both divide and unify this unit.

3.9.1 PART I — ALL THINGS ANEW (31:23-34)

3.9.1.1 Section 1 — *Blessing Anew* (31:23-26)

The final unit of Jer 30-31 opens, like Poem I (30:5), with Yhwh quoting the people. In 30:5 (Poem I) he quotes a present saying, one which expresses the people's experience, while in 31:23 he refers to their future words (*'wd y'mrw*). The emphatic position of *'wd*[424] makes clear the two-dimensional referent — past and future — and thus introduces

---

[421] *'wd* is found as frequently in these 18 verses as in the rest of the two chapters (the other 46 verses); *hnh ymym b'ym* or other expressions using *ywm* and pointing toward the future are found 5 times in these verses, 5 times in the remainder of these two chapters.

[422] Apart from this unit, there are a few first person-third person insertions in what is otherwise a text of predominantly first person-second person style.

[423] The presence of this expression in 31:37 does not indicate a major division.

[424] Cf. G-K § 142g; Joüon § 155p; T. Muraoka, *Emphatic Words*, 43, notes (though regarding narrative text) that "the fronting of the adverb is unmistakably for the sense of emphasis or contrast."

the notion of continuity with the past which plays a major role in this prose conclusion.[425]

The God who speaks here is not simply *yhwh* but *yhwh ṣb'wt 'lhy yśr'l*, the God who is not only powerful[426] but also identified with the people. He is Lord of Israel as well as Lord of creation. In taking up the words of the people Yhwh repeats their pronouncement of a blessing on the land: *ybrkk yhwh nwh-ṣdq hr hqdš* (31:23), a blessing which cannot be separated from Yhwh's deed of restoring fortunes and of bringing back to the land (*b'rṣ yhwdh wb'ryw bšwby 't-šbwtm*).[427]

Although the meaning of *nwh-ṣdq* and *hr hqdš* is unambiguous, the referents of the several words are not clear. These two expressions are usually interpreted as a double vocative referring to the 2 m.s. (object) suffix of *ybrkk*. Nevertheless, the context points to Yhwh as the antecedent of *nwh-ṣdq*.[428] The Masoretic accents indicate that *nwh-ṣdq* is in apposition to *yhwh* (the subject)[429] leaving *hr hqdš* as vocative. Another argument in favor of this interpretation is that Jer 50:7, the only other occurrence of *nwh-ṣdq* in the MT, clearly understands it to be an attribute of Yhwh.

Some ambiguity also exists concerning the locus of righteousness (*ṣdq*) which some scholars hold to be the city[430] while others consider it to be the whole land.[431] Such a differentiation is not of great importance since the city often represents the nation. Some exegetes disagree about whether the attributes *ṣdq* and *hqdš* are to be ascribed to Yhwh or to the place.[432] If the entire expression *nwh-ṣdq* is considered to refer to Yhwh,

---

[425] The notion of continuity, though not developed for the entire unit 31:23-34, has been noted and discussed concerning 31:31-34. Cf., e.g., B. W. Anderson, "The New Covenant and the Old" in B. W. Anderson, ed., *The Old Testament and Christian Faith*, London: SCM Press, 1964, 232-39; R. Martin-Achard, "Quelques remarques sur la nouvelle alliance chez Jérémie (Jérémie 31,31-34)" in C. Brekelmans, ed., *Questions disputées d'Ancien Testament. Méthode et Théologie*, BEThL 33, Grembloux: Editions J. Duculot; Leuven: Leuven University Press, 1974, 157; W. Lemke, "Jeremiah 31:31-34" *Int* 37 (1983) 186-87.

[426] Cf. above, p. 40 and n. 89.

[427] The reference to *yhwdh* indicates the exilic provenance of this text. Cf. Giesebrecht, 170; Rudolph, 199. S. Böhmer, *Heimkehr*, 71, opts for exilic provenance though saying it could well have been earlier. Weiser, 283, sees no textual basis for assigning this a date after 587, since there is no mention of destruction.

[428] Cf. Sym and Aq and, more recently, Thompson, 577, who states: "The context seems to require that these phrases be used of Yhwh."

[429] *yhwh* is joined by the conjunctive accent *merka* to the following *nwh-ṣdq* which has the disjunctive *tibḥa*.

[430] Cornill, 342; Giesebrecht, 170; Condamin, 225; Weiser, 263; Carroll 605-606; and H. Ringgren, "*nwh*," *TWAT* V, 297. Bright, 282, restricts it to the temple mount.

[431] *hr hqdš(-y)* is used as a reference to Zion but also as an attribute of the land in Is 11:9; 57:3; 65:25. Cf. Volz, 278; Rudolph, 198-99.

[432] Cf. Carroll, 605.

the word *ṣdq* would clearly be ascribed to him. However, the relationship between *hqdš* and *yhwh* is somewhat different. Since *nwh-ṣdq* is in apposition to *yhwh* which precedes it and also has much the same content as *hr hqdš* which follows, it forms a kind of hinge expression,[433] linking *hr hqdš* with *yhwh* as the locus of his presence.

Yhwh often blesses people with prosperity, progeny, food, health, political power,[434] or, to use a more general expression, he blesses the people with increase.[435] He acts in favor of the people, so that in reality the one blessed is always a person (or persons) rather than a thing.[436] Only in this text (Jer 31:23) and in Gn 2:3 and Ex 20:11, where Yhwh blesses the Sabbath, is he said to bless a thing without it explicitly mediating a blessing for the people.[437] The same notion of blessing found in Gn 2:3 and Ex 20:11 fits well in Jer 31:23 where the blessing of *hr hqdš* by Yhwh can be understood as his setting the place apart not only for himself, but especially as a point of contact between himself and the people.

This wish, then, expresses the hope that Yhwh's presence be found in the midst of the people, that it touch their lives more deeply and more closely, and thus gives explicit continuity with the past. The blessing, pronounced once, will be repeated, implying that the land will once again be the locus of Yhwh's presence for the people.[438]

Those who will live there encompass the whole of society (*yhwdh wkl-ʿryw yḥdw ʾkrym wnsʿw bʿdr*, 31:24), as indicated by merismus.[439] The group is specified by its place of dwelling: some live within the city walls (*wkl-ʿryw*), others, by virtue of their profession (*ʾkrym wnsʿw bʿdr*[440]),

---

[433] Both *hr* and *nwh* refer to places, locations. The two expressions are syntactically identical, both being *nomen regens* plus *nomen rectum*. Both *ṣdq* and *qdš* are concepts related to Yhwh and his presence.

[434] Dt 7:13-14 is a typical example of such blessing; cf. J. Pedersen, *Israel* I-II, 204-212, for a lengthy exposition of the concept.

[435] This increase takes many forms: e.g., bread and water (Ex 23:25); fruit of body and soul (Dt 28:4); basket and kneading trough (Dt 28:5); growth of the earth (Ps 65:11).

[436] Cf. H. Mowvley, "The Concept and Content of 'Blessing' in the Old Testament" *BT* 16 (1965) 77-78.

[437] In Gn 2:3 and Ex 20:11 Yhwh blesses the Sabbath. The content of the blessing is that the day be set apart, made different from the others. Ex 20:11 makes it clear that the day is set aside by Yhwh, and thus for the people, as a time of closer contact with him.

[438] Thompson, 577.

[439] Merismus seems an apt term to describe the device used here, although J. Krašovec does not include this text among his examples in either *Der Merismus im Biblisch-Hebräischen und Nordwestsemitischen*, BibOr 33, Rome: Biblical Institute Press 1977, or "Merism – Polar Expression in Biblical Hebrew," 231-39. However Cornill, 343, Volz, 278, Weiser, 283, and Rudolph, 199, all see this expression as indicating the totality of the returnees.

[440] Read *wnsʿw* according to the MT, interpreting it as a relative clause without *ʾšr*, following G-K §138e and §155n. Some (BHS; Cornill, 343; Giesebrecht, 170; Volz, 278)

dwell outside the walls. The expression *yhwdh wkl-ʿryw*, expanded from a similar expression in 31:23, indicates that the people are made up of more than the city-dwellers. The totality of the nation, whatever their profession or original place of residence, will together inhabit the land which is here declared a holy place.

The allusion to blessing found in the simple statement *wyšbw bh* is developed and specified in the following verse where an emphatic *ky* (indeed)[441] introduces Yhwh's actions on behalf of the people: *ky hrwyty npš ʿyph wkl-npš d'bh ml'ty* (31:25). The presence of a syntactic chiasm[442] tends to make the double object, with its repeated noun and similar sounding adjectives[443] and meaning,[444] merge into a single object. This serves to highlight Yhwh's deeds of *rwh* and *ml'*.[445]

Continuity with the past, stated explicitly by the use of *ʿwd* in 31:23, has now changed to implicit discontinuity. There will certainly be a change.[446] Yhwh will reverse the situation of his people; he will satiate (*rwh*) those who need refreshment and will fill (*ml'*) those who languish (cf. 31:13-14). The people will be not only kept alive but filled to the limit, until there is no want or lack. They will experience not merely adequacy but satiety. Discontinuity with the past is clearly indicated, though not stated as such.

Although it is exegetically or textually clear, the closing line of this first subsection (31:26) is, like 31:22b, very enigmatic.[447] Even the identification of the speaker is difficult, for although the immediate context indicates it to be Yhwh,[448] modern commentators deny the possibility that the statement could have been his. Rather they assign these words to a variety of human subjects. Some consider it an indication that the prophecy was received in a dreamlike state or

---

repoint it as a participle. Both Bright, 276, and Rudolph, 198, acknowledge the validity of either choice.

441 J. Muilenburg, "The Particle *ky*," 145.

442 Verb-object-object-verb.

443 The sonoric similarity is true of both consonants: /ʿ/ – /'/; /p/ – /b/; /h/ – /h/ (guttural; plosive; aspirate) and vowels: /ă/ – /ā/; /ē/ – /ă/; /ā/ – /ā/.

444 *ʿyph* means weary, in need of refreshment (cf. Dt 25:18; 2 Sm 17:29) or in need of water (cf. Is 29:8; Ps 143:6); *d'bh* means languishing, wasting away, moving toward non-existence or death (cf. Ps 88:10). Read *d'bh* as in the MT, i.e., *qal* perfect 3 f.s. used (a) in an incomplete relative clause whose attributive relation is expressed by simple co-ordination (G-K § 155b) and (b) in place of an adjective (G-K § 155f).

445 E. Zurro, *Procedimientos iterativos*, 151-52, considers the repetition of the same noun with semantically similar adjectives to be a poetic means of intensification of an idea.

446 Note the use of the perfect tense with future meaning, understood as an assured future or *perfectum confidentiae* (G-K § 106n).

447 Cornill, 344, gives a clear statement of the problem.

448 The fact is that the whole has been in 1 s. speech of Yhwh thus far and now appears to continue without change.

ecstasy[449]; others hold it to be a marginal gloss added by some reader who was delighted with the text[450]; still others suggest it is the citation of some hymn refrain.[451]

The basis for imputing these words to a human subject is the belief that the idea cannot be predicated of Yhwh.[452] Yet the verb *qyṣ* (awake) is attributed to him in Ps 44:24 and 78:65. In both of these instances his 'waking' is a metaphor for his becoming aware of the people's need and acting in their favor. Another problem lies in ascribing to Yhwh *šnty ʿrbh*, which is almost always translated as 'my sleep was sweet.' Yet since *ʿrb* can also mean 'overtake,' 'become darkness,' and 'fail,'[453] if the latter sense were accepted as a possible meaning for *ʿrbh* of 31:26, one could also admit *šnty ʿrbh* as words of Yhwh. In this case they would reflect his sorrow or regret at past inaction (expressed by the metaphor of sleep), inaction which he remedies by his care for his people (expressed in the metaphor to awaken).

Perhaps these are words uttered by Yhwh or words of the prophet,[454] but to whomever they may be attributed, they reinforce the implicit discontinuity: being awake and aware (*hqyṣty w'r'h*) the speaker recognizes the past for what it was (*wšnty ʿrbh ly*). With this enigmatic saying, the first sub-section closes.

3.9.1.2 Section 2 — *A New Proverb* (31:27-30)

The tension of continuity-discontinuity becomes more marked in this section which explicitly states both. First continuity is expressed through the use of *k'šr ... kn* (31:28) and then discontinuity is proclaimed with *l' ... ʿwd* (31:29).

The section opens with the formulaic *hnh ymym b'ym*, which gives a formality and an oracular force to what follows by assuring the action of Yhwh at some unspecified future moment.[455] Such an intervention of Yhwh, aimed at effecting change in the future, forms the broad definition of 'eschatology.'[456]

---

[449] Giesebrecht, 170. Volz, 278, however, denies even the possibility of such an understanding since Jeremiah did not receive the word of Yhwh in sleep.

[450] Volz, 278; Condamin, 228; Bright, 282.

[451] Weiser, 283; Rudolph, 200.

[452] I have failed to locate a specific reason for this commonly held opinion.

[453] Cf. C.C. Torrey, "Studies in the Aramaic of the First Century A. D." *ZAW* 65 (1953) 240, who notes that the Hebrew verb *ʿareb* 'enter, go under' was familiar in the tropical sense 'fail, perish,' as used in Is 24:11.

[454] It is difficult to ascribe them to a glossator since a gloss generally explains a text, making it more, rather than less, clear.

[455] Cf. G. von Rad, "*hēmera*," *TDNT* II, 946; H. Kosmala, "'At the End of the Days'" *ASTI* 2 (1963) 29; H.D. Potter, "The New Covenant in Jer xxxi:31-34" *VT* 33 (1983) 355.

[456] Cf. above, p. 29, n. 32.

Progeny are promised. Yhwh will act: *wzrʿty ʾt-byt yśrʾl wʾt-byt yhwdh zrʿ ʾdm wzrʿ bhmh.*[457] *zrʿ* is clearly a key word[458] as indicated by the root repetition (verb once, noun twice). It recalls the promise to the patriarchs that their progeny (*zrʿ*) will inherit the land.[459] 'Sowing' might also allude to the re-establishment of relationship between Yhwh and his people, an image set out in Hos 2:25. Since the multiplication of the people, implied in 'sowing,' is considered a sign of renewal after judgment in Jer 3:16; 30:19,[460] *zrʿ*, then, contains an implicit reference to renewed relationship.

The people have a future, for Yhwh will sow / will 'seed' (*zrʿ*) both cattle (*zrʿ bhmh*) and progeny (*zrʿ ʾdm*).[461] Yet even if they can look forward to a future, they cannot deny their past for their descendants will be stamped by who and what their fathers were,[462] as the proverb of 31:29 makes evident.

Although the promise of progeny (*zrʿ*) is guaranteed by comparison with the past (*kʾšr ... kn*, 31:28), it will, nevertheless, be very different. Although the fact of Yhwh's action as *šqd ʿlyhm* is consistent in both past and future, the content of *šqd* differs: in the past his deed was negative while in the future it will be positive. The basis for future assurance is Yhwh's past vigilance *lntwš wlntwṣ wlhrs wlhʾbyd wlhrʿ*.[463] Israel's past negative experience is the guarantee of her positive future. There is a note of discontinuity between past and future, implicitly present in the opposition of the infinitives which complete *šqdty* and *ʾšqd* (31:28), and explicitly present in the *lʾ ... ʿwd* of 31:29.

The five infinitives which give specificity to Yhwh's past vigilance (*šqdty*) proceed with increasing severity: first, 'to uproot' (*ntš*),[464] which in itself does not necessarily imply destruction (in Exile the people existed though they were uprooted); then, 'to pull down' (*ntṣ*) which indicates a lack of protection afforded by walls of house or city; then, 'to lie in ruins'

---

457 This is a reversal of the situation pictured in 4:25 where *ʾyn hʾdm wkl-ʿwp hšmym nddw*.

458 W. G. E. Watson, *Classical Hebrew Poetry*, 279, 287-88.

459 To Abraham, Gn 12:7; 13:15; to Isaac, Gn 26:4; to Jacob, Gn 28:13; 35:12.

460 Weiser, 284; Thompson, 578; Carroll, 607.

461 This is another instance of merismus, according to J. Krašovec, *Der Merismus*, 75.

462 Cf. H. D. Preuss, "*zrʿ*," *TWAT* II, 686.

463 Here and elsewhere in Jeremiah the negative aspect is much more highly developed than the positive, reflecting, perhaps, the overriding negativity of the book as a whole. It is indicated here by the five infinitives which express negative action. This is the only instance in Jeremiah where these five verbs are found together. Although the five are not found together elsewhere in Jer, the first four are also in 1:10; *ntš*, *ntṣ*, and *ʾbd* are in 18:7; *ntš* and *hrs* in 24:6, 31:40 and 42:10.

464 *ntš*, to pluck up or 'un-plant,' destruction due to lack of rootedness, is an image in opposition to *zrʿ* of the previous verse. Cf. J. Hausmann, "*ntš*," *TWAT* V, 730.

(*hrs*)[465] or no longer exist as a people; finally, 'to annihilate' (*'bd*)[466] or destroy the people's existence as individuals. The final infinitive summarizes the whole in a single action of Yhwh: *hr'*, 'to do harm' or 'to do evil,' or, as is predicated of Yhwh in Jer 25:6,29, 'to punish'[467] (the only other instance of this usage in Jer). Rather than being merely repetitious,[468] this list is a nuanced development in which the meaning of each succeeding word increases the negative element, with the last predicating of Yhwh a destructive deed.

The certainty of Yhwh's vigilance with which the people are familiar through personal experience of punishment is now extended to embrace his positive action. Although the positive verbs used are only two (*bnh* and *nṭ'*), they invert the negative imagery of the five preceding infinitives in its totality. *bnh* reverses the destruction of walls, buildings, houses, expressing the opposite of *ntṣ* and *hrs*; similarly, *nṭ'* is the opposite of *ntš*. What was 'un-built' will again be built, what had been 'unplanted' will again be planted. Whether in the sphere of agriculture and nature or of building and city, Yhwh gives assurance of his constructive future actions.[469] The two positive verbs (*bnh* and *nṭ'*) also reverse the general actions expressed by *h'bd* and *hr''*. When something is planted or built, one may no longer speak of annihilation.

Even more important than the act itself are its results.[470] In the days when Yhwh will 'seed' (*zr'*) Israel and Judah, in the days when he will *bnh* and *nṭ'*, in those days there will be a change. The series of actions is used metaphorically, rather than literally, expressing the hope in a future saving deed, the beginning anew of a "Heilsgeschichte."[471] Since there is a development from negative to positive acts, the list of verbs is an expression of a hope which sees future salvation replacing lack of salvation.[472]

---

[465] *ntṣ* and *hrs* picture a more urban scene, expressing the idea of 'pull down' or 'un-build' as one would do to the walls of a house or a city. *ntṣ* quite literally means 'to pull down the walls' (cf. Ch. Barth, "*ntṣ*," *TWAT* V, 717-18) while *hrs*, beyond this, also means 'to lie in ruins' or 'to no longer exist' (cf. G. Münderlein, "*hrs*," *TWAT* II, 499-500).

[466] *h'byd* means 'exterminate, eradicate, annihilate, destroy' so that no traces will be left, and often has people as object. Cf. B. Otzen, "*'bd*," *TWAT* I, 21-22.

[467] Such a statement, predicated of Yhwh, is rare in the OT. Cf. H. J. Stoebe, "*r''*," *THAT* II, 803.

[468] W. G. E. Watson, *Classical Hebrew Poetry*, 33, places lists among stylistic devices in poetry.

[469] Note that these images also mirror the concepts of city/country used in identifying the people in 31:24.

[470] R. Bach, "Bauen und Pflanzen" in R. Rendtorff und K. Koch, ed., *Studien zur Theologie der alttestamentlichen Überlieferungen*, Fs. G. von Rad, Neukirchen Kreis Moers: Neukirchener Verlag, 1961, 18.

[471] Cf. G. Münderlein, "*hrs*," *TWAT* II, 501.

[472] There is a certain logic to the presence here of these words, despite S. Herrmann's statement to the contrary (Cf. *Die prophetischen Heilserwartungen*, 167).

The first change is *l'-y'mrw ʿwd*: they will no longer say what was said in the past. The proverbial statement (found also in Ez 18:2), which will not be repeated 'in those days,' is a metaphor for collective guilt: the sons will suffer the consequences of the father's actions (*'bwt 'klw bsr wšny bnym tqhynh*).

This proverb has been interpreted as a complaint of the exiles who are dissatisfied with their own fate, the loss of the land due to their fathers' sins.[473] Whether or not one accepts an eschatological context as that which gives these lines consonance,[474] they do appear to be part of an attempt to explain the relationship between the exilic and pre-exilic generations. They hold out hope for the exiles in a way similar to that ascribed to Ez 18:2.[475] Both the proverb of the past and that of the future have their roots in earlier traditions.[476] Yet the emphasis here is on change (discontinuity) as presented textually with the adversative, contrastive sense carried by *ky ... 'm*.[477] Discontinuity is also present in the literary transformation which exists in the text. There is a tripartite change: first, a shift from a positive (*k'šr ... kn*, 31:28) to a negative statement (*l' y'mrw*), accenting change which now becomes the standard; second, a shift from more factual statements which concern physical reality (*y'mrw*, 31:23; *wyšbw*, 31:24; *hrwyty*, 31:25; *wzrʿty*, 31:27; *'šqd*, 31:28) to descriptive imagery (*šny bnym tqhynh*, 31:29-30) more closely allied to relationships; and, third, a shift from emphasis on the collectivity or community to concern for the individual.

Discontinuity with the past gains precedence, yet always with an eye to what will remain: Yhwh's deed of *šqd* and the death of the sinner perdure.[478]

3.9.1.3 Section 3 — *A New Covenant* (31:31-34)

This short section of the poetic cycle of Jer 30-31, the one most studied and quoted, has made the Little Book of Consolation famous, for

---

473 Giesebrecht, 171; Bright, 283; Weiser, 285; Thompson, 578.

474 So, H. G. May, "Individual Responsibility and Retribution" *HUCA* 32 (1961) 114-15.

475 L. Rost, "Die Schuld der Väter" in *Studien zum Alten Testament*, BWANT 101, Stuttgart, Berlin, Köln, Mainz: W. Kohlhammer, 1974, 71.

476 The proverb of the past is rooted in the threat of Ex 20:5; Dt 5:9; that of the future in Dt 24:16; 2 Kg 14:16. Cf. G. von Rad, *Das 5. Buch Mose. Deuteronomium*, ATD 8, (3., unveränd. Auflage) Göttingen: Vandenhoeck & Ruprecht, 1978, 109, who maintains that the notion of personal guilt and individual responsibility for sin was not a late development but part of the early tradition of Israel.

477 Cf. J. Muilenburg, "The Particle *ky*," 142.

478 Whether this should be seen as "eine kleinmütige Verengerung der gewaltigen Verheissung von 31-34" (Rudolph, 201) depends on whether the text is considered sequentially (i.e., as 31:31-34 being a development which follows 31:27-30).

it is the only OT text which uses the expression 'new covenant.' Although often studied apart from its literary context, 31:31-34 is in close relationship with the two preceding sections with which it forms the unit 31:23-34. 31:31-34 opens, like 31:27-30, with *hnh ymym b'ym n'm-yhwh* (31:31) and concludes with a *l' ... ʿwd* statement (31:34), repeated twice, once referring to the deeds of the people, once to the deeds of Yhwh. It reflects the concern with continuity-discontinuity noted in the previous section. Here, however, the accent is on discontinuity which is presented explicitly four times: *bryt ḥdšh* (31:31), *l' kbryt* (31:32), *l' ylmdw ʿwd* and *l' 'zkr-ʿwd* (31:34), while continuity is only implicitly present.

The opening statement points to an unspecified future when Yhwh will act with and for the entire people, both the Northern and the Southern Kingdoms.[479] To them *bryt ḥdšh* is promised.

A much debated term,[480] *bryt* holds a position of importance in this text.[481] Although some scholars consider it to be a late theological concept, originating with the 8th century prophets,[482] and others interpret it to be a very early notion, reaching back as early as Sinai and Exodus,[483] for the purposes of this study the date of origin has little importance. What is certain is that 'covenant' was an important theological concept throughout the history of Israel, whether its link to 'treaty' was early or late.[484]

The necessary identification of *bryt* with the treaty form[485] has been superseded by a broader understanding,[486] due to the wide discussion concerning the type of relationship established by *bryt*. Kutsch's definition of *bryt* as 'Verpflichtung' (obligation)[487] has its validity.

---

[479] Some commentators who eliminate *'t-byt yhwdh* as a later addition consider *yśr'l* a reference to the populace of what was once the united kingdom. Cf. Cornill, 353; Bright, 283; Weiser, 286; Carroll, 610. Rudolph, 201, on the other hand, considers it addressed to the North alone.

[480] E.W. Nicholson, "Covenant in a Century of Study since Wellhausen" in *Crises and Perspectives: Studies in Ancient Near Eastern Polytheism, Biblical Theology, Palestinian Archaeology and Intertestamental Literature*, OTS 24, Leiden: E.J. Brill, 1986, 54-63, summarizes the changing emphases in the understanding of *bryt* since Wellhausen (1878) through the identification of *bryt* with treaty and back to a more theological understanding.

[481] It is used four times in two verses.

[482] E.g., J. Wellhausen, *Prolegomena to the History of Ancient Israel*, Gloucester, Mass.: Peter Smith, 1973 (reprint of 1957 ed.), 417-19.

[483] E.g., G. Mendenhall, *Law and Covenant in Israel and the Ancient Near East*, Pittsburgh: The Biblical Colloquium, 1955, 37.

[484] Cf. D.J. McCarthy, *Treaty and Covenant* (rev. ed.), AnBib 21A, Rome: Biblical Institute Press, 1978, 14.

[485] G. Mendenhall, *Law and Covenant*, 36-39.

[486] Cf. E.W. Nicholson, "Covenant in a Century of Study," 65.

[487] Cf. E. Kutsch, "Gottes Zuspruch und Anspruch," 71-90.

Nonetheless such obligation is often mutual and presupposes an existing agreement or relationship for which it seeks a legal foundation.[488] It is precisely this relational aspect of *bryt* which has precedence in Jer 31:31-34.

31:22 describes the covenant from which the *bryt ḥdšh* is distanced as the one established at the time of the Exodus (*l' kbryt 'šr krty 't-'bwtm bywm hḥzyqy bydm lhwṣy'm m'rṣ mṣrym*). Although this may be a reference to the Sinai covenant,[489] still, rather than focusing on legal bonds or the laws of that covenant, the text presents that *bryt* as one constituted by a relationship: *w'nky b'lty bm* (31:32).[490]

The simple statement *'šr-hmh hprw 't-bryty w'nky b'lty bm* (31:32) clarifies the importance of this relationship. Since both *hmh* and *'nky* are subject pronouns used with finite verbs (i.e., superfluous elements) they indicate an intense concern with or focus consciousness on the referents of the pronouns,[491] in this case Yhwh and the fathers. In addition, *waw* with the subject (*w'nky*) introducing a verbal clause points to an antithesis between the two groups thus described.[492] Since the action of the people (*hprw*) is clearly negative, this antithetical use of *waw* suggests that Yhwh's deed (*b'lty*) must be positive.[493] The contrast between the broken covenant and Yhwh's lordship is indicated not only by the pronoun subjects but also by the presence of *bryt* which, as a resumptive noun in the relative clause,[494] implies a close connection between *bryt* and *b'lty*.

---

[488] M. Weinfeld, "*Berît* – Covenant vs. Obligation" (Review article of Kutsch's *Verheissung und Gesetz*) *Bib* 56 (1975) 124-25; D. J. McCarthy, "*Berît* and Covenant in the Deuteronomistic History" in G. W. Anderson, *et al.*, ed., *Studies in the Religion of Ancient Israel*, SVT 23, Leiden: E. J. Brill, 1972, 84-85. *Ibid.*, *Treaty and Covenant*, 19-22, 292, 297.

[489] Cornill, 350; Volz, 293; Weiser, 286; Rudolph, 201; Thompson, 580; J. Mejía, "La problématique de l'Ancienne et de la Nouvelle Alliance dans Jérémie xxxi 31-34 et quelques autres textes" in J. A. Emerton, ed., *Congress Volume: Vienna 1980*, SVT 32, Leiden: E. J. Brill, 1981, 270.

[490] The text here refers to the *bryt l'bwtm* which could well mean the covenant made with Abraham, Isaac, and Jacob, rather than the Sinai covenant. Cf. R. Martin-Achard, "Quelques remarques sur la nouvelle alliance," 152-53.

[491] T. Muraoka, *Emphatic Words*, 48.

[492] G-K § 142d.

[493] This is not a universally held opinion, as can be seen by a glance at the commentaries. Rudolph, 201-202, considers *b'lty* to be lordship which is punitive; while Cornill, 354, Giesebrecht, 172, and Condamin, 230, following the LXX, emend *b'lty* to *g'lty* ("I rejected them").

[494] The presence of a noun as resumptive (Lambdin § 70 uses this term, while both Joüon § 168g-i and G-K § 155f-m opt for 'retrospective') in a relative clause is rare. Joüon § 158h, n. 2, counts only two examples of a resumptive noun, though the resumptive pronoun is very common.

Both the general context of this poetic cycle which includes the relationship determined by *ḥsd* and *'hb*, introduced in 30:14 and developed in 31:3, and the familial relationships expressed in 31:15-22 indicate the fact that *b'l* might better be understood as 'husband' than as 'lord.'[495] *b'l* was often used to portray the marital relationship, for the husband was clearly the master and his wife subservient.[496] Yet one must not overemphasize the aspect of power or possession since the relationship of *b'l* "presupposes a psychic community, ... an intimate relation" within whose limits power is exercised.[497] Thus in the context of this poetic cycle *b'l*, while certainly meaning 'lord,' can also mean 'husband,' a lordship in intimacy and authority rather than power, accenting not a punitive but a caring authority. Such an interpretation is consistent with covenant language, since the relationship legalized by *bryt* extended beyond the notion of political agreement or vassal treaty to include adoption and marriage among others.[498]

In light of this, the broken covenant could be equated with a wife's rejection of her husband, an image used in Jer 2-3 and Hos 2-3 to express the people's rejection of Yhwh. With the aspect of discontinuity with the past now set out, the description of the newness begins:

l'	*kbryt 'šr krty*	(31:32)	is replaced by
ky z't	*hbryt 'šr 'krt*	(31:33).	

The break with the past is not absolute, for *bryt* remains, yet with a difference,[499] now to be defined.

bryt is placed in a future which repeats that of *hnh ymym b'ym* but in different words: *'ḥry hymym hhm*.[500] It refers to a future time, though to what specific moment is unclear.

---

[495] For the interpretation of *b'l* as husband, cf. Carroll, 609. Both Bright, 283, and Thompson, 581, use 'Lord' but admit the possibility of 'husband.'

[496] R. de Vaux, *Les institutions de l'Ancien Testament* I, Paris: Editions du Cerf, 1958, 48.

[497] J. Pedersen, *Israel* I-II, 62-63. E. Neufeld, *Ancient Hebrew Marriage Laws with Special References to General Semitic Laws and Customs*, London, New York, Toronto: Longmans, Green and Co., 1944, 232, denies a philological basis for Pedersen's inclusion of a sense of intimacy in the word *b'l* though he does agree that the fact of intimacy in marriage was a part of the actual relationship.

[498] For covenant as expressing these relationships, cf. R. de Vaux, *Les institutions*, 58-59; M. Weinfeld, "The Covenant of Grant in the Old Testament and in the Ancient Near East" *JAOS* 90 (1970) 200; *ibid.*, "*Berît* — Covenant vs. Obligation," 125; and P. Kalluveettil, *Declaration and Covenant*, 79-80 and 107-11.

[499] Cf. R. Martin-Achard, "Quelques remarques," 157.

[500] Rudolph, 202-203, refers this time to the return to the land, seen as an eschatological moment. Giesebrecht, 172, Condamin, 230, Bright, 227, Weiser, 264, construe it in a general way as 'after / at that time.' Cornill, 610, refers it back to the end of 31:32.

The first deed of Yhwh which gives content to this new covenant is presented in a chiasm

ntty ’t-twrty
bqrbm
wʿl-lbm
’ktbnh

in which only the nominal object appears to disturb the structure, thus drawing attention to itself. Since it includes Yhwh's *twrh*, the new covenant is indeed in continuity with the previous one. The content of the new covenant is the same as that of the old — same Torah, same partners.[501] The newness appears not in the content but in the manner of establishing the relationship and in its consequences of unmediated knowledge of Yhwh.

Yhwh's *twrh* will be inscribed not on stone tablets as in the Sinai tradition but *ʿl lbm*.[502] This image reverses that of Jer 17:1 where sin was inscribed on the people's hearts. There the sin was linked to the worship of false gods which would result in the loss of the land. Now they will have on their hearts the law of Yhwh which is understood both as the teaching given in his name which includes a knowledge of his action in history and as a rule of life,[503] or as the totality of divine revelation[504] which the rabbis considered the source of freedom, of honor and of life itself.[505] Yhwh will do this, and the certainty of the fact is expressed by the *perfectum confidentiae* of *ntty*.[506]

As a literary expression this statement is both a syntactic chiasm and a semantic parallelism. The chiastic structure, as noted above, focuses on *twrty*, while the parallelism serves as a means to disambiguate the first member.[507] *ntty ... bqrbm* is a general expression which could well mean 'to place in the midst of them,' i.e., in the midst of the community, externally, much as stone tablets might be placed. However, the second member specifies that what will be done is not an external deed but one which reaches the depth of their interiority (*ʿl-lbm*)[508] and which will have lasting effects (*ktb*).

---

[501] Rudolph, 202; B.W. Anderson, "The New Covenant and the Old," 236-37; R. Martin-Achard, "Quelques remarques," 156.

[502] Cf., e.g., Volz, 293.

[503] S.R. Driver, s.v. 'law' in *Hastings Dictionary of the Bible* III, 66; P. Buis, *La notion d'alliance dans l'Ancien Testament*, Lectio Divina 88, Paris: Editions du Cerf, 1976, 182.

[504] S.S. Cohen, s.v. 'torah,' *Universal Jewish Encyclopedia* X, 267.

[505] Cf. b Ab VI, 2-7; M Ps 1:18.

[506] G-K § 106n.

[507] Cf. A. Berlin, *Dynamics of Biblical Parallelism*, 96-97.

[508] *lb* is the locus not only of feelings but also of rational activity, thus that which is specifically human; cf. H.W. Wolff, *Anthropology of the Old Testament*, 46-55.

The result of such an act is expressed in the relationship articulated by the covenant formula: *whyyty lhm l'lhym whmh yhyw ly l'm* (31:33). Although the relationship itself is not new, it has an element of newness. The contrast between the use of *hmh* in this statement (31:33) and its use in 31:32 highlights the difference. In the past they broke the covenant (*hmh hprw 't-bryty*, 31:32); in the future they will be Yhwh's people (*whmh yhyw-ly l'm*, 31:33). The broken *bryt* is replaced by a relationship of belonging expressed in the covenant formula.

The two *l'* ... *'wd* statements clarify the relationship; the first speaks of the people, the second, of Yhwh. Both determine a future different from the past. They will no longer teach the knowledge of the Lord (*d'w 't-yhwh*, 31:34) because this will be part of their existence. There is no indication that all human teaching will cease,[509] but the promised knowledge of the Lord guarantees both the possibility and the certainty of adherence to the Torah.[510] Every action of the people will both be consistent with and express their acknowledgement of Yhwh as Lord.[511] In this context, with the former *bryt* expressed by *b'lty* (be husband to), *yd'* could well carry its most profound connotation of intimate personal knowledge.[512] It is clear that *yd'* includes more than cognitive knowledge, for it expresses participation in the life of or a deep concern for the object of knowing.[513]

Every person will be changed; the merismus *lmqṭnm w'd-gdwlm*[514] expresses totality by two extremes as well as by polysemy. Thus both young and old, together with all levels of society from the lowest to the highest are included.

If it were merely a question of completeness of thought, the section might end here on the note that all will know Yhwh. But the text moves forward. The final line is not accidental.[515] It gives the source, the actuating principle for what has been mentioned in the preceding line.

This section ends not with the activity of the people but with that of Yhwh. They will know him because he has acted first: *ky 'slḥ l'wnm wlḥṭ'tm l' 'zkr-'wd* (31:34).

Introduced by a climactic *ky*, the concluding line is an announcement of the deed which will establish the relationship,[516] the forgiveness of sin. The repetition of the same idea in a positive and then a

---

509 Cf. B.W. Anderson, "The New Covenant and the Old," 234-35; *pace* Carroll, 611.

510 Condamin, 231; P. Buis, "La nouvelle alliance" *VT* 18 (1968) 10; J. Mejía, "La problématique," 271.

511 Cf. the few occurrences of *yd' 't-yhwh/'lhy ('bwt)* in the MT, especially 1 Sm 2:12; 3:7; Hos 5:4 and 1 Chr 28:9.

512 Cf. Thompson, 581.

513 W. Schotroff, "*yd'*," *THAT* I, 685-91.

514 J. Krašovec, *Der Merismus*, 140.

515 Volz, 283; Rudolph, 202.

516 B.W. Anderson, "The New Covenant and the Old," 230.

negative formulation, together with the concluding *l'* ... *'wd* predicated of Yhwh both serve to emphasize the coming forgiveness. *l'* ... *'wd* reinforces the notion that a change will occur, not only in the lives of the people and their attitude toward Yhwh but also in his attitude toward them. This latter change is the basis for the former one. Individual guilt and punishment expressed in the *ky-* clause of 31:30 is no longer the norm; the *ky* clause of 31:34 assures forgiveness. The decisive deed is not sin (*'wn*, 31:30) but forgiveness (*slḥ*, 31:34).

Throughout 31:31-34 the focus is on the activity of Yhwh. He establishes a new covenant which touches the people's interiority (*ntty twrty* ... *'ktbnh*, 31:33) and reestablishes relationship (*whyyty* ... *whmh yhyw*). Yhwh's forgiveness (*'slḥ* ... *l' 'zkr 'wd*, 31:34) has made it all possible. The emphasis is placed on Yhwh's deeds, deeds of might and power for the first covenant and deeds of mercy for the new one.

With this, the first section (31:23-34) draws to a close. It has brought to light many aspects of both the continuity and the discontinuity which Yhwh promises. The text moves from what the people will say (blessing, 31:23) to what they will no longer say ("know the Lord," 31:34), from that which touches their exteriority and physicality (food, dwelling, progeny, 31:24,25,27) to that which touches their interiority and spirituality (being for Yhwh, knowing him, 31:33-34). It begins with positive comparisons (*'wd*, 31:23) and ends with negative ones (*l' 'wd*, 31:29,34), preparing for a change in the future toward which one is constantly drawn by textual references.

3.9.2 PART II — A GUARANTEED FUTURE (31:35-40)

The second part of the prose conclusion is composed of two smaller units, the first (31:35-37) introduced by *kh 'mr yhwh*, the second (31:38-40), by *hnnh ymym (b'ym) n'm-yhwh*. The first, clearly poetic,[517] accents the aspect of continuity, while the second, more prosaic, emphasizes discontinuity.

3.9.2.1 Section 1 — *Existence Assured* (31:35-37)

The first section, hymnic in tone,[518] opens with a presentation of Yhwh in his role as creator: *ntn šmš* ... *rgʿ hym* (31:35), recalling the first acts of the Genesis account (Gn 1:3-7). Through this image it introduces the two *'m-gm* statements which follow: the first by a reference to *hḥqym* (31:36), the second by a reference to heights and depths (31:37).

[517] Despite the presence of a poetic portion, 31:23-40 is called a prose conclusion because of the predominance of prose elements. This is similar to the situation of the poems, which, despite the predominance of poetic discourse, contain prose elements.

[518] Cf. Volz, 295; Weiser, 288-89; Rudolph, 204; Carroll, 615.

Yhwh is initially presented as the one who is responsible for light: the sun for day and the moon and stars for night. The evident parallelism between

ntn šmš l'wr ywmm

and *ḥqt yrḥ wkwkbym l'wr lylh*

in 31:35a has led some exegetes and translators to make *ntn* and *ḥqt* equivalent, requiring emendation of *ḥqt*.[519] Others, following the LXX, simply suppress it.[520]

The participle which is parallel to *ntn* is not *ḥqt* (i.e., proposed *ḥqq*) but *rg'*.[521] Schematically it appears thus:

yhwh					
	ntn	*šmš*			*l'wr ywmm*
		ḥqt	*yrḥ*		
			wkwkbym		*l'wr lylh*
	rg'	*hym*			
yhwh					

This clear parallelism, which emphasizes Yhwh's direct and indirect control of creation,[522] favors retaining the MT.[523] *ḥqt* of the MT also accentuates the permanence of what has been established and introduces *hḥqym* of 31:36.

Yhwh's stirring up the seas (*rg' hym*) results in an action of the water itself (*wyhmw glyw*). This action demonstrates his tremendous power, destructive as well as creative. The sea can roar with potential for destruction[524] or can be, under the power of Yhwh, the sign and source of blessing.[525] The power of Yhwh, as creator God, is reiterated by the attribution *ṣb'wt* added to his name, at the end of the description.[526]

---

[519] Both Weiser, 264, and Rudolph, 204, follow BHS emending *ḥqt* to *ḥqq* (participle) in order to maintain a strict parallelism with the preceding *ntn*.

[520] Cornill, 354; Giesebrecht, 173; Condamin, 232; Bright, 227; Thompson, 582.

[521] Cf. Thompson, 582; Carroll, 615.

[522] D. Barthélemy, *Critique textuelle* II, 689-90, upholds the MT because "la modulation nuancée des ténèbres et de la lumière qui se déroule durant les nuits est assurée par les mécanismes subtils et délicats des phases de la lune, ainsi que par la connexion des étoiles en constellation et les mouvements complexes des astres."

[523] Cf. Carroll, 615.

[524] Cf. P. Reymond, *L'eau, sa vie*, 183-84; R. Luyster, "Wind and Water: Cosmogonic Symbolism in the Old Testament" *ZAW* 93 (1981) 1. Examples of this can be found in Ps 46:4; Jer 5:22; 6:23; 50:42.

[525] P. Reymond, *L'eau, sa vie*, 196-98.

[526] Cf. above, p. 40, n. 89.

If he has authority over the laws and powers of nature, then his words will surely be effective.[527] As in the first section (31:23-34) where future hope is based on a series of comparisons with the people's past experience, here (31:36-37) future hope is founded on the people's knowledge of what is humanly unthinkable. In both instances the protasis of the unreal condition is a known natural phenomenon alluded to in the attributes of Yhwh in 31:35.

Although *'m* is generally used to express a fulfilled or at least possible condition,[528] it can be used instead of an expected *lw* to express a condition considered impossible,[529] as is the case here.[530]

In 31:36 the protasis refers to *hḥqym h'lh*, the statutes of the created universe, the 'laws' of the sun and the moon mentioned in 31:35. If these should cease to stand before the face of Yhwh, a clearly unthinkable case, then the *zr' yśr'l* will cease from being *gwy* before Yhwh.

The repetition of *mlpny/lpny*, once in the protasis and once in the apodosis, focuses these lines on Yhwh's presence. Thus the use of *gwy* to describe the people appears somewhat strange since *gwy* is linked closely to Israel's existence as a political entity, as a nation among other nations, rather than to its specific personal relationship with Yhwh.[531] Such a political existence before Yhwh[532] assumes his approval and support and will continue as long as the *zr' yśr'l* exist.[533] Thus *hḥqym* is a guarantee of the people's existence as a nation. The *zr' yśr'l* exist not only as *'m* for him but also as *gwy* before him; their political existence is thus assured.

Although 31:37 is not a separate unit, it is introduced by *kh 'mr yhwh*,[534] reiterating the fact that these words are the words of Yhwh and not of another. The *'m ... gm* statement of 31:37 is, like that of 31:36, an unreal condition used to give assurance to the people. Yet between the two there is also a difference, highlighted by the close parallelism. Though both *'m* clauses are presented impersonally, the first (*ymšw hḥqym*, 31:36) portrays an event which lies solely in the realm of nature,

---

527 Weiser, 288-89.

528 G-K § 159l.

529 G-K § 159m.

530 The same *'m ... gm* construction found in 31:36-37 is found in two other texts of the MT, both of which clearly have *'m* introducing what is impossible. In Gn 13:16 Abraham is told that *'m* a person can count the dust of the earth (clearly impossible), *gm* his descendants will be able to be counted. Similarly in Jr 33:20-21,25-26, the *'m* clause again presents an unthinkable statement: *'m* night and day can no longer be distinguished.

531 A. Cody, "When Is the Chosen People Called a *gôy*?" *VT* 14 (1964) 5; R.E. Clements u. G. Botterweck, "*gwy*," *TWAT* I, 971-72.

532 Weiser, 289, n. 1.

533 Most uses of the expression *kl-hymym* refer to the lifetime of an individual (32 uses), the others (13 uses) mean for all the generations of a group as long as they endure as a group.

534 This same phenomenon was noted for 31:16.

while the second describes (*ymdw šmym ... wyḥqrw mwsdy-'rṣ*, 31:37) an occurrence which would involve human participation. Both actions are related to the description of Yhwh in 31:35. *'m-ymšw hḥqym* (31:36) refers back to *ḥqt* (31:35) of which Yhwh is the author. *'m-ymdw šmym* (31:37), by mentioning the heavens, alludes to the lights of 31:35 while *mwsdy-'rṣ*, 'the depths,' makes reference to the seas, both of which are controlled by him. Thus the actions of Yhwh described in 31:35 can be said to introduce what follows. Both the link between 31:35 and 31:37 and the description of Yhwh's dominion create an implicit comparison between the power of Yhwh on the one hand and the powerlessness of creation and humanity before him on the other.

Both measuring the heavens from above and exploring the foundations of earth to the depths are clearly impossible. Just as impossible, then, would be Yhwh's rejection of all the descendants of Israel (*kl-zrʿ yśr'l*) because of all they have done (*kl-'šr ʿśw*).[535] It appears that the *kl* in *kl-zrʿ yśr'l* assures a limit to the punishment Yhwh will place upon Israel.[536]

All this is true, but it is not the whole picture. The literary function of *kl* is more expansive. Just as 31:36 repeated *l/mpny* to focus on the importance of Yhwh, here *kl* is repeated to accentuate totality: *all* the people, *all* their deeds. The 'all' on the one hand is in striking contrast to the 'one' presented in *gm-'ny*: Yhwh. His action is not consistent with all the deeds of all the people. It is the one versus the many, but the one is given heightened importance in 31:35 and 31:37. This is accomplished in 31:35 by the many attributes given to Yhwh, in 31:37, by the contrast with *kl* as well as with the expected response of punishment which would be consistent with *'m-'yš bʿwnw ymwt* of 31:30. By moving beyond the punishment assured in 31:30, 31:37 reiterates still more forcefully what 31:34 states: Yhwh's forgiveness and forgetting of sins.

3.9.2.2 Section 2 — *Life Changing* (31:38-40)

The final section (31:38-40) of the second part opens with *hnh ymym (b'ym) n'm-yhwh*[537] presenting a future which will be in discontinuity

---

[535] The LXX omits *kl*; Bright follows the LXX without explanation.

[536] The whole of Israel will not be destroyed even if part is punished. Cf. Rudolph, 204-05, and D. Barthélemy, *Critique textuelle* II, 690-91.

[537] *b'ym*, lacking in the MT, is to be added, based on the fact that this is a formulaic statement, used 14 times in Jer, always with *b'ym*; its lack can easily be explained as haplography due to the following *n'm*. Cf. BHS; Cornill, 355; Giesebrecht, 174; Volz, 280; Bright, 278; Weiser, 264; Rudolph, 206; Thompson, 583; Carroll, 617.

with the past.[538] The imagery of 31:38-40 is physical and geographical,[539] but its referent appears to be the interiority of the people.[540]

The city will be built *lyhwh,* which grammatically could be 'for Yhwh' (dative), 'of Yhwh' (genitive), or 'by Yhwh.'[541] The actual, physical city of Jerusalem known to the people was 'for Yhwh' and 'of Yhwh.' And if one admits that Yhwh is the God of history as well as of creation, then he would also ultimately be responsible for building the city. Since the people were called *ʿyr* in 31:24, then it might be said that they, in a particular way, would be built by him.[542] The expression *ʿyr lyhwh,* as the conclusion to a poetic text, could well be an instance of polysemy. In that case *ʿyr lyhwh* should remain ambiguous, referring to both people and place, both of which are given existence thanks to Yhwh and both of which belong to him.

Since certain terms, e.g., Corner Gate, Horse Gate, refer to the actual physical city of Jerusalem, many scholars consider this statement to be an indication of the limits of the geographical city which is to be rebuilt.[543] But the measuring line moves out to places not known apart from this text; *grb* and *gʿth*[544] make it difficult to say with certainty that this describes the city of Jerusalem as it is to be rebuilt.[545]

Since *grb* is found in Lv 21:20 and 22:22 in reference to "itching disease" which makes a priest or a sacrificial animal unclean before Yhwh and unacceptable to him, it is possible that *grb* of 31:39 refers to a hill of uncleanness[546] to be included in the precincts of the city.

The following (and final) verse makes a more shocking statement. That which will be holy to the Lord (*qdš lyhwh*) is the valley of cadavers and fatty ashes, the valley of death,[547] also known as the Hinnom valley,

---

538 As did the *hnh ymym bʾym* statements of 31:27-30 and 31:31-34.

539 Like 31:23-30 which portrays the place and population, the gifts and blessings in concrete images.

540 Like 31:31-34 which emphasizes relationships.

541 Only Rudolph, 206, admits all these possible interpretations.

542 This is also the idea expressed by *ʾbnk* of 31:4.

543 Cf. J. Simons, *Jerusalem in the Old Testament. Researches and Theories*, Leiden: Nederlandsch Archaeologisch-Philologisch Instituut voor het Nabije Oosten, 1952, 231-33; and most commentators: Cornill, 355-56; Giesebrecht, 174; Volz, 280; Bright, 283; Weiser, 289; Rudolph, 205-06; Thompson, 583.

544 Bright, 283; Weiser, 290; Rudolph, 205; Thompson, 583; Carroll, 617; J. Simons, *Jerusalem*, 232.

545 Although J. Simons, *Jerusalem*, 231, calls this a "complete outline of the city" he also says that "this boundary description is hardly or not at all intelligible" except insofar as one posits it as the description of a single hill.

546 Cf. C. F. Keil, *The Prophecies of Jeremiah* II, trans. from German by J. Kennedy, Grand Rapids: Wm. B. Eerdmans, 1980 (reprint date), 44.

547 MT *hšrmwt* should be read *hšdmwt* (cf. M. Lehmann, "A New Interpretation of the Term *šdmwt*" *VT* 3 [1953] 361-62; J. S. Croatto and J. A. Soggin, "Die Bedeutung von *šdmwt* im AT" *ZAW* 74 [1962] 49). As such it follows the pattern thus far presented and is

and the Topeth, where the idols and unclean cultic items were burnt by Josiah.[548] What is striking and startling is not the rebuilding nor the extension of the city, but rather the transformation of the unclean places into ones holy to Yhwh. The city extends beyond its natural boundaries, and what had once been rejected now becomes not only acceptable but sacred.

If the designation of the people as city (31:24) is maintained, then the people might be understood metaphorically to be holy to the Lord, even in their uncleanness and sinfulness. The city is circumscribed with the measuring line, which determines the limits of the city, reaching two unknown locations as well as the places of death and uncleanness (*wkl-h'mq hpgrym whdšn* // *wkl-hšrmwt*). All the descriptive elements of these verses are related to death, yet even this will become *qdš*! Not only the aspects that had previously been seen as clean or holy, but even those that were cause for separation are now the source of union with Yhwh. And this will not be rooted up or torn down again — ever!

The whole of 31:38-40 is organized around Yhwh, opening with *h'yr lyhwh* (31:38) and closing on the note of *qdš lyhwh* (31:40) which also makes reference to *'yr* with all it includes. The city will be built (*wnbnth*), as was predicated of the people in 31:3 and 31:28. Similarly Yhwh's action in the past, expressed as *šqd lntwš ... wlhrs* in 31:28, is denied for the future: *l' yntš wl' yhrs* (31:40). This discontinuity with the past is both explicit and enduring: *'wd l'wlm* (31:40).

The second section of the prose conclusion assures the future based on the creative power and activity of Yhwh: his power over heavens and seas. First the people are guaranteed existence as a nation, a deed then shown to be totally gratuitous. Their sinfulness is not denied, but it no longer determines Yhwh's attitude toward them.

Finally, the notion of measuring, introduced in 31:37, is taken up, here not in a cosmic context but in a political, geographical one. A city is described which transcends the limits of the known and the possible. This is accomplished by the interplay of the known and the unknown, the possible and the impossible, the juxtaposition of death (*hšrmwt*) and the holy (*qdš*).

The prose conclusion presents the tension of continuity-discontinuity as a theme which underlies Yhwh's activity for Israel. She is guaranteed a future patterned according to what she knows of the past: as Yhwh acted for her then, he will do so once again. Yet the experience of the past, of sin and punishment, will be altered. Newness and radical change are promised, but always in relationship with Yhwh.

---

now seen not as a field that needs cultivation so much as a barren land which in fact has been used for burial, as both of the above-mentioned articles note.

[548] J. Simons (*Jerusalem*, 233, n. 4) excludes the possibility that Topeth would be included in the city which will be "holy to Yhwh."

CHAPTER 4

UNIFYING ELEMENTS IN JER 30-31

As a poetic cycle, Jer 30-31 is more than a mere anthology of poems and prose units. Whatever the original provenance of the individual poems or segments, the final (and present) form exhibits obvious connections between contiguous poems and throughout the whole. This continuity constitutes the subject of the following pages.

First, lexical links and other connective devices between two poems will be identified, showing that each poem is related to the preceding and the following one in a very concrete way through repetition of words, roots and structural elements. Then motifs and themes will be traced through the entire poetic cycle, taking note of their occurrence and, at times, their absence.[1]

This analysis, although it can never replace the text, can help to focus on certain aspects which make the reader, in turn, more attentive to the written word as it now stands.

4.1 CONNECTIVE DEVICES AMONG THE POEMS

4.1.1 *Poems I–II*

The first line of Poem II echoes the same major sounds as the last line of Poem I: the sibilants /s/ and /š/ of *wysrtyk lmšpṭ* (30:11) are repeated in the /š/ of *'nwš lšbrk* (30:12) while the palatals /q/ and /k/ of *wnqh l' 'nqk* (30:11) are reproduced in the /ḥ/ and /k/ of *nḥlh mktk* (30:12). This homophony closely links the two poems to one another and also reinforces the image of correction (*wysrtyk lmšpṭ*, Poem I, 30:11) which is symbolized by illness (*'nwš lšbrk*, Poem II, 30:12) and characterized in 30:14 (Poem II) as the chastisement of a cruel one (*mwsr 'kzry*). Both poems open with an image of distress (stanza 1) and close with the assurance of salvation (stanza 2). Their emphasis, however, is different, as reflected in the number of lines each devotes to the themes of distress and salvation: in Poem II seven lines are given to distress, four lines to salvation; in Poem I six lines are devoted to distress, ten lines to salvation.

---

[1] Rather than reduplicate information or fill the text with footnotes which refer to Chapter 3 (Close Reading), this chapter has been left virtually free of notes.

This same opposition between distress and salvation exists on the lexical level in root repetition. In Poem I *šbr* appears in verbal form as an action of Yhwh to free the people from oppression (30:8); in Poem II, the same root *šbr*, this time a substantive, indicates the suffering imposed by Yhwh on the people (31:12,15). Similarly the root *ysr* is found in Poem I to express both bonds of oppression (30:8) and chastisement by Yhwh (30:11), while in Poem II it is used to describe the punitive but 'cruel' deed of Yhwh (30:14), synthesizing the two ideas set forth in the previous poem. In Poem I (30:7) *ṣrh* describes a moment or time of distress, while in Poem II (30:16) Yhwh promises to destroy those who were *ṣr* in relation to his people. The lexical connections, made with *šbr*, *ysr* and *ṣrr*, reinforce the thematic unity of the two poems: distress in stanza 1 and salvation in stanza 2.

Both 30:5 (Poem I) and 30:15 (Poem II) present the sound or cry of distress. In 30:14-15 (Poem II) the suffering, expressed in a cry, is due to the sins and offenses of the 'woman.' The reason for the sound of terror in 30:5 (Poem I) is not given, unless it is perhaps caused by the assured correction and punishment of 30:11 (which presupposes sin).

Just as Poem I promises the destruction of Israel's enemies (*'ʿšh klh bkl-hgwym ...*, 30:11), so Poem II develops at greater length the same concept in 30:16: *y'klw ... bšby ylkw ... lmšsh ... 'tn lbz*. And like Poem I, Poem II also moves from an image of distress to one of salvation. The first poem ends on a note which attenuates the promised salvation, since punishment is assured. In a similar manner, Poem II ends on a note of joy which is subsequently lessened by the reason for her healing: she has been abandoned; none seek her.

4.1.2 *Poems II–III*

Poem II ends on a note of hope: the wound will be healed (30:17) for Sion has been left alone and called 'desolate.' The removal of her desolation is the dominant image of Poem III through the development of *šwb šbwt*: the city is rebuilt, the people are numerous and honored (30:19).

Yet even with the accent on the favorable deeds of Yhwh for his people, the third poem concludes with a short stanza depicting the results of Yhwh's wrath (*ḥrwn 'p-yhwh*, 30:24). The evildoer will suffer the consequences of Yhwh's anger and the designs of his will, embodied in the natural symbol of a storm wind (*sʿr*, 30:23). Whereas Poem II develops the notion of Israel's punishment with the image of wounds and illness, Poem III expresses the punishment of evildoers (*ršʿym*) in the image of a storm, without specifying whether *ršʿym* refers to Israel or to other nations.

There is no vocabulary repeated between these two poems, and their imagery is quite different, yet thematic links do exist since both develop the concept of distress as punishment (30:12-15 and 30:23-24). Both illustrate Yhwh's presence and deeds in favor of his people, expressed symbolically in 30:16-17 and concretely in 30:18-21. Both poems also assure the punishment of Israel's foes (30:16 and 30:20b).

Despite certain similarities between the two poems, their emphasis is reversed. Poem II develops the negative, punitive image in four verses and the opposite image of salvation in two; Poem III represents the positive deeds in four verses, the contrary deeds in two.

4.1.3 *Poems III–IV*

Poem IV, like Poem III, elaborates the positive deeds of Yhwh for his people, presenting two interconnected aspects through the repetition of *bnh*. Poem III declares that the city will be built (*bnh*, 30:18) while Poem IV applies this same verb to Yhwh's deed for 'virgin Israel' (*btwlt yśr'l*, 31:4), an expression which can refer to either the city or the people. The notion of multiplying the people contained in the building up of the virgin is also present in Poem III, but with different terminology: 'I will make them many' (*whrbtym*, 30:19) and 'their progeny will be as before' (*whyw bnyw kqdm*, 30:20).

The sounds of joy introduced in Poem III (*wyṣ' mhm twdh wqwl mśḥqym*, 30:19) are repeated in Poem IV (*wyṣ't bmḥwl mśḥqym*, 31:4) and given greater precision by the mention of timbrels (*tpyk*) and dance (*bmḥwl*, 31:4). The nation's existence and growth, which were developed at length (city, numbers, honor, assembly before the Lord, leaders from their own group, 30:18-21) and given a permanent status in Poem III (*twkn*, 30:20), are presupposed by Poem IV since vines will be planted and their fruit enjoyed (31:5).

The motion toward Sion and toward Yhwh, expressed as physical displacement in Poem IV (31:6), is presupposed in its spiritual dimension by Poem III with the twofold use of the 'covenant formula' (30:22; 31:1).

4.1.4 *Poems IV–V*

After describing the return to the land (stanza 1), Poem V mentions the pilgrimage to *ṣywn* (31:12), to which the people were called at the end of Poem IV (*qwmw wn'lh ṣywn*, 31:6). One of the assurances of the future given in Poem IV, the planting of vineyards and enjoying the fruit (31:5), is repeated in Poem V, though by reference to new wine (*tyrš*) as one of Yhwh's gifts (31:12). The joy expressed in dance (*wyṣ't bmḥwl mśḥqym*), promised 'virgin Israel' in Poem IV (31:4), is mentioned again in Poem V where the virgin rejoicing in dance (*tśmḥ btwlh bmḥwl*, 31:13) suggests the change which Yhwh will effect.

Both poems repeat *rḥq* which has a similar meaning in both yet with different nuances. In Poem IV it describes Yhwh's relationship to the people (*mrḥwq*, 31:3); in Poem V it refers to the distance overcome by Yhwh's deed of 'bringing back' (*mmrḥq*, 31:10).

The joy of the people is made public in Poem IV through their actions: being built, dancing in joy, planting vineyards, going up to Sion. Although Poem V also highlights the making public of joy, it does so predominantly in words and announcements, without, however, excluding actions.

4.1.5 *Poems V–VI*

There are several semantic connections between Poems V and VI, although they are not expressed predominantly by root repetition. Both poems have two stanzas which open with *šmʿ* even if the usage is quite different. In Poem V *šmʿ* is twice present in the imperative (once the *hiphil*, once the *qal*) as a call or command to the people to announce and listen to what Yhwh has done or will do (31:7,10). In Poem VI, on the other hand, what is heard is a human voice, first that of Rachel (31:15) and then that of Ephraim (31:18). Rachel's voice is one of weeping (*qwl bky*, 31:15,16). She sheds tears of sorrow and even of desperation over the plight of her sons, tears which, as supplication, Yhwh hears. The tears of Poem V (*bky*, 31:9), on the other hand, are tears of joy or supplication which accompany the people's return to the land.

The consolation (*nḥm*) promised by Yhwh to the returnees in Poem V (31:13) is refused by Rachel (31:15) but experienced by Ephraim (31:19). Similarly, the return described in Poem V as a deed of Yhwh who gathers the people from distant lands (*hnny mby' 'wtm m'rṣ ṣpwn wqbṣtym myrkty-'rṣ*, 31:8) is assured for Rachel's progeny in Poem VI (*wšbw m'rṣ 'wyb*, 31:16).

If in Poem V (31:8-9) the return is described, in Poem VI (31:21-22) the opposite, the non-return or refusal to return (though used metaphorically), is the foundation for the imperatives *hṣyby* ... *śmy* ... *šty lbk* ... *šwby* ... *šby*.

The parent/child (mother/son, father/son, (father)/daughter) relationships which run as a thread through Poem VI had been introduced in Poem V by the expression father/first-born (*'b*/*bkry*) applied to Yhwh/Ephraim (31:9). This relationship, merely stated in Poem V, is developed in Poem VI in the terms 'precious son' (*bn yqyr*), 'darling child' (*yld šʿšʿym*), as well as by an expressed emotional attachment (*hmw mʿy lw rḥm 'rḥmnw*, 31:20).

Poem V describes intense joy and enjoyment of Yhwh's many gifts — the return, the food, the being many and being with him. Poem VI pictures the opposite — the sorrow at being few and far from Yhwh, the need and desire to turn to him and move back from being at a distance. Yet in both there is a sense of the caring and tenderness of Yhwh toward Ephraim.

4.1.6 *Prose Conclusion*

The prose conclusion repeats many of the words and ideas found in the poems, connecting one with another, repeating certain elements and changing others.

The conclusion opens with a statement (31:23) which recalls the introduction by repeating *dbr*, the key word of 30:1-4. While the introduction has the word of Yhwh as the center of attention, 31:23 focuses on the word of the people. The people will pronounce a blessing on the land (31:23). The blessing of the prose conclusion, repeated from the past (*ʿwd*), recalls the blessings which Poem IV mentions as occurring again (*ʿwd*): again will the virgin Israel be built (31:4), again will she express her joy (31:4); again will the people plant vines (31:5). These are the foundation for the blessing on the land with which the conclusion opens.

Such blessing is possible because Yhwh will have restored the fortunes of the people (*bšwby ʾt-šbwtm*, 31:23). This restoration of fortunes, a major motif in this cycle, is also found in the introduction (30:3) and Poem II (30:18). Poems I (30:10), V (31:8) and VI (31:16,17,18,19,21) allude to the same reality with the simple verbal statement *šwb*.[2]

The restoration of fortunes includes satisfying those who are in need, as described by the verb *rwh* (31:25), which is also found twice in Poem V (31:12,14), and in each case *rwh* has *npš* as object. Yhwh will 'satiate' the people, fill the lives even of those who languish (*dʾbh*, 31:12,25). One aspect of the 'fullness' is described in 31:27 as the deed of *zrʿty* ("I will 'seed' "), a reference to an increase in the people, explicitly stated in Poem III but in other words: Yhwh will make them many (30:19), and their sons will be like before (i.e., numerous) (30:20). Yet it is not merely their progeny that will be multiplied, for their wealth in flocks and herds will also increase, as 31:12 (Poem V) implies by its use of a similar phrase (*bny-ṣʾn wbqr*) to depict Yhwh's blessings. The same *zrʿ* are assured of continued existence in 31:36,37, a fact alluded to already in Poem I (30:10) with Yhwh's promise to bring their progeny (*zrʿk*) back from captivity.

Such assurance of blessings is presented metaphorically in the conclusion as 'building and planting' (31:28), deeds which appear in their literal significance in Poems III and IV. *bnh* is predicated (in the *niphal*/passive) of the city in Poem III (30:18) as well as in the final

---

[2] This is developed at greater length under the motif 'return.' Cf. below, p. 138.

section of the prose conclusion where the city is specified as *lyhwh* (31:38). It is not only the city which experiences the action of Yhwh. In Poem IV (31:4) the virgin Israel will be 'built' (*'bnk wnbnyt btwlt yśr'l*), a metaphorical usage of *bnh* similar to that of 31:28. The other verb used metaphorically in 31:28, 'to plant' (*nṭ'*), is also found in Poem IV in its literal sense. Repeated three times in a single line, *nṭ'* is the actual deed of planting vineyards, made possible only with the dwelling in the land. New wine (*tyrš*, 31:12), the result of planting, is found among Yhwh's gifts mentioned in Poem V.

The prose conclusion treats not only of blessings but also of responsibility for sin and personal guilt, as portrayed in the proverb of 31:29-30. The same guilt, deserving of punishment, is the reason for the suffering described in Poem II. In both instances sin (*'wn*) finds a response in punishment. In Poem II (30:14,15) the guilt appears to be collective, that of the people as a whole, while in the conclusion (31:30) it is particularized, resting on the shoulders of the individual sinner. This same sin, expressed by *ḥṭ't* as well as by *'wn* (both substantives are found twice in Poem II), is the object of Yhwh's forgiveness in 31:34, a forgiveness which is an essential part of the new covenant.

The fathers (*'bwt*), the consequences of whose sin fell on their sons (31:29), were responsible for the breaking of the former covenant (31:32). In the conclusion, Yhwh's relationship to the fathers is pictured as negative. In the prose introduction, on the other hand, the link with the fathers is positive: he will give the land again, just as he did in the past to *'bwtm* (30:3).

Since the covenant concluded in the past has been broken, Yhwh promises a new one: *bryt ḥdšh* (31:31). The adjective (*ḥdšh*) is the same one used to describe the creative act of Yhwh at the conclusion of Poem VI (31:22): *ky-br' yhwh ḥdšh b'rṣ*. In both instances there is an element of discontinuity with the past which does not, however, mean something totally unknown.

Evident links from one poem to the other on the level of structure, content and lexical repetitions have been shown. If one maintains, with N. Lohfink,[3] that the prose conclusion is a later reinterpretation of the original poetic cycle, its connection with the poems is not at all surprising. But this analysis has also shown the less obvious connections between one poem and the next, indicating the actual, if redactional, unity of Jer 30-31. This unity will be considered in a more global manner with the study of motifs and themes which are found throughout the Little Book of Consolation.

---

[3] N. Lohfink, "Der Gotteswortverschachtelung," 106-11.

4.2 MOTIFS

Besides the clear connections, lexical and other, between one poem or section and the following one, the poetic cycle of Jer 30-31 is also unified around seven motifs.[4] These are: 1) the feminine image; 2) voice and listening; 3) suffering and punishment; 4) turn or return; 5) city or settlement; 6) mountain and Sion; and 7) covenant. The following pages will examine each of these images or motifs in turn, noting especially how each is used throughout the entire poetic cycle. While there is no claim that the motifs here mentioned are the only ones present, they can be recognized as an organizing principle for the whole.

4.2.1 *Feminine Imagery*

The use of the feminine address in Jer 30-31 is striking because it alternates according to a regular pattern with the masculine address from poem to poem, and in Poem VI, from stanza to stanza. Within the entire OT, this phenomenon is found only here with such regularity. The remarkable presence and systematic repetition of the feminine image call for a closer study, which is offered in the next chapter. As one of the seven motifs, it ought to be included here, but to avoid unnecessary repetition the development of this image has been left entirely to chapter five where it will be considered in its historical and psychological context.

4.2.2 *Voice and Listening*

This motif is found in a semantic field which includes the verbs *dbr*, *'mr*, *šmʿ*, *zʿq* and the nouns *dbr*, *qwl*.

From the beginning, with the prose introduction (30:1-4) whose key word is *dbr*, importance is given to communication in both speaking and its converse, listening. The main speaker of the whole cycle is Yhwh, made clear by the repeated use of *dbr* which has him as subject in 30:1,2,4, as well as by the repetition of *(ky) kh 'mr yhwh* (30:2,5,12,18; 31:2,7,15,23,35,37) and *n'm yhwh* (30:3,8,10,11,17,21; 31:1,14,16,17,20,27, 28,31,32,33,34,36,37,38). It is this word of Yhwh which is to be heard and

---

[4] 'Motif' is here understood to be a word or a pattern of thought which recurs in the poetic cycle, one which can be expressed quite concretely and is, in itself, polyvalent. This 'definition' accords with that of J. Shipley, *Dictionary of World Literary Terms*, *ad loc.*; O. Ducrot et T. Todorov, *Dictionnaire encyclopédique des sciences du langage*, Paris: Editions du Seuil, 1972, 282-83. It is not used in the sense common to folklore, where motif and theme are terms referring to expected elements of content which recur in variable forms in different tales. (Cf. A. B. Lord, *The Singer of Tales*, Harvard Studies in Comparative Literature 24, Cambridge: Harvard University Press, 1960, 68-98, 198; R. C. Culley, *Oral Formulaic Language in Biblical Psalms*, Toronto: University of Toronto Press, 1967, 17-19, 100.)

spoken by the people (Poem V, 31:7,10): *hšmyʿw ... wʾmrw*; *šmʿw dbr-yhwh ... wʾmrw*.

Yet the communication is not one-sided, for throughout the poems the voice of the people is heard. Poem I opens with the sound of distress: *qwl ḥrdh šmʿnw* (30:5). The same distress is 'heard' in Poem II in the question 'Why do you cry out over your wound?' (*mh-tzʿq ʿl-šbrk*, 30:15). It appears that the cry is directed to Yhwh, since he responds with this question.

The sound heard in Poem III is quite the opposite from that of the earlier poems, for it is the sound of joy (*qwl mśḥqym*, 30:19), the same sound which would be heard in the 'dance of joy' in 31:4 (*tʿdy tpyk wyṣʾt bmḥwl mśḥqym*). Another joyful sound is the cry of the watchmen (*qrʾw nṣrym*) who call the people to go in pilgrimage to Sion (31:6). Poem V includes the sound of rejoicing on Sion (*wrnnw bmrwm ṣywn*, 31:12) and the sound of the virgins' dance (*ʾz tśmḥ btwlh bmḥwl*, 31:13) already mentioned in 31:4 and alluded to in 30:19.

After the voice of distress in Poems I-II becomes the sound of joy and gladness in Poems III-V, Poem VI returns to the sound of distress with its opening words: *qwl ... nšmʿ nhy* (31:15). The change from the sound of distress to that of salvation which was noted in the first five poems is reflected in the portrayal of Rachel in Poem VI. She is told to cease her weeping (*mnʿy qwlk mbky*, 31:16) for 'there is hope.' The second stanza of Poem VI describes the sound of Ephraim's voice heard by Yhwh: *šmwʿ šmʿty ʾprym mtnwdd* (31:18). Ephraim's words, in their ambiguity, balance between distress and hope. They end on a positive note made explicit in Yhwh's deed of remembrance which cannot be separated from his words (*dbr*, 31:20) in favor of Ephraim.

This motif of voice and listening plays a less important, even a secondary, role in the prose conclusion where it is articulated in the words which the people will again say or will no longer say. The words the people will repeat (*ʿwd yʾmrw ʾt-hdbr*, 31:23) are a blessing while those they will not repeat (*lʾ-yʾmrw ʿwd*, 31:29; *lʾ-ylmdw ʿwd ... lʾmr*, 31:34) include the proverb which shifts punishment for guilt onto the next generation (31:29) and the teaching one another to know the Lord (31:34).

The voice is a major motif of this cycle of poems: voice of Yhwh and voice of the people; sound of distress and sound of salvation; words which repeat the past or speak something new. The people must listen to Yhwh, but he also listens to them.

4.2.3 *Suffering and Punishment*

As already noted under the motif 'voice,' the sound heard throughout these poems is as often that of distress as it is of joy. The suffering, the punishment and the guilt are expressed by many words. While there is little lexical repetition from poem to poem, the motif is present either implicitly, by reference to what the people are saved from, or explicitly, in a longer or shorter exposition.

The overriding image of Poem I, stanza 1 (30:5-7), is that of distress both in an aural form (*qwl ḥrdh ... pḥd*, 30:5) and in a visual manifestation (*kl-gbr ydyw ʿl ḥlṣyw kywldh wnhpkw kl-pnym lyrqwn*, 30:6). Even when salvation is assured the people through the utter destruction of their enemies, their hope is always limited by the punishment which they cannot escape (*wysrtyk lmšpṭ wnqh lʾ ʾnqk*, 30:11).

Similarly Poem II accents the suffering of the people, using the physical image of blows and wounds which are without healing (*ʾnwš lšbrk*, 30:12,14; *nḥlh mktk*, 30:12; *mkt ʾwyb, mwsr ʾkzry*, 30:14). The accumulation of images leaves no doubt that the situation is virtually hopeless. The pain is obvious, and there appears to be no escape.

Poem III takes up again the idea of punishment, but here perhaps in a more secondary sense, in that it focuses on the source of punishment rather than on its results. Yhwh is presented as one whose commands are established by *sʿrt yhwh ḥmh* (30:23) and *ḥrwn ʾp-yhwh* (30:24), one whose punishment falls on evildoers (*ršʿym*, 30:23).

By implicit reference Poem IV includes the motif of suffering, contained in the phrase *ʿm śrydy ḥrb* (31:2). As 'saved from the sword,' the people faced at least a threat of suffering in the past. With similar allusions, such as the need to be gathered (*qbṣ*, 31:8,10), the fact of having been scattered (*mzrh yśrʾl*, 31:10) and the transformation of want (*ldʾbh*, 31:12) and sorrow (*ʾblm*, 31:13), Poem V carries through an undertone of past distress.

The final poem develops suffering and punishment in the first two stanzas, but it accents psychological or spiritual rather than physical pain. The dominant image of the first stanza is Rachel weeping inconsolably, repeated with several different expressions: lamentation (*nhy*, 31:15), bitter tears (*bky tmrwrym, mbkh*, 31:15,16; *mdmʿh*, 31:16), without consolation (*mʾnh lhnḥm*, 31:15). She who has done nothing to merit punishment suffers the deep pain of loss. In the second stanza Ephraim speaks of his correction by Yhwh (*ysrtny wʾwsr*, 31:18) and his shame over his past deeds (*bšty wgm-nklmty ky nśʾty ḥrpt nʿwry*, 31:19). He, too, suffers, but his was a deserved punishment.

In the prose conclusion, with the metaphor of sour grapes setting teeth on edge, death is linked to individual misdeeds (*ʾm-ʾyš bʿwnw ymwt*, 31:30). Twice again the theme of punishment for sin is mentioned, but in its denial: Yhwh will no longer remember the sins and offenses of Israel (*ʾslḥ lʿwnm wlḥṭʾtm lʾ ʾzkr-ʿwd*, 31:34), nor will he punish them for their deeds (*ʾmʾs ... ʿl-kl-ʾšr ʿśw*, 31:37), implying that they deserve punishment.

The image of pain is developed in its physical and psychological aspects in the poems and is linked to the sins of the people. The punishment of Yhwh is presented as deserved but also educative. Consistently, he promises to bring an end to distress and suffering, as the prose conclusion makes explicit by its emphasis on the forgiveness of sins.

4.2.4 *Turn–Return*

After Yhwh's punishment, the people will 'return' to him and to their land. These two chapters repeat this motif many times, above all by the repeated use of *šwb* and by references to the land, both the land from which (*m'rṣ*) and the land to which (*'l-h'rṣ*) they are brought.[5]

In the prose introduction Yhwh promises to restore the fortunes of the people (*wšbty 't-šbwt*, 30:3) by bringing them back to the land (*whšbtym 'l-h'rṣ*, 30:3). *šwb šbwt* constitutes the opening phrase of and thus the introduction to Poem III (30:18) which develops at length the implications of return. In a similar way the prose conclusion employs this expression in the first line (31:23) before describing the specific deeds included.

šwb refers to the historical deed of Yhwh who will effect the people's return from enemy land (*wšbw m'rṣ 'wyb*, 31:16). This same action of bringing the people from a place is also expressed with other verbs: bring from the land of the north (*mby' ... m'rṣ ṣpwn*, 31:8), gather from the ends of the earth (*wqbṣtym myrkty-'rṣ*, 31:8), save from the land of captivity (*mwšy'k mrḥwq w't-zr'k m'rṣ šbym*, 30:10). A similar notion is found in the reference to the first covenant and the Exodus event where no mention is made of the finality or goal of the event but merely the point of departure: *lhwṣy'm m'rṣ mṣrym* (31:32). Since Yhwh acts to bring the people 'from' someplace, he also acts to bring them 'to' a place. This positive deed is also expressed by *šwb* in Poem VI. The people return to their own territory (*wšbw bnym lgbwlm*, 31:17) and return to their own cities (*šby 'l-'ryk 'lh*, 31:21); the former is given as a promise, the latter as a command. The group which will return is, according to Poem V, a great assembly (*qhl gdwl yšwbw*, 31:8), gathered and led by Yhwh.

Return to the land has close ties with turning to or returning to Yhwh, made explicit only in Poem VI with Ephraim's petition to be 'turned around' by Yhwh (*hšybny w'šwbh*, 31:18). While Ephraim's request implies that Yhwh is the one who accomplishes *šwb*, in stanza 3 virgin Israel is told to take the initiative in this regard, to stop wandering (*'d-mty tthmqyn*) and to return (*šwby ... šby*, 31:21).

---

[5] Cf., e.g., S. Böhmer, *Heimkehr*, 81; Thompson, 76-81; J. Lust "'Gathering and Return' in Jeremiah and Ezechiel" in P.-M. Bogaert, ed., *Le Livre de Jérémie*, 127, 131-33; J. Bracke, "*šwb šbwt*: A Reappraisal," 236-40.

Only in the conclusion are the land and its cities explicitly mentioned (*b'rṣ yhwdh wbʿryw*) as the goal of *šwb šbwt* (31:23), although the fact that this is the place where the returnees will dwell (*wyšbw bh yhwdh wkl-ʿryw*, 31:24) has already been described in the prose introduction and in Poem III. The notion of 'return' is developed in a way that leaves room for ambivalence and thus justifies an interpretation which bears more than one level of meaning.

The return Yhwh effects, expressed by *šwb (šbwt)* as well as by other words, is a dominant motif which, in its polyvalence, includes both an actual historical experience and its spiritual counterpart. Return to the land and return to Yhwh are inseparable, the latter depending on the people, the former on their God.

4.2.5 *City–Settlement*

Another image present in Jer 30-31 is that of the city or settlement of the people. It is explicitly stated in the roots *ʿyr* and *yšb* which are found in Poems I, III, VI and the prose conclusion, but it also comes to expression in Poems IV and V, although not with these specific words. First introduced in 30:3 by a reference to *h'rṣ 'šr ntty l'bwtm wyršwh*, the idea of 'city' is taken up in 30:10 in the series of verbs which depict peaceful existence: *wšb yʿqb wšqṭ wš'nn*, the only reference to 'dwelling' in Poem I.

The first explicit mention of the city is in Poem III. With the restoration of fortunes comes the rebuilding of the city as well: *wnbnth ʿyr ʿl-tlh w'rmwn ʿl-mšpṭw yšb* (30:18). Not only will the city with its buildings be restored, but the people themselves will again become great.

Poem IV mentions the city only indirectly in 31:5-6, since both the planting of vineyards with the enjoyment of their fruit (31:5) and the presence of watchmen (*nṣrym*, 31:6) presuppose settlement in the land. A similar allusion to settlement is found in Poem V in the reference to the results of agriculture: grain, wine, oil (31:12) as the gifts given by Yhwh. Since agricultural products take time to grow, the implication is that the people belong to a settled society.

The first stanza of Poem VI suggests settlement since it promises that Rachel's sons will enjoy their inheritance which, as 'territory' (*lgbwlm*, 31:17), can also refer to a city. In the final stanza, Israel is told quite explicitly *šby 'l-ʿryk 'lh*, 31:21. It is not merely to the land, but specifically to her cities, that she is to return.

The prose conclusion develops the idea of 'city' more fully than any other part of Jer 30-31. The introductory line locates the voice of restored fortunes in the city as well as in the land (*b'rṣ yhwdh wbʿryw*, 31:23), for return and restoration imply the existence of cities. The description of the population in 31:24 once again refers to Judah and her cities as one part of a merismus whose other member is ‘farmers and those who go with the flocks’ (*’krym wns‘w b‘dr*, 31:24). The city is both the place of dwelling and a metaphor for the people.

At the very end of the prose conclusion, the idea of *‘yr* is taken up again. The city is described in its extension which is so broad it includes the burial ground as far as *qdrwn*. The whole is *qdš lyhwh* and will stand *l‘wlm* (31:40).

The image of settlement and city is traced implicitly and explicitly through the whole of these two chapters where it ranges from allusion to detailed description. Israel will possess the inheritance of the fathers (30:4; 31:17), the place where all the people will dwell (31:25), but also the place of Yhwh’s dwelling and thus the locus of his good gifts (31:5,12). The city is both the place where Yhwh’s deeds are recognized (31:23) and the result of his saving activity (30:18; 31:38-40).

It is not a return to the wilderness experience (cf. Hosea) which is the basis for hope in the future, but a coming together in their *own* city which both reflects and teaches the people about Yhwh’s caring and saving acts.

4.2.6 *Mountain–Sion*

The image of the mountain or Sion is present throughout these chapters specifically in the words *ṣywn* and *hr*. When this motif first appears at the end of Poem II it is as ‘Sion’ (*ṣywn*, 30:17b) who will be protected, consoled and healed by Yhwh. Poem III only alludes to this motif in the statement that the city will be built on its mound of ruins (*‘l-tlh*, 30:18), which implies a raised area.

The first appearance of *hr* is found in Poem IV in a double reference to the mountain(s) as *bhry šmrwn* (31:5) and *bhr ’prym* (31:6). The first is the place where vines will be planted, the place of settlement and joy; the second is the place from which the watchmen call out and thus the place where the people are to be found. A possible reference to the remnant of Israel, it is closely tied to their existence as settled in the land. The cry of the watchmen is a call to arise and go up to *ṣywn ’l-yhwh ’lhynw* (31:6), explicitly identifying *ṣywn* with the presence of Yhwh.

This call to go up to Sion finds a response in Poem V where the pilgrimage *bmrwm ṣywn* (31:12) is described. Here the people are made glorious by the blessings of Yhwh toward which they stream (*wnhrw ’l-ṭwb yhwh*, 31:12).

In Poem VI Rachel’s voice emanates from the heights (*brmh*, 31:15), the only reference to a hill as the locus of a negative action. Elsewhere in this poetic cycle the hill or mountain is the place where Yhwh and his gifts are to be found.

In its opening line, the prose conclusion uses the expression *hr hqdš* (which *may* refer to Sion). It contains a blessing directed toward the land with which the holy mountain is here identified. In the final verses, the holy city (*hʿyr lyhwh*) is located on an unknown hill, *gbʿt grb* (31:39), although the measuring line goes out to include low-lying areas (*hʿmq*, 31:39-40) as well as heights.

Throughout this poetic cycle, there is an upward motion toward Yhwh, toward his city, toward the heights, i.e., toward the locus of his presence and his blessing. At the end of the cycle the image of city on the height comes into focus, but as incomplete in itself, to be completed by its opposite (possibly hinted at in the sound of Rachel's cry from the heights), for the holy place now includes the low (and unclean) areas as well as the heights.

4.2.7 *Covenant*

Assuming 'covenant' to be the expression of a relationship between two parties, in this case that between Yhwh and the people Israel/Judah, one can speak of a persistent covenant image throughout these two chapters. First seen in *yhwh 'lhy yśr'l* (30:2) and *ʿmy yśr'l* (30:3) of the prose introduction, the covenant motif is developed in the image of *ʿbd* and *yhwh 'lhyhm* (30:9-10) in Poem I. Although absent in the imagery of Poem II, the motif is repeated twice in Poem III in the complete or classic 'covenant formula' of two clauses (e. g., *whyytm ly lʿm w'nky 'hyh lkm l'lhym*, 30:22 and 31:1). In both cases this 'covenant formula' concludes the description of a relationship, the first, that of Yhwh's building up the nation and taking their leader into his confidence, the second, that of wrath falling on the wicked (though not without Israel understanding the event).

The call to go up *'l-yhwh 'lhynw* (31:6) of Poem IV is also an expression of how the people see themselves in regard to Yhwh and thus is an allusion to covenant insofar as it is the expression of a bond between the two parties.

The father-son relationship in 'covenant formula' structure, found in Poem V (*hyyty lyśr'l l'b w'prym bkry hw'*, 31:9) is yet another instance of this same understanding, here expressed by an adoption formula. Similarly, Ephraim's words in Poem VI, *'th yhwh 'lhy* (31:18), appear to be a cry of confidence, while Yhwh's response reflects a love often considered covenantal (*hbn yqyr ly*, 31:20).

Besides the covenant allusion contained in the name given Yhwh (*'lhy yśr'l*, 31:23), the prose conclusion employs the term *bryt* four times in 31:31-33. Moreover, this last named verse includes a classic example of the covenant formula: *whyyty lhm l'lhym whmh yhyw-ly lʿm.*

The covenant and 'covenant formula' are used from the beginning to the end of Jer 30-31 to summarize and make explicit the relationship between Yhwh and Israel, a relationship on which all the promises and all the deeds of Yhwh are based.

These several motifs are specific and concrete instances of the prophet's message which speaks of the mutual encounter between Yhwh and his people, an encounter made possible only by his continual presence, both 'destructive' and creative. These concrete images indicate the broader perspectives of Jer 30-31 which are treated in the following section on themes.

4.3 THEMES OF JER 30-31

The theme of a literary work is almost universally understood to be the subject of the discourse, the dominating idea which accounts for the content, structure and development of the work. Unlike a motif, which can often be expressed in a single word or phrase, a theme is of a higher degree of abstraction and can, in fact, reach expression in many other ways than those of the given text.[6] To state a theme is not to give a summary of the literary work but rather to focus attention so that the modifications and extensions of meaning within the text itself can be more fully appreciated.[7]

Three major unifying themes have been noted in Jer 30-31: transformation of reality; gratuitousness of Yhwh's salvific deed;[8] and future events as based upon, yet different from, the known (past and present).[9] The following analysis will consider each theme separately, although these three elements are not independent but rather are interwoven to form the fabric of the whole text.

---

[6] Cf. J. Shipley, *Dictionary of World Literary Terms*, *ad loc.*; C. Brooks and R. Warren, *Understanding Poetry*, 560; O. Ducrot et T. Todorov, *Dictionnaire encyclopédique des sciences du langage*, 283-84; D. J. A. Clines, *The Theme of the Pentateuch*, JSOTS 10, Sheffield: JSOT Press, 1978, 18-21.

[7] C. Brooks and R. Warren, *Understanding Poetry*, 343. The statement of a theme does not imply that the author had this particular idea in mind. A theme is a concept necessary for the critic or reader who seeks a way into the work, rather than for the artist, for whom the theme may have come into being in the process of literary creation. Cf. D. J. A. Clines, *The Theme of the Pentateuch*, 21.

[8] T. M. Raitt, *A Theology of Exile. Judgment/Deliverance in Jeremiah and Ezechiel*, Philadelphia: Fortress Press, 1977, 130-34, 145, 175-80, makes similar observations concerning the element of transformation in oracles of deliverance in general, including specific mention of short oracles contained in Jer 30-31. He also mentions the gratuitousness of salvation in his development.

[9] For a general discussion of this concept cf. B. S. Childs, *Myth and Reality in the Old Testament*, SBT 27, London: SCM Press, 1960, 79. S. Böhmer, *Heimkehr*, 87, mentions it in relation to Jer 30-31.

4.3.1 *TRANSFORMATION*

4.3.1.1 *Prose Introduction* (30:1-4)

The idea of transformation is first introduced in the opening verses of Jer 30 with the twofold use of *šwb*. In Yhwh's words, *wšbty 't-šbwt ʿmy ... whšbtym 'l-h'rṣ* (30:3), is a promise of change from the present to the future. The actual physical reality of the people will be changed since the place of their dwelling will be the land of their fathers to which they shall return.

4.3.1.2 *Poem I* (30:5-11)

The opening poem reflects transformation in both its structure and its images. The initial stanza hints at transformation in the simile 'every male ... like a woman in labor' (*kl-gbr ... kywldh*, 30:6), indicating a change which is both impossible and undesirable. The same stanza also states it explicitly with the verb *wnhpkw*, which is part of a metaphor expressing imminent destruction. In the first stanza of Poem I transformation reflects the change from life to death, initially by using the image of giving birth as a metaphor for helplessness and weakness, and then by employing the parallel image of ashen or deathly faces.

The idea of transformation is made more explicit in the second stanza, beginning with Yhwh's breaking the yoke of oppression (*'šbr ʿlw mʿl ṣw'rk*, 30:8) which results in *wl'-yʿbdw-bw ʿwd ... wʿbdw* (30:8-9). The modification of the actual situation is accented by the repetition of a single root: *ʿbd*, negated for one circumstance (serving foreigners) and predicated of another (serving Yhwh). Even the manner of expression adds emphasis to the idea of change, since the first use of *ʿbd* (*yʿbdw*) has foreigners (*zrym*) as grammatical subject, though the meaning is that the Israelites are the slaves of their foes. The second use of *ʿbd* (*wʿbdw*) has the Israelites as subject (understood) both grammatically and thematically.

The physical change of place introduced in 30:3 is repeated in 30:10 with Yhwh's promise to save them *from* afar and their progeny *from* the land of captivity (*mwšyʿk mrḥwq ... m'rṣ šbym*). The change is made explicit in the result, in Jacob returning and finding tranquility, as well as in *wšb* (30:10).

The most striking transformation in this first poem occurs in the existence and experience of the people reflected in the relationship between the two stanzas of the poem. Stanza 1 opens on a note of intense pain and suffering, articulated in both aural and visual images. Both images evoke the possibility, though not the certainty, of imminent death. The second stanza goes on to describe at length the saving deeds of Yhwh. The opposition is striking. The poem moves from an engaging description of distress and destruction to a developed notion of peace and security as the result of Yhwh's deed of *yšʿ*. The transformation is total. Distress and fear are turned into tranquility and peace.

4.3.1.3 *Poem II* (30:12-17)

The second poem, like the first, moves from a very negative, almost hopeless, tone in the first stanza to a more positive one in the second.

This poem opens with Israel's suffering and develops it in seven lines by reiterating the incurableness of her wounds and the fact that this is due to her sins (30:12-15). In the brief second stanza (four lines) her healing is first hinted at indirectly by assuring the destruction of her enemies (30:16), and then is made explicit in a single line which reverses the image of incurableness with a promise of healing (30:17). This reversal is all the more striking since much the same vocabulary used to describe the suffering in 30:12-13 is used to reverse the image in 30:17.

Poem II, however, adds another element to the idea of transformation with its shift from the physical to the spiritual plane. Although the language refers to the physical reality of woundedness and incurableness, the underlying reality is spiritual, as made clear in 30:14 which explains the "incurable wound" in terms of Israel's 'lovers' (*m'hbyk škḥwk*) and again in 30:17 where the transformation is based upon, and is also a reversal of, the fact that she is called desolate — none seek her (*ndḥh qr'w lk ... drš 'yn lh*). Her woundedness, linked with her being alone and without relationship, is transformed.

Both Poem I and Poem II reflect the same structure: distress turned to joy, threat of death to life, and both by Yhwh's deeds. In each case the negative element is developed without hope, only to be unexpectedly reversed in the second stanza.

4.3.1.4 *Poem III* (30:18-31:1)

The third poem expresses in detail the changes to be brought about by Yhwh, beginning with the general *šb šbwt* and then enumerating his specific deeds: the rebuilding of the city and the citadel (30:18), and a promise of increased numbers and glory (30:19-20). This transformation is portrayed in terms of a change in Israel's national existence; the nation will become what it is not yet. All will be accomplished by the action of Yhwh.

Within the poem itself the variation in tone between the first and second stanzas is remarkable. While the first stanza portrays a situation of light and peace, alluding to Israel's existence as a nation among nations (*whrbtym ... whkbdtym*, 30:19) and mentioning her existence as a people before Yhwh (30:20-21), the second stanza pictures punishment, in the form of Yhwh's wrath on the heads of the wicked (30:23-24). Unlike the first two poems, this poem does not describe a change in the situation of the same people, yet, like the first two poems, the second stanza takes on a tone which is the opposite of the first.

What emerges as striking in the development of the idea of transformation is the relationship between Poems II and III, for these two poems present the same ideas with opposite emphases. Poem II first accents the negative, punitive action of Yhwh and the sinfulness of the people, and then goes on to change that concept to its opposite. It ends on a note of hope, presenting a God who listens to the cries of the suffering and heals them. Poem III first develops the expressed hope in great detail, by giving specificity to the caring and saving deeds of Yhwh; but then, after a first mention of the covenant formula, it also recalls him as not merely saving, or rather not saving unconditionally, but also as punishing those who deserve it.

4.3.1.5 *Poem IV* (31:2-6)

The theme of transformation clearly appears in two elements of Poem IV: the change described in the opening lines and the repetition of *ʿwd*. The initial statement refers to a past situation (Exodus) in which the threat of the sword was changed to favor (*mṣ' ḥn bmdbr ʿm śrydy ḥrb*). The positive aspect is expanded by the triple *ʿwd* implying that the positive experiences of the past, though lacking in the present, will be part of the future. The contrast between the threat of the past and the promised blessings for the future is remarkable even though it is more intimated than described.

This is, perhaps, the poem where the theme of transformation is least explicit and least developed, yet even here the undertone of change effected by Yhwh informs the whole.

4.3.1.6 *Poem V* (31:7-14)

The transformation spoken of in Poem V is first described as the return of the people (31:8), secondly, as the satiety which will not end (31:12) and finally, as the change from sorrow to joy (31:13). The image of return is developed in 31:8 with a description of Yhwh as the one who brings from the north and gathers from distant lands (*mby' ... m'rṣ ṣpwn wqbṣtym myrkty-'rṣ*). The change is *from* the land of the north without a destination being specified. The focus is, rather, on the size and composition of the group (*qhl gdwl*, 31:8).

The satiety granted the people by Yhwh is yet another element which establishes a difference between present (or past) and future: *wl' - ywsypw ld'bh ʿwd* (31:12). The implication is that the situation of *d'bh*, a common experience, is now changed by the promise of Yhwh and will become part of their past. All will be filled to overflowing.

Finally this poem moves beyond the physical plane. The change which Yhwh effects not only concerns the place of residence and an abundance of food for the people but even reaches to the depths of their spirit, turning their sorrow into joy (*whpkty 'blm lśśwn*, 31:13). This, the only explicit mention of change in Poem V, summarizes what precedes, for this change in their spirit will flow from the other, material, changes.

Both stanzas speak of actual physical displacement. In both, one of Yhwh's major activities is *qbṣ*: he gathers the people who have been scattered (31:8,10) and brings them to his good gifts. The first stanza accents the motion of return or moving *away* from that which is or was threatening, while the second gives emphasis to motion *towards* the gifts of Yhwh.

The imagery is predominantly that of physical, geographical change. Yet as physical transformation it is a symbol of a deeper spiritual reality, one which is present not only in the mention of *npš* (with its possible spiritual referent) as the recipient of Yhwh's deeds, but also in the explicit change of mourning turned into joy (31:13b). The promised transformation will touch every level of the people's existence.

4.3.1.7 *Poem VI* (31:15-22)

The theme of transformation is highly developed in this poem by the repeated use of *šwb* with its various nuances. In the first stanza *šwb* signifies return from the land of the enemy and return to their inheritance (31:16,17). Although the verbs are active (*qal*) and have as (implied) subject Rachel's sons, the one who effects such change is Yhwh, and in both instances the change is spatial and geographical. In the second stanza the same verb *šwb* is used, but this time it expresses an interior, spiritual change and a return of heart and attitude toward Yhwh (31:18). Yhwh is presented as the one who initiates such change, but Ephraim's union with this deed implies that he too participates actively and is not merely a passive recipient. In the third stanza the virgin Israel is addressed by a series of imperatives, including a double *šwby*/*šby* (31:21). She is told to return (*šwby*), but it is not clear whether she is called to a physical, geographical turning back (as in the first stanza) or an interior, spiritual one (as in the second stanza). However, the fact that she is addressed as 'back-turning daughter' (*hbt hšwbbh*, 31:22) seems to indicate the latter rather than the former interpretation.

Clearly, *šwb* is used in Poem VI to express the physical return to the land, as well as the motion of the heart or spirit of an individual toward Yhwh. In the first stanza the concept leans more to the physical/geographical view, while in the second, it connotes a more interior/spiritual content. The third stanza contains sufficient ambiguity to bring the two aspects together, including both physical and spiritual motion, all the while accenting the latter.

The expression of transformation and change is certainly contained in *šwb* but it is not limited to this verb. There are other ways in which this theme is developed in Poem VI.

Rachel, inconsolable (31:15), is told to stop her weeping since the reason for her lament will come to an end (31:16). The sons who are not, over whose demise she weeps, will once again exist in their land. Her present situation will be transformed into its opposite.

In stanza 2, Ephraim has already experienced a transformation in his own existence. He has known the educative presence of Yhwh (*'wsr*, 31:18) which has led him to the experiences of *nḥmty* and *spqty 'l-yrk* (31:19). It is his attitude, his spiritual self, which has undergone change. Ephraim is no longer the person he once was, for in recognizing his dependence upon Yhwh (trained/taught by him) and his own personal sinfulness (*bšty wgm-nklmty*, 31:19), he has undergone an interior transformation.

The third stanza is a cry to return, a call to the virgin Israel (the people) to shift the locus of her life. The initial imperatives are a call to a different existence, because the setting-up of waymarks or roadmarks (31:21) is the preparation for a change of circumstances, for going along the road to another place. The double *šwby* makes explicit what has been merely implied thus far. Yet the basis for the call to return is the deed of Yhwh: *br' yhwh ḥdšh b'rṣ*. That which is accomplished is new, different from what was known in the past. A new creation implies a new reality. The newness is striking as well as enigmatic, for it includes or results in *ngbh tswbb gbr*.

Nothing remains the same. The reason for Rachel's lamentation has been eliminated. Ephraim is no longer separated from Yhwh — he has recognized his own sin and is now the beloved son. The virgin Israel is no longer isolated but has the possibility of return. Creation itself takes on a new face.

4.3.1.8 *Prose Conclusion* (31:23-40)

The prose finale of this Little Book of Consolation develops the theme of transformation beyond anything found in the cycle of poems. The opening verse (31:23) reiterates the already-used expression *šwb šbwt* as attributed to Yhwh. He will effect a major change in the lives of the people, including their actual return to Judah and her cities. The empty or languishing soul will be filled (31:25), which implies an alteration of circumstances such that all need or want will be abolished. Transformation, however, reaches beyond the people. It not only has its source in Yhwh but is also *his* experience: 'he awakened and his sleep was darkness to him' (31:26), a metaphor for his shift from inaction to action on behalf of his people. The content of Yhwh's *šqd* will also change. No longer will he accomplish negative deeds but now he acts positively for his people (31:28, cf. 31:26).

If there is a modification in what Yhwh does, there is also an alteration in the people's perception of reality. Their understanding of sin and its consequences will no longer be what it once was; they will no longer believe that punishment can be inherited from one generation to another.

Yhwh also relates another element of newness: there will be a transformation in the covenant he makes with them. This is made explicit in the series of statements which redefine the covenant (*wkrty ... bryt ḥdšh, l' kbryt 'šr krty, ky z't hbryt*, 31:31-33). This new covenant is the underlying element of a new and transformed life, described by his action of *ntty 't-twrty bqrbm w'l-lbm 'ktbnh* (31:33). The change will be in the way the people come to know Yhwh, no longer through teaching (*wl' ylmdw 'wd*), but by his law inscribed on their hearts. There is also a modification in Yhwh's action; his former way of being was punishment of sin (cf., e.g., 30:12-15; 30:23-24) but now his hallmark is forgiveness.

The final verses (31:38-40) present an extraordinary picture of change and transformation. Not only will the city be rebuilt but the valley of the cadavers and fatty-ashes (offerings to idols?) will be *qdš lyhwh*! That which is most profane and unclean becomes not only clean but actually holy — and this *l'wlm* (31:40). This is, in effect, a new creation, which changes the understanding of reality at its most basic level.

The theme of transformation found throughout these two chapters is expressed not only in the words and thematic development but even in the structure of the poems, with one stanza reversing the dominant image of the preceding one. Distress and fear become peace, want is satisfied, and oppression is replaced by freedom. More concretely still, wounds are healed, those at a distance return to the land, sorrow is turned into joy. The experience of punishment is replaced by forgiveness. The need to teach and learn is replaced with infused knowledge and forgiveness of sins. Most startling of all, however, is that the unclean becomes holy. Yhwh acts to transform the whole of life, not only to establish a new covenant but, in some way, to effect a new creation.

4.3.2 *GRATUITOUSNESS OF SALVATION*

An important, if secondary, theme of these two chapters is the gratuitousness of Yhwh's deeds for his people. Although it is not equally present in every part of Jer 30-31, it does appear in several places and is developed at the end.

Neither the prose introduction nor the first poem is concerned with this theme, but at the same time neither makes any statement to the contrary.

4.3.2.1 *Poem II* (30:12-17)

Poem II accents the distress and suffering of the people, twice linking it to their sin and evil (30:14,15). After establishing the fact that their distress flows from their own sin, this poem promises healing, based not on any deed of theirs but on Yhwh's reaction to what he has heard others say of them (30:17). His action of healing and care comes uniquely and totally from himself and is not based on the people's deserving it.

4.3.2.2 *Poem III* (30:18-31:1)

Poem III develops at length the actions of Yhwh for the people: the rebuilding of the city, the repopulation of the nation, the renewal of their honor and glory before others, their re-establishment as a congregation before Yhwh, the raising up of a leader from among them (30:18-21). The last line of the first stanza (excluding the covenant formula) reiterates the gratuitousness of these deeds for it states quite clearly that no one dare draw near to Yhwh, not even the leader he has chosen from among the people (30:21). It is Yhwh's prerogative to act or not in favor of the people. His deeds are in no way based upon their positive response to him.

It becomes ever more clear in Poems II and III that the negative or sinful deeds of the people do in fact cause distress and suffering. Yhwh does punish the evildoer (30:15,23-24). On the other hand there is no deed of the people that can move him to act in their favor. His caring and saving acts are totally beyond the people's control. They are gratuitous, given to whomever he chooses, with no foundation in the people's deeds.

4.3.2.3 *Poem IV* (31:2-6)

Poem IV does no more than allude to the gratuitousness of Yhwh's deeds by attributing *ḥsd* and *'hbh* (31:3) to him, attitudes which are generally held to be undeserved by the recipients.

4.3.2.4 *Poem V* (31:7-14)

In a way similar to that of Poem IV, Poem V alludes to Yhwh's gracious deeds to an undeserving people. The expression *w'prym bkry hw'* in 31:9b implies a comparison between the story of Gn 48:8-20 and the present relationship of Yhwh with his people. In blessing his grandsons who were the sons of Joseph, Israel/Jacob placed the younger son, Ephraim, before the firstborn, Manasseh, despite the best efforts of their father to prevent such a thing from happening. This choice was a gratuitous gift of birthright given by Israel to Ephraim. Yhwh, like Jacob, has chosen Ephraim as first-born of the people. His deed is similar to that of Jacob and similarly gratuitous.

4.3.2.5 *Poem VI* (31:15-22)

Poem VI, with its reference to Ephraim and Rachel, makes allusion to Gn narratives as a point of reference for understanding Yhwh's deeds for his people. The mention of Rachel calls to mind her story and the fact that she was the favored and beloved wife despite her barrenness. Having borne Jacob no children, she was loved gratuitously by him. As a symbol of the people, 'Rachel' suggests a similar gratuitous love on the part of Yhwh. In like manner the appearance of Ephraim in stanza 2 recalls Gn 48. But Poem VI explicitly mentions Yhwh's gratuitous care, his assuring Ephraim of continued mercy. The only reason given is that he is loved (*hbn yqyr ly ... 'm yld š‘š‘ym*, 31:20). Ephraim has done nothing which is deserving of such treatment and care. It is pure gift for the one who is beloved and precious.

4.3.2.6 *Prose Conclusion* (31:23-40)

The conclusion develops the theme of gratuitousness both explicitly and implicitly. The explicit mention is most clear in 31:37 where Yhwh states that even if the depths could be plumbed and the heavens measured, even then he would not act according to what Israel has done. This is by far the clearest indication that his deeds on Israel's behalf are in no way determined by what she has done.

Less explicit but nonetheless important is Yhwh's assurance in 31:34 that he will forgive the people's sins and no longer remember their offenses, as the basis of their new covenant with him. It is not the people's motion toward Yhwh to which he responds, but rather Yhwh himself initiates the deed which results in the relationship.

31:36 repeats a similar idea, noting the impossibility that *zr‘ yśr'l* might ever cease being *gwy lpny*. Although no mention is made of the gratuitousness of Yhwh's deed nor of the forgiveness of the people's sins in 31:36, the striking parallelism between 31:36 and 31:37 indicates that one might read back into 31:36b the statement of 31:37b,[10] that he will not act according to the deeds of Israel. Yhwh's promise that Israel will

[10] A. Berlin, *The Dynamics of Biblical Parallelism*, 13, 73.

remain a people before him flows from his choice of them rather than from their behavior.

Jer 30-31 as a whole is concerned with the gratuitousness of Yhwh's saving deeds, even though the theme is not found in every poem. Although less dominant than 'transformation,' this theme is no less important, for it indicates the source of the transformative deeds as none other than Yhwh. Rather than focus on what is done, as does the theme of transformation, gratuitousness of salvation highlights the basis for the deed, as well as the one who initiates it. It distances the deeds of Yhwh from those of the people, demonstrating the inability of their efforts to effect their own salvation or even influence Yhwh in their favor.

4.3.3 *CONTINUITY AND DISCONTINUITY BETWEEN PAST AND FUTURE*

The poetic cycle of Jer 30-31 dwells very little on the present. Rather, it emphasizes the future, often in relationship to the past to which it is connected by both continuity and discontinuity.

4.3.3.1 *Prose Introduction* (30:1-4)

In the introductory verses the link between past and future is alluded to for the first time by the expression *wšbty 't-šbwt* (30:3), implying that the future will in some way reflect what had been previously experienced. The deed which Yhwh will accomplish in the future, bringing them back to the land, is explicitly connected to what happened in the past to their fathers (*whšbtym 'l-h'rṣ 'šr-ntty l'bwtm wyršwh*, 30:3). The same God gives the same land to the same people (though of different generations) at different moments in history. The future is connected with the past.

4.3.3.2 *Poem I* (30:5-11)

Poem I links the future both positively and negatively with the present (and perhaps the past as well) by the change expressed in *wl'-y'bdw-bw 'wd zrym w'bdw* (30:8-9). The people will no longer be the servants of foreigners, but they will serve Yhwh, their God, and David, their king. The reference to the historical personage David connects the future with the past, while the repetition of *'bd* indicates that the activity of 'serving' will continue. Despite the expressed continuity with the past, the change from a negative to a positive statement, the change of subject, and finally the change of implied object, all indicate that in the similarity there will also be a difference. The future is both a continuation of and a break with the past.

4.3.3.3 *Poem II* (30:12-17)

By the repetition of the same root in both the subject (participle) and the predicate (verb or object), found three times in 30:16, a link between past and future is clearly established. Those who acted against Israel (expressed in the participial subjects: *'klyk*, *š'syk*, *bzzyk*) in the past/present will, in the future, suffer the same fate they had inflicted on Israel (*y'klw*, *lmšsh*, *lbz*). The deeds of *'kl*, *šss*, *bzz* will continue, but both the subjects and the objects of these actions will change. Those who had been the subject will now be the object, though the reverse is not true. Thus a continuity exists between past and future action, but with a change in the recipients of this activity, a change to be effected by Yhwh.

4.3.3.4 *Poem III* (30:18-31:1)

The link between past and future in Poem III can be seen in the explicit comparison set out in 30:20: *whyw bnyw kqdm*. The future will reflect a positive past; the increase in numbers will not be a novelty but the repetition of a known experience, with no element of change mentioned.

4.3.3.5 *Poem IV* (31:2-6)

This short poem makes some of the most striking and explicit connections between past and future through the triple repetition of the particle *'wd* to introduce three successive lines (31:4a,4b,5). The use of this adverbial particle directs attention to the future, but always by repeating a past event. *Again* Yhwh will 'build up' the virgin Israel; *again* she will go out in joy; *again* vineyards will be planted and enjoyed. The future will be in continuity with the past, a repetition of the good things enjoyed at an earlier time.

4.3.3.6 *Poem V* (31:7-14)

The only reference in this poem to a link between the past and the future is found in 31:12b; it speaks of the future by a negative reference to the past as a time which included the experience of want and of emptiness (*ld'bh*). In the future this will no longer occur, as the negation (*l'* ... *'wd*) makes clear, predicating a discontinuity between past and future.

4.3.3.7 *Poem VI* (31:15-22)

The past-future connection in Poem VI is found implicitly in the repetition of the imperative *šwby* (31:21), implying that the future *can* have a link with the past, that the people *can* repeat a past experience, although there is no assurance or certainty that this will occur.

There is also an implicitly expressed element of *dis*continuity with the past in the statement that Yhwh is creating something new (*br' yhwh ḥdšh b'rṣ*, 31:22). The present/future differs from the past, since there is a new aspect to creation; yet this newness is not further specified, but merely hinted at.

4.3.3.8 *Prose Conclusion* (31:23-40)

The prose conclusion develops the past-future tension in a way not done in any of the poems, by a series of comparisons which run through the entire passage.

In one instance the people will repeat in the future a saying of the past (*ʿwd y'mrw*, 31:23), while in another their words will be different (*l' y'mrw ʿwd*, 31:29). The saying that will repeat a past expression is a blessing on Yhwh and his abode, while the one that will differ from what was said is the proverb which sees punishment for sin as inherited. The positive will be repeated; the negative, changed.

31:28 expresses the fact that Yhwh will continue his watchfulness (*k'šr šqdty ... kn 'šqd*) but change the content, for the infinitives which are the object of *šqdty* (perfect) are negative, punitive or destructive actions, while those which are the object of *'šqd* (future) are positive, constructive deeds. Continuity exists in Yhwh's watchfulness but changes in his actual deeds, which are no longer chastising but salvific.

The 'new covenant' is yet another element which enters into this theme of continuity-discontinuity. Continuity is found in the fact of a covenant while discontinuity is expressed by the fact that the new covenant will be different from the first (*l' kbryt 'šr krty*). One distinction is that the future covenant, unlike the former, will not be broken (*l' kbryt ... 'šr-hmh hprw*). With the new covenant, teaching one another to know the Lord will cease, as will Yhwh's remembrance of sins (*l' ylmdw ʿwd* and *wlḥṭ'tm l' 'zkr-ʿwd*, 31:34). The future will be radically different from, but understood in light of, the past.

The building of *hʿyr lyhwh* (31:38-40) is also in continuity with what occurred formerly, for the measuring line will go out again (*wyṣ' ʿwd qwh*, 31:39). The city will *again* be built up. Yet this city will have greater extension than the former one and will not suffer the destruction which had been its fate: *l'-yntš wl'-yhrs ʿwd lʿwlm* (31:40). Similarity with the past is found in the positive aspect (the existence of the city); dissimilarity to the past is expressed in the negative aspect (its destruction).

Throughout this cycle of poems there is constant reference to a future understood in terms of past experience, with the positive or salvific elements repeated. The saving presence of Yhwh, known once, will again be known. The suffering, punishment, and distance from the land which were part of the past distress will come to an end. The future, while radically new, has its roots in Yhwh's enduring presence.

These three themes are interwoven to form the single fabric of the Little Book of Consolation. Salvation is promised in the theme of transformation, a transformation which touches both the interiority and exteriority of Israel's life. Its source is Yhwh, who grants this gratuitously and makes it possible by forgiveness of sin. His deeds are new yet not totally unknown, for he always acts consistently. A knowledge of the past can indicate the way of the future, without confining it to past experience. The people can hope for joy, forgiveness, salvation, not only because they have known these in the past but also because Yhwh creates anew.

Chapter 5

FEMININE ADDRESS AND IMAGERY IN JER 30-31

One very striking aspect of the Hebrew text of Jer 30-31 is the movement back and forth between masculine and feminine address. Of the six poems in these two chapters (30:5-31:22), three are addressed exclusively or predominantly to a feminine 'you,' three to a masculine. Although feminine address is not uncommon,[1] its presence in Jer 30-31 is striking in its regularity, in what appears to be a studied usage, the feminine alternating with the masculine address from beginning to end.

The first poem (30:5-11), addressed to Jacob and Israel (30:10a), opens with the image of *gbr* compared to *yldh* (30:6), introducing the feminine at the beginning of this cycle of poems as a point of comparison (if a negative one). In the second poem (30:12-17) the feminine is not merely a point of comparison but the one to whom the poem in its entirety is addressed.[2] Like the first poem, the third (30:18-31:1) is directed toward a masculine audience,[3] without so much as an allusion to a feminine being, unless one so considers the reference to the city in 30:18. As the third poem reflects the gender usage of the first, so the fourth reflects that of the second, for in the fourth poem (31:2-6) the one addressed is feminine[4] as specified by *btwlt yśr'l* (31:4a). Poem V (31:7-14), like Poems I and III, addresses a masculine audience, although there is reference made to women as part of the returning assembly (*hrh wyldh*, 31:8) and as part of the rejoicing community (*tśmḥ btwlh*, 31:13). The final poem (31:15-22) directs two of its three stanzas toward a feminine being: 31:15-17 presents a description of the inconsolable Rachel and Yhwh's response to her, while 31:21-22 once again addresses *btwlt yśr'l*, now called *hbt hšwbbh*.[5] The prose conclusion is about and addressed to a masculine audience, though there are a few allusions to a feminine being.

This alternation is a fact which bears investigation, since in the prophetic books the people are more usually addressed with the masculine

---

[1] It is found throughout Jer 1-23, Dt-Is, Trito-Is, and also in Hosea, Micah, Nahum, Zephaniah.

[2] In the second poem the 2 f.s. suffix is found twenty-three times; a 2 f.s. verb, once.

[3] The 3 m.(s. and pl.) is used consistently except in 30:22, 24b where 2 m.s. is found.

[4] Note the fourfold use of the 2 f.s. suffix as well as the four 2 f.s. verbs.

[5] This last stanza uses a 2 f.s. verb seven times and the 2 f.s. suffix four times.

form. The repetition of the feminine image warrants consideration in order to determine why it was used and how an understanding of its use affects our comprehension of the text as a whole.[6]

The feminine image as applied to the people in Jer 30-31 differs from the one most commonly found elsewhere in the prophets and even elsewhere in the book of Jeremiah, that of the harlot or adulterous woman.[7] In Jer 30-31, while the negative side (harlotry or adultery) is alluded to in 30:14 and 31:22, it is never developed or stated explicitly.

Given the highly developed and somewhat unusual presentation of the feminine image (at least for the book of Jer) in Jer 30-31, it seems justified to consider it as an interpretive key for the entire two chapters. It is an image which not only spans the whole passage but also reflects a broad concept of woman's role in Israelite society.

This feminine image will be considered on three levels: literary, historical and psychological. Then, on the basis of such an analysis, some hypotheses will be proposed for its use in this poetic cycle. As hypotheses they are no more than suggestions of possible motivation for its presence. Yet, as such, they may open the way to further considerations of the feminine which go beyond the simple proposal that it reflects speech directed toward the capital city (never the nation), though at times the city is used as a symbol of the people.[8] Even if the origin of the feminine

---

[6] J. J. Schmitt, "The Gender of Ancient Israel" *JSOT* 26 (1983) 122, makes a similar comment regarding Jer 2 where "there is a careful structuring of masculine and feminine forms ... I claim that the editors purposively structured the passage, identifying the figures with their respective gender and number ... The effect the editors intended is lost if the care they took with grammar is not observed."

[7] In Jer 1-29 feminine address is used in reference to (a) the harlotry of the people in 2:2,17-25,33-37; 3:2-13,19-20; 4:30-31; 5:7-11; 11:15-17; 13:20-27; 22:20-23; (b) their suffering: 4:14,17-18; 6:2-8,25-26; 7:29; 8:18-9:1; 18:13; 21:13-14; and (c) only twice, the people as deserving of pity: 14:17; 15:5-6. The positive use, in promises of salvation, is found in Dt-Is, a fact which will be given further consideration below.

[8] A. F. Fitzgerald, "The Mythological Background for the Presentation of Jerusalem as Queen and False Worship as Adultery in the OT" *CBQ* 34 (1972) 414-15, in looking for the origin of the female image as it is applied to cities, says that the cities, powerful forces in human life, were seen as goddesses, identified with the patron deities of the particular people or city. In a later article, A. F. Fitzgerald ("*BTWLT* and *BT* as Titles for Capital Cities" *CBQ* 37 [1975] 170, 177) treats specifically *bt* and *btwlt* and argues that these terms are applied almost without exception to a capital city or a nation and not to a people, though he does admit that a great deal of ambiguity exists and that the city could indeed be a symbol for the people. J. J. Schmitt ("The Gender of Ancient Israel") holds that feminine address such as that used here in Jer 30-31 must be directed not toward the nation Israel (which is always addressed in the masculine) but toward Jerusalem, which as a capital city is personified by a female figure since Israel as an individual (patriarch), and thus as a name, is consistently masculine.

address as used here is to be found in a personification of the city, of greater importance than its origin is the literary purpose of the image.[9]

5.1 LITERARY USE OF THE FEMININE IMAGE

From a literary viewpoint the feminine image is one means of evoking a response from the readers, real or 'mock'.[10] Historically directed to exilic Israel, the text could be an encouragement for the people to identify themselves with the ideal woman and thus to respond to Yhwh in much the same way as the ideal woman responds to her husband.[11] Since the relationship of an Israelite woman to her husband is in many ways analogous to, and thus can be an image of, that of the nation to Yhwh, a careful consideration of woman's role is needed in order to indicate the close parallelism. The portrayal of the feminine in Jer 30-31, as used in address to the people, includes several essential elements of the Israelite understanding of woman.

5.1.1 *Dependence*

The Israelite woman was essentially dependent on the male segment of society and usually treated as a minor. She could not be a legal witness, and even her private vows were subject to the approval of her father or husband.[12] She had no right of inheritance from her husband or her father except under unusual circumstances. If, for example, her father had no male issue, she could inherit property[13] but only to preserve it in the family until a male descendant was born.[14] Even if she owned property, her husband had the usufruct of it. She was, in all public areas

---

[9] This fact was recognized by A. F. Fitzgerald in his 1975 article "*BTWLT* and *BT*," 183: "The reason why these Canaanite titles for capital cities became Israelite is that the Israelite poets found them useful for their own literary purposes."

[10] This terminology is used by W. Gibson in "Authors, Speakers, Readers, and Mock Readers" in J. P. Tompkins, ed., *Reader-Response Criticism. From Formalism to Post-Structuralism*, Baltimore and London: Johns Hopkins University Press, 1980, 1-6.

[11] *Pace* J. J. Schmitt, "Gender of Ancient Israel," 119, 124, who states that the marriage image is an inadequate description of the divine-human relationship for in fact 'Israel' is a masculine rather than a feminine being. He denies a feminine attribution to Israel in Jer 3:6,8,11,12, because, among other reasons, it "would offend against the *proposed* [emphasis is mine] universal rule that the noun Israel is masculine and its adjectives are masculine" (p. 122). (He does not consider the feminine address of Jer 30-31 in his analysis.)

[12] Num 30:3-15.

[13] Num 27:8.

[14] R. Loewe, *The Position of Women in Judaism*, London: SPCK, 1966, 34; P. Bird, "Images of Women in the Old Testament" in R. R. Ruether, ed., *Religion and Sexism. Images of Women in the Jewish and Christian Traditions*, New York: Simon and Schuster, 1974, 53; P. Trible, "Woman in the Old Testament," *IDBS*, 964.

and in many private ones, subject to her husband or father. This is reflected in the laws of Israel, both apodictic and casuistic, which define and protect above all the rights and authority of the male.[15]

It is obvious that the woman was dependent on her husband for protection, care, material support.[16] This dependence is made quite explicit in Poem II, where the female figure is described as suffering from incurable wounds which include the fact that her lovers have forsaken her (*kl-m'hbyk škḥwk 'wtk l' ydršw*, 30:14). She depends on them (or on some other) for wholeness and fulfillment. Yhwh steps in with healing because she has been called *ndḥh*, with none to seek her (30:17). He heals her by filling the role of presence which has been left vacant by others. She cannot be left alone; her dependence is clear.

The other reference to dependence is found in 31:4 with its statement that she will be 'built.' Since the life of the woman was directed toward marriage and the bearing of male progeny to her husband and his family,[17] the woman depends on her husband for sons and thus for her happiness. It is he who brings her the fulfillment which she seeks. It is he who 'builds' her; she cannot achieve this alone.

In Jer 30-31 it is Yhwh who gives material support to, shows his protection of and care for, Israel by healing their wounds (30:17), giving them numbers and status (30:19), raising up a leader for them (30:21), building them up (31:4), feeding them to satiety (31:12-14), giving them hope in their sons (31:16-17), increasing them (31:27), watching over them for the good (31:28) and forgiving their sins (31:34). Such care should lead to a knowledge of themselves as dependent on Yhwh and of living accordingly.

5.1.2 *Intimacy*

But a woman's dependence on her husband (or some male family member) is not merely that of servility or of being a possession, for the woman is often seen as the beloved one. In fact there are many recorded instances of marriage being a relationship of love between the spouses,[18]

---

[15] Cf., e.g., Ex 20:10; Dt 5:14; 21:18-22; Num 5:11-31. P. Bird, "Images of Women," 49-51.

[16] Cf. Ex 21:10.

[17] This is perhaps the most commonly found statement concerning the role and status of Israelite woman. Cf. A. Rainey, s.v. "Woman," *EncJud* XVI, 623; C. Breyfolge, "The Social Status of Woman in the Old Testament" *BW* 35 (1910) 108-09; J. Pedersen, *Israel* I-II, 70; A. Tosato, *Il matrimonio israelitico. Una teoria generale*, AnBib 100, Rome: Biblical Institute Press, 1982, 105-06. R. Loewe, *The Position of Women in Judaism*, does not state this explicitly although it is presupposed in his emphasis on marriage law and the role of the woman in the family.

[18] Cf., e.g., Hannah and Elkanah (1 Sm 1:5,8), Rachel and Jacob (Gn 29:18,30).

with the contract often understood as a protection of the woman's rights.[19] Although the operative word in marriage was *bʿl*[20] which includes the fact that the husband was lord or master of his wife,[21] still it was a lordship based on relationship and intimacy rather than on mere control.[22]

Such intimacy is portrayed in Poem IV (31:3-4) which describes not only the husband's duty of giving the woman children, but first the love she has received. The woman is portrayed as the beloved of her husband, the one who elicits sentiments of caring and concern. The same concern with love in relationship is alluded to in the reference to Rachel, the mere mention of whose name in 31:15-17 (Poem VI) evokes this idea of woman as loved, since Rachel was the beloved wife of her husband Jacob, long before she bore him any children.[23]

The woman in Jer 30-31 is one who experiences both intimacy and subordination. She is beloved (31:3; 31:15) and thus cared for, given children and made to fulfill her primary role in society. Yet she will be built only if and when she is 'built' by another; her experience of intimacy is closely tied to her subordination/dependence.

5.1.3 *Exclusivity*

Despite the apparent permissiveness of the law concerning the rights of the husband, in the best of marriage relationships in Israelite society the woman was beloved of her husband and intimate with him alone. This, according to Jer 30-31, is the attitude Israel must develop in her stance before Yhwh. She shall no longer serve foreigners (*zrym*) but rather her own God and leaders (*yhwh ... dwd*, 30:9). This is reflected in the fact that the assembly of Israel will exist not for its own sake but before Yhwh (30:20). The leader of the people will also have a special connection and intimacy with Yhwh who alone can effect it (30:21). The relationship of mutual belonging is repeated three times: Yhwh – our/your God // Israel – his/my people (30:22; 31:1; 31:33), a relationship which presupposes the exclusivity presented elsewhere.[24] The prose conclusion reiterates this important aspect. The people are no longer to respond to Yhwh as they once did, repudiating his *bryt* and the fact that

---

[19] A. Tosato, *Il matrimonio israelitico*, 105-06.

[20] Cf. Dt 21:13.

[21] Cf. Hos 2:18 (MT) which opposes *bʿl* to *'yš*, accenting the latter as the preferred loving relationship.

[22] Cf. above, p. 120 and A. Tosato, *Il matrimonio israelitico*, 161.

[23] Cf. Gn 29:18-30.

[24] The exclusivity of a marriage relationship is also mirrored in the uniqueness of the tie between a father and his first-born or beloved son (31:9) or that with a dearly beloved child (31:20) as Yhwh describes his relationship with Ephraim in Poems V and VI.

he is *b'l* (31:32) but they will live in the condition of 'knowing' him (*ky-kwlm yd'w 'wty*, 31:34), which in a marriage context is an expression of a profound intimacy.[25] Israel is called not only to intimacy with her God, but also to exclusivity in this relationship, as seen throughout this poetic cycle.

5.1.4 *Legal Obligations*

Women in Israel were equally liable with men under criminal law[26] and were equally bound by the negative prescriptions concerning cult and worship (no Sabbath work, no idolatry).[27] They were not, however, responsible for keeping the positive time-bound prescriptions though they were encouraged to participate when possible.[28] They could not be counted as part of an official minyan, though they were not discouraged from passive participation in liturgies and other cultic ceremonies and were even encouraged to take part with their husbands in the three annual religious feasts.[29]

This makes it clear that the woman's response to Torah was more interior and of her free choice than was that of the man. Such emphasis on choice in the service of Yhwh is alluded to in Jer 31:34 which states that no longer will an Israelite teach his brother or his neighbor, for the Torah will be inscribed on the hearts of all. This is a clear movement toward greater interiority. The law is now written not on external objects to be kept because of external sanctions, but is rather inscribed on the heart, in the interior of the person, to be enforced by desire and choice rather than by constraint. This is yet another way in which Israel's stance before Yhwh reflects that of the Israelite woman who was encouraged and given the possibility to follow Yhwh's requirements, but with few if any pressures.

5.1.5 *Suffering*

The woman as the image of suffering and travail is closely linked with that of the woman in her essential role of mother. The pangs of childbirth were considered to depict the greatest agony of the human being, for they bring helplessness and terror, agony which is both physical and psychological.[30] This attitude of suffering is explicit in 30:6

---

[25] Cf., e.g., Gn 4:1,17,25; Jdg 11:39; 1 Sm 1:19.

[26] Num 5:6-7.

[27] Dt 17:2-7.

[28] b Ber 20b.

[29] Cf. Dt 16:11-16; 1 Sm 1:1-28; 2:19; 2 Kg 4:23; and R. Loewe, *The Position of Women*, 44-45.

[30] P. Bird, "Images of Women," 62.

(Poem I) which describes the warrior in terms of the woman's weakness and fear before childbirth. The seriousness of the situation is clear, since a common treaty curse of the ANE was that warriors would become like women.[31]

The woman is the one who bears life and yet, in this act of power, shows her weakness (30:6; 31:8). She is the picture of one who is overwhelmed by weakness, fear, helplessness, yet from whose very helplessness comes forth life (30:6). Pregnant or nursing, she is weak and needy because of her maternity; yet in her weakness she forms part of the assembly whom Yhwh brings back (31:8).

In 31:15-17 (Poem VI) the mother suffers not because of the pain of childbirth but because she has lost the sons she once bore, those who brought her honor and status in society. The plight of being alone is also the source of her suffering in 30:12-17 (Poem II). Unsupported and wounded, she cries out to Yhwh.

In Jer 30-31 suffering generally reflects the negative or reverse of the ideal relationship, although from a more positive stance, it does accent dependence which is portrayed as the source of suffering in several of these poems.

5.1.6 *Representative of Society*

One area in which the woman had clear responsibility in Israelite society was in noncultic religious activities[32]: processions, laments,[33] and festal dances of victory or harvest,[34] all of which are mentioned in Jer 30-31. In 31:4 it is said that *btwlt yśr'l* will put on her tambourines and go out in a dance of joy. This expression recalls what is said of Miriam who celebrated Yhwh's victory over the Egyptians with a song and dance of praise (Ex 15:20-21). The statement which follows in Jer 31:5 speaks of planting vines and enjoying their fruit, an allusion to a harvest celebration in which women also danced.[35] Similarly in 31:13 the *btwlh* will rejoice in a dance together with the young men and the elders in response to receiving the good things of Yhwh, which could well refer to

---

31 D. Hillers, *Treaty Curses*, 66-68.

32 Women were required to offer sacrifices on certain occasions, though for personal rather than community reasons. Cf. Lev 12:6-8; 15:19-23; and C. Breyfolge, "The Religious Status of Woman in the Old Testament" *BW* 35 (1910) 405-19; I. J. Peritz, "Woman in the Ancient Hebrew Cult" *JBL* 17 (1898) 111-48; C. Vos, *Woman in Old Testament Worship*, Delft: Judels & Brinkman, s.d., 61,73.

33 Cf. Jer 9:16-19.

34 Cf. Ex 15:20-21; Jdg 11:34; 1 Sm 18:6-7. W. O. E. Oesterley, *The Sacred Dance*, 31-43.

35 W. O. E. Oesterley, *The Sacred Dance*, 39-41 and 141-44. Cf. Jdg 21:19-21 as a possible scriptural indication.

both harvest and cult (harvest, because of the agricultural products mentioned; cult, because the priests will be sated with *dšn* as well). 31:15-17 with its reference to Rachel's weeping and lamenting also recalls the women's participation in noncultic community activity. Their role in lamenting was important as Jer 9:16-19 testifies.

Woman is thus portrayed as one who is in touch with and reflects the high and the low points of societal life. She rejoices with those who rejoice (31:5; 31:13) and weeps with the sorrowing (31:15-16). She is indeed an integral part of the most intensely lived moments of her people.

5.1.7 *Responsibility*

Despite their seemingly secondary status in the society, women are portrayed as persons of intelligence and will, capable and persuasive individuals who can have a positive or a negative influence on their male counterparts.[36] Although they may, at times, be depicted as unscrupulous, they are seldom if ever considered frivolous or foolish.[37] Perhaps this is why wisdom was personified by a feminine figure in the book of Wisdom. The ideal wife is intelligent, beautiful, discreet, loyal, prudent, quick-witted, resourceful, capable of independent action, yet one who always acts on behalf of her husband.[38]

In Midrash and Jewish legends,[39] the intelligence and the religious devotion of woman have also been praised. Despite the many negative traits attributed to her, the woman was also recognized as having been given more understanding (*binah*) than the man, and she developed this gift at an earlier age than her male counterpart.[40] Her religious devotion was held in esteem as evidenced in the story about God's giving the Torah to Israel. God told Moses to give it first to the women, who would then persuade the men to accept it. One of the reasons proposed for this is that women are more scrupulous in observance of religious precepts.[41] In a similar vein, the rabbis said that after the reception of the Law in the

---

[36] Cf. S. Amsler, "La sagesse de la femme" in M. Gilbert, ed., *La Sagesse de l'Ancien Testament*, BEThL 51, Gembloux: Editions Duculot et Leuven: Leuven University Press, 1979, 112-16.

[37] Cf., e.g., the story of Tamar in Gn 38; P. Bird, "Images of Women," 70.

[38] P. Bird, "Images of Women," 65. Cf., e.g., Abigail, 1 Sm 25:2-42.

[39] It is true that Midrash was recorded several centuries after the time of Jeremiah, but Judaism shows a certain atemporality in its beliefs and practices. R. Loewe, *The Position of Women*, 13, speaks of Judaism's nonacceptance of a western concept of time which colors their view of history, law and institutions and sees them in a synchronistic framework. Thus even if these ideas are 'late' they almost certainly reflect an attitude which existed much earlier or was already existing seminally.

[40] GenR 18,1; b Nid 45b. Cf. L. Ginzberg, *The Legends of the Jews* I, trans. from German by H. Szold, Philadelphia: The Jewish Publication Society of America, 1909, 67.

[41] L. Ginzberg, *The Legends of the Jews* III, 85.

wilderness, it was the women who remained faithful to Yhwh while their husbands rebelled and built the golden calf.[42] And it was thanks to the righteous women of that generation that Israel was redeemed from Egypt.[43]

The woman, beloved or not, was considered intelligent, persuasive, at times manipulative. This aspect of the feminine image is portrayed in 31:15-17 (Poem VI) where Rachel's tears and cries are successful in drawing Yhwh's attention, with the result that he effects a change for her benefit: the restoration of her sons. It is she who is responsible for this: *ky yš śkr lp'ltk* (31:16b).

Thus 'woman' in Jer 30-31 is one who can have an effect on others and can determine how they react to her. She evokes a response from Yhwh by her tears, her weeping, and her extreme desolation which find active expression (31:15-17). Yet she can also elicit a response simply by her need. In 30:12-17 it is her incompleteness which evokes compassion and action on the part of Yhwh. He comes to her aid because she is desolate (*ndḥh*, 30:17). The simple fact that she is alone and needy leads the other to respond to her.

If she can change her circumstances by affecting the action of others, as 31:15-17 suggests, she can also act for her own benefit as is made clear in 31:21-22 (Poem VI) where she is addressed by five imperatives. She not only 'turns' and 'returns' (*šwby* – twice), but she also constructs, sets up, and in a certain sense builds her own future by physical deeds (*hṣyby lk ṣynym, śmy lk tmrwrym, šty lbk lmslh*).

This accent on the independent status of the woman and her autonomy, when applied to Israel, reflects the need for Israel to take an autonomous and responsible stance before Yhwh. He is the one who encourages this. She is called to find her way, to set up roadmarks, to turn back, that is, to act by herself and for herself.

Besides her responsibility for change in the future, she is also responsible for her present and past. Poem II (30:12-15), for example, twice states that she suffers as a consequence of her own deeds: *'l rb 'wnk 'ṣmw ḥṭ'tyk ... 'l rb 'wnk 'ṣmw ḥṭ'tyk 'śyty 'lh lk*. She may be dependent in many areas but she is, at the same time, responsible for her own situation.

Such responsibility is the foundation of her sinfulness. She has sinned, multiplied her own sins (30:12-15) and turned away continuously (31:22). And only the person who is responsible can be counted sinful.

The changed proverb of 31:30 also reflects personal responsibility for one's deeds and their consequences, which is one aspect of an independent existence. Each person will suffer the consequences of his/her

---

[42] L. Ginzberg, *The Legends of the Jews* III, 121-22, 393.

[43] ExR 1,12.

own sin; each has his/her own independent existence. Yet all are dependent on Yhwh for he is the one who guarantees their future, whatever their past may have been (31:36-37).

Throughout these poems the woman is presented as both dependent and independent, attitudes which are important for an adequate relationship with God. Thus the feminine figure represented as both weak and strong, meek and fearless, dependent and autonomous, is an image which Israel is encouraged to imitate in her relationship to Yhwh.

The portrayal of Israel according to feminine categories is an effective means of alluding to the desired relationship with Yhwh. Israel is not a 'possession' of Yhwh any more than a woman is the property of her father or husband. There is obvious dependence on the male yet this dependence is not absolute. Love and intimacy determine the husband's deeds for his wife while at the same time she acts with responsibility and even a certain autonomy. Such a situation adequately reflects Israel's stance before Yhwh. She is dependent on him yet also responsible for what befalls her. She is free to act, be it according to or contrary to the ideal of intimacy and exclusivity, yet her happiness and freedom lie in living in conformity with her knowing herself dependent on Yhwh and loved by him.

If the Exile was considered a punishment for the sins of the people, then Jer 30-31 sets out a blueprint for a life which, more in harmony with the ideal relationship, points to a new beginning.

5.2 HISTORICAL HYPOTHESIS

The historical situation and background, the fact that Israel was in exile in Babylon at the time of the final writing of this poetic cycle, suggests another way in which the use of such extraordinary feminine imagery might be understood.

Babylon, part of the larger Mesopotamian culture, had developed in such a way that the woman played an important role in all aspects of society.[44] Without ever attaining full equality with the male, she had an

---

[44] The description of woman in Ancient Mesopotamia is based largely on J. Bottéro, "La femme dans l'Asie occidentale ancienne: Mésopotamie et Israël" in P. Grimal, ed., *Histoire mondiale de la femme*, Vol. I: *Préhistoire et antiquité*, Paris: Nouvelle Libraire de France, 1965, 156-247. Much the same information is available in more summary fashion in E. Boulding, *The Underside of History. A View of Women through Time*, Boulder, Colo.: Westview Press, 1976. The Nuzi tablets also concur with many of the attitudes found in Mesopotamia. Cf., C. Gordon, "The Status of Woman Reflected in the Nuzi Tablets" *ZA* 43 (1936) 147-69. J. Bottéro's description of the social situation in Mesopotamia has been criticized by R. Harris, Review of *Histoire mondiale de la femme* in *JESHO* 9 (1966) 308-09, as a generalization which does not distinguish the difference in the status of woman between the old and neo-Babylonian periods. Similarly, A. L. Oppen-

active part in the economic as well as the familial structures and thus gained a high level of independence (even if this independence did not touch equally all strata of society nor did it affect all women in each stratum).[45] It would be hard to imagine that Israelite women, living side by side with the Babylonian/Mesopotamian, could have escaped the influence of these ideas of greater autonomy and a wider role in society.[46]

5.2.1 *Babylon*

Since the basic component of the society in Ancient Mesopotamia was the family which centered around the male, the woman's role was defined essentially in relation to that of the man, specifically her husband.

Marriage was essentially "la prise de possession d'une femme par un mari"[47] that she might join the family of her husband in order to bear male children to him and his family and thus perpetuate the line.[48] This attitude toward woman as an object of exchange for the benefit of the husband is clear in the marriage contract which was drawn up between two parties without requiring the presence or the consent of the future wife.[49] In fact it was often done while she was still a minor, before she reached menarche and was still under the care of her father.[50] She remained in his house until she was nubile, at which time she went to the house of her husband. Thus her role was essentially that of wife as

---

heim, *Ancient Mesopotamia. Portrait of a Dead Civilization*, Chicago and London: University of Chicago Press, 1964, 77, makes reference to a changed status of woman between the two periods without giving particulars or documentation. However, one indication of a continuity between the periods is the existence of some fragments of the Code of Hammurabi in neo-Babylonian script, making it likely that it was still in effect. (Cf. P. Garelli et V. Nikiprowetzky, *Le Proche-Orient asiatique. Les empires mésopotamiens. Israël*, L'histoire et ses problèmes, 2 bis, Paris: Presses Universitaires de la France, 1974, 161.) B. Meissner, *Babylonien und Assyrien* 1. Band, Heidelberg: Carl Winters Universitätsbuchhandlung, 1920, 388, states that the neo-babylonian period saw women with greater freedom and rights than at the time of Hammurabi. A similar positive judgment is given by E. Ebeling, s.v. "Frau," *Reallexikon der Assyriologie und Vorderasiatischen Archaëologie* III, 103-04.

45 Clearly those who could attain a high level of culture and education had both leisure and the wealth which such leisure presupposed. Thus the independent woman could exist only in the upper class of Babylonian society. Cf. J. Bottéro, "La femme dans l'Asie Occidentale," 160.

46 Cf. S. W. Baron, *A Social and Religious History of the Jews*, Vol. I: Ancient Times, Part I, New York: Columbia University Press, 1952 (2nd rev. ed.), 111-12.

47 J. Bottéro, "La femme dans l'Asie occidentale," 184.

48 R. Harris, "Woman in the Ancient Near East," *IDBS*, 961; J. Bottéro, *Mésopotamie. L'écriture, la raison et les dieux*, Paris: Editions Gallimard, 1987, 237.

49 Code of Hammurabi 159-61, *ANET*, 173.

50 J. Bottéro, *Mésopotamie*, 225.

child-bearer, a fact emphasized in the images of woman that have come down to us in figurines and other plastic art which accentuate her sexual attractiveness both physical and spiritual.[51]

Though she may have been in many instances a 'possession' of her husband, as wife the woman had certain rights and responsibilities. She had the right to food, shelter, and all physical necessities being met by her husband and his family. Even if she fell ill and was unable to fulfill her conjugal duties, she could not be repudiated or divorced by her husband; she retained the right to be cared for, although he could take a secondary wife or a concubine to bear him children.[52] (In Nuzi some marriage contracts forbade a man taking a second wife or a concubine even if his first wife was barren.[53]) The wife had the right to dispose of her own material wealth (dowry, etc.)[54] as well as that of the household, according to her own designs, even to the ruin of the family. She alone was responsible for the running of the house, although she might also have to work outside this realm in order to help the family survive. Fidelity to her husband was of primary importance, though adultery was not unknown.

The woman was responsible for the early education of both male and female children, though male children passed to the tutelage of their father at about the age of seven or eight years. Despite her essential role in bearing and rearing children, these children belonged not to her but to their father.[55] Still she was honored by them and they often cared for her if she was widowed. (In many instances there is a clear similarity with customs of the Israelite society.)

Although in theory the male was considered the master, the one who was truly independent within the society, in fact women in Mesopotamia (and also in Nuzi[56]) arrived at a status which was hardly less than that of their "lords and masters."[57] Women were considered juridical persons (they could have their own seal), though how frequently they exercised their rights is not clear. A woman could possess property[58] and make use of it in any way she wished: give it as a gift, rent it, or sell it. She could lend money at interest, borrow money, buy whatever she pleased, or take a lease on a piece of property.[59] She had the same right as a man to adopt

---

[51] J. Bottéro, "La femme dans l'Asie occidentale," 168.

[52] Code of Hammurabi 148, *ANET*, 172.

[53] C. Gordon, "The Status of Women," 159.

[54] Neo-Babylonian Laws 11-13, *ANET*, 197.

[55] Code of Hammurabi 135, *ANET*, 171.

[56] C. Gordon, "The Status of Women," 164-66.

[57] J. Bottéro, "La femme dans l'Asie Occidentale," 204-05.

[58] Code of Hammurabi 38, *ANET*, 167-68; Middle Assyrian Laws 35, *ANET*, 183; R. Harris, "Woman in the Ancient Near East," 961.

[59] R. Harris, "The *nadītu* Woman" in R. D. Briggs and J. A. Brinkman, eds., *Studies Presented to A. Leo Oppenheim*, Chicago: University of Chicago Press, 1964, 129-30.

children or adults[60] (either real adoption or sale-adoption, to use the expressions of Gordon concerning the Nuzi practice[61]); she could free slaves or reduce a free person to slavery at whim. She could be a witness, legally guarantee the authenticity of a document, or make an oath. She could take legal action not only outside the control of her husband but actually against him. She had a high status in society and possessed equal powers with men before the law in many circumstances.[62]

Interestingly, despite the high importance given to motherhood, celibacy was not unknown in this society nor was it held in contempt. Besides the group of women who were single by accident, others, the *nadītu*, remained so by a freely chosen religious vow,[63] though it is impossible to say whether the reason for the vow was economic or religious.

Another striking fact is that there were women scribes in Mesopotamia since the third millennium. This meant that women had access to the entire body of science and culture of the society as it was kept and passed on in writing. And since this was a profession which required long years of preparation, these women professionals presumably remained unmarried or, if married, free of domestic duties at this time. Above all, the existence of women scribes presupposed a well-developed intellectual ability and an acceptance of the fact that women were capable of intellectual pursuits.

Since women could be scribes, it is less surprising to discover that women also played an important role in the economic life of the country. Some operated drinking houses (perhaps because they were responsible for the production of beer, the national drink) which in nonurban areas served also as a type of general store in which merchandise was often sold on credit.[64] Besides these local commercial ventures, women, including the *nadītu*, were involved in buying and selling, importing and exporting goods as well as in negotiating work contracts.[65]

In political life women exercised power mainly through their influence on the male members of their family, husband or son. Still, there were instances where the king's daughter, in her role as high

---

[60] This is mentioned in relationship to the *nadītu* in R. Harris, "The *nadītu* Woman," 119, 123.

[61] C. Gordon, "The Status of Women," 150.

[62] This was also true at Mari. Cf. B. F. Batto, *Studies on Women at Mari*, Baltimore and London: The Johns Hopkins University Press, 1974, 5.

[63] R. Harris, "The *nadītu* Woman," 135, states that this group existed only during the First Dynasty of Babylon, although their memory was retained by later generations.

[64] Code of Hammurabi 108, *ANET*, 170.

[65] B. Meissner, *Babylonien und Assyrien*, 387; R. Harris, "The *nadītu* Woman," 130.

priestess of a city, was the official representative of the king in that locale.[66] (This occurred from 2350 until 539 B.C.)

While women did serve in roles of cultic leadership, these functions were most often carried out by men. This is very likely due to the fact that in the Mesopotamian pantheon, which was composed of both male and female deities, the god at the head was always male.

However, it was the female figure with her natural functions of love and maternity who became the key to understanding the origin of life in the universe. If she played a secondary role in certain aspects of society, she nonetheless achieved a great deal of independence and virtual equality with her male counterpart in many areas of society and culture.[67] This was the social situation which the Israelites confronted on a daily basis during the Exile. They were continually faced with a society which gave woman greater freedom and legal autonomy than they had been accustomed to.

5.2.2 *Israel*

There are indications that already at the time of Jeremiah, and even before the Exile, women held a position of a certain importance within Israelite society (though whether this was accepted by the society at large is not at all clear). One indication of an acceptance of women's authority appears in 2 Kg 22. When he discovered the book of the law in the temple, Josiah called upon Huldah the prophetess to make a judgment on it (2 Kg 22:14-20). Huldah was chosen for this important duty, and not Jeremiah (assuming that he was already exercising his prophetic role) nor any other male prophet, though it is clear that other prophets existed.[68] The choice of a woman for such a deed suggests that she must have had a great deal of influence and thus gives an instance of a positive judgment on the role of women at that period.

Several times in the book of Jeremiah the women of Israel are found blameworthy for their worship of the Queen of Heaven (Jer 7:16-20; 44:15-19,24-28). Peritz observes, interestingly, that they were not condemned for their participation in worship, but rather for directing their cultic activities to the wrong god.[69]

Whether or not Peritz's observations are correct, it is clear that the women of Jeremiah's time were taking initiative in cultic matters.

---

[66] An example can be seen in the Mari texts. Cf. B.F. Batto, *Studies on Women at Mari*, 42-44.

[67] G. Furlani, *La civiltà Babilonese e Assira*, Roma: Istituto per l'Oriente, 1929, 383.

[68] The existence of other prophets is indicated by the references to prophets (plural) in 2 Kg 23:2; Jer 23:9-15; 26:7-16; 27:16-18 as well as in Jeremiah's confrontation with the prophet Hananiah (Jer 28:1-17).

[69] I.J. Peritz, "Woman in the Ancient Hebrew Cult" *JBL* 17 (1898) 126.

Although such an attitude toward cultic affairs, which would lead to participation in the cult, would not have been acceptable in monarchic and post-monarchic Israelite society,[70] it would have been common in Babylon. This could perhaps be a reflection of the influence Mesopotamian society had on Israel, an influence that would have been intensified during the Exile. Even if the worship of the Queen of Heaven had arisen quite apart from the influence of Mesopotamian culture, the daily confrontation with Babylonian practices during the Exile would certainly have impinged on the Israelite women's awareness of their role in society.

The Israelite woman was thus faced with two interlocking realities: a present, observable experience of other women (those of Babylon) who enjoyed an active role in their own society, and the remembrance of their own historical forerunners who also had a great deal of power and autonomy in Israelite society (Miriam, Deborah, etc.).

Given this background, one hypothesis for the use of the feminine image by the author (or redactor) is that it was a way of including the women (the feminine element of society) in the community. It is clear that Jeremiah, in 44:24-25, addresses the men and women in Egypt, a fact that reflects the importance (if not the equality) of the women. By the explicit mention of women as included in the assembly (31:8) and as responsible for the return (31:21-22), as well as by the repeated use of feminine address, Israel was reminded of the fact that she was composed not only of males but also of females. The women no longer needed to consider themselves excluded from an active role in their own society and drawn instead to the practices of the surrounding Babylonian culture. Nor did they need feel that their exclusion from the Israelite cult necessitated their turning to the worship of goddesses (Queen of Heaven) in order to experience their own importance. They were important in themselves as an essential part of the society, not only in their dependence (so highly developed in Israelite culture) but also in their autonomy (more notable in the lives of their Mesopotamian sisters). Thus they would be encouraged in their positive role as an integral part of their own society by their inclusion as an integral part of the poems.

Such an hypothesis would also help explain the alternation between masculine and feminine address. It was the community as composed of two groups, distinct but united, which was addressed by Yhwh through the prophet.

Throughout prophetic literature, the presence of feminine address in promises of salvation is found only in texts of assumed exilic or post-exilic origin. Such positive imagery appears frequently in Dt-Is

---

[70] This is true even if Peritz is correct in saying that it was a common attitude in the earliest years of Israel. Cf. I. J. Peritz, "Woman in the Ancient Hebrew Cult," 114.

(40:2; 49:14-26; 51:3,17-23; 52:1-2; 54:1-10; 54:11-17) and Trito-Is (60:1-22; 62:1-12) as well as in Is (22; 32), Micah (4:8-13), Zephaniah (3:14-20). The cited passages of these last three books are, according to Fohrer,[71] later additions to pre-exilic texts. All other references to the people in feminine terms (i.e., all the pre-exilic texts) use the image of harlotry or sinfulness of the woman. This fact appears to confirm the proposal that during the exilic period the feminine was given added prominence and held in greater honor in a response to the socio-cultural milieu which influenced the Israelite community.

5.3 PSYCHOLOGICAL HYPOTHESIS

It is not only on the literary and historical levels that the feminine image plays a role. This image is also operative on the psychological level. Such would seem to be the case if Jung is correct in maintaining that all thought rests on general images which he calls archetypes, that is, functional schemes which unconsciously form thought.[72]

As typical modes of apprehension and as organizing forces of the unconscious, archetypes exist in the pre-conscious of humans of whatever age or culture and are expressed in specific symbols and images which are colored by their own socio-historical situation.[73] The archetype *an sich* is a "*facultas praeformandi*; a possibility of representation which is given *a priori*."[74] It is, according to Jung, "an inborn mode of psychic apprehension"[75] which belongs to entire peoples and epochs, if not to all times and all races. The discovery of an archetype and its use in a given circumstance helps our understanding of certain fundamental aspects of *homo sapiens* revealed in the particular situation.

As an organizing and dynamic force in the human psyche, archetypes are manifested in art and literature throughout the ages. Jung himself notes that both myth and fairy tales are expressions of the

---

[71] G. Fohrer, *Introduction to the Old Testament*, trans. from German by D. Green, London: SPCK, 1970, *ad loc.*

[72] C. G. Jung, *Psychological Types*, The Collected Works of C. G. Jung, vol. 6, Revision by R. F. C. Hull of a translation by H. G. Baynes, Bollingen Series XX, Princeton: Princeton University Press, 1971, 381.

[73] C. G. Jung, "Instinct and the Unconscious" in *The Structure and Dynamics of the Psyche*, Collected Works, vol. 8, 135-38 and *ibid.*, "A Psychological Approach to the Dogma of the Trinity" in *Psychology and Religion: West and East*, Collected Works, vol. 11, 148-49.

[74] C. G. Jung, "Psychological Aspects of the Mother Archetype" in *The Archetypes and the Collective Unconscious*, Collected Works, vol. 9.1, 79.

[75] C. G. Jung, *Psychological Types*, 356.

archetype,[76] and he uses literature as one source for demonstrating the universal presence of the archetypes and how they touch all aspects of human being and expression. Maude Bodkin has studied the presence of various archetypes in literature both ancient and modern, with specific emphasis on tragedy.[77] W. Scott notes the influence of Jung on that branch of literary criticism which has shown interest in the cultural patterns and myths recurring in literature.[78] More recently, Gilbert Durand has developed a system of symbolic presentation which presupposes and uses the archetypes as they appear in literature.[79] Thus what came to expression and clarity over a long period in Jungian psychology, the existence and importance of archetypes, is seen as an organizing element for images and symbols in both art and literature.

While it is true that archetypes in general and the feminine archetype[80] in particular are most often studied in their more developed or specific manifestations (e.g., the feminine in literature and art, the virgin-mother in myth[81]), it seems that one could justifiably consider them in their more generic representation based on Jung's 'definition' of an archetype as "an irrepresentable factor ... which ... arranges the material of consciousness into definite patterns."[82]

The consensus maintains that the two major concrete representations of the feminine archetype are the mother and the virgin, both of which often find expression in different goddess figures. Through these and other specific images and symbols one can go back to the basic characteristics which inform all the expressions of the archetype and uncover the organizing axes for the conscious image. For the feminine archetype these have been determined as the elementary and the transformative 'characters.'[83] It is at this level, toward these characters,

---

[76] He makes reference to Nietzsche's *Zarathustra*, *The Shepherd of Hermes*, Rider Haggard's novels, *She*, *The Return of She* and other works of literature, throughout *The Archetypes and the Collective Unconscious*, Collected Works, 9.1 (cf. pp. 5, 37, 71).

[77] M. Bodkin, *Archetypal Patterns in Poetry. Psychological Studies of Imagination*, New York: Vintage Books, 1958.

[78] W. S. Scott, "The Archetypal Approach: Literature in the Light of Myth" in *Five Approaches of Literary Criticism*, 247-57.

[79] G. Durand, *Les structures anthropologiques de l'imaginaire*, Collection Etudes Supérieures, Poitiers: Bordas, 1969.

[80] Jung himself speaks not of the 'feminine' but of the 'mother' archetype. However, students of Jung and later writers use the term 'feminine archetype' with the mother image as a specific manifestation of the feminine, much as is done in these pages.

[81] M. Bodkin, *Archetypal Patterns*, 148-210; E. Neumann, *The Great Mother. An Analysis of the Archetype*, trans. from the German by R. Manheim, Bollingen Series XLVII, Princeton: Princeton University Press (2nd ed.), 1963, 89-336; G. Durand, *Les structures anthropologiques*, 225-320.

[82] C. G. Jung, "A Psychological Approach to the Dogma of the Trinity," 148-49.

[83] E. Neumann, *The Great Mother*, 24-38; A. B. Ulanov, *The Feminine in Jungian Psychology and in Christian Theology*, Evanston: Northwestern University Press, 1971, 157-62.

and before they take further expression in specific images, that the present study is directed.

The *elementary* character is that aspect of the feminine which contains, holds, and protects all that springs from it. It is the foundation of the conservative, stable and unchanging part of the feminine which gives security and protection. As such it tends to assure, to maintain reality as it is known, to give a sense of stability.[84] The *transformative* character, on the other hand, places the accent on the dynamic element of the psyche which drives toward motion and change. It does not let things remain as they are but moves them to new life, to birth and rebirth.[85]

This feminine archetype is at play in Jer 30-31, not in the symbol of the female goddess or the Great Mother (neither of which was an important symbol for the Israelite religion, though both appear in the culture of Mesopotamia), nor even in the less defined image of mother, but in the more general features and character of woman or the feminine.

Jer 30-31, with its extraordinary presence of the feminine, evokes the feminine archetype not so much in a specific image or symbol, much less in a given myth, but in its generality as an organizing factor of human thought. Given the elementary and transformative character of the feminine, the unusual (at least for Jeremiah) repetition of the feminine as is found in these chapters cannot help but elicit a reaction from the audience.

If it is true that the feminine archetype (as other archetypes) informs the whole of our experience of and attitude toward reality even though at a subconscious level, it could well be that the use of the feminine imagery has an effect on the psyche of the reader / hearer. Since the feminine is the archetype which includes the idea of transformation, the presence of feminine imagery used consistently and repetitively might well evoke, even subliminally, this aspect of transformation. It could set up in the reader a subconscious predisposition to understanding and assimilating the more explicit details of the text: transformation of reality not as divorced from the past but as linked with it, in continuity with the known.

The fundamental notions of the feminine archetype (elementary character = protection; transformative character = change) also constitute the underlying theme of Jer 30-31 (continuity with the past; change for the future). The transformation and security which find their source in the feminine as their underlying primordial image are developed in Jer 30-31 by a series of images, symbols and modes of expression. The Little Book of Consolation does indeed communicate the promise of transformation — in ways both subliminal and articulated.

---

[84] E. Neumann, *The Great Mother*, 25-26; A. B. Ulanov, *The Feminine*, 157-58.
[85] E. Neumann, *The Great Mother*, 29; A. B. Ulanov, *The Feminine*, 159-60.

CONCLUSION

The foregoing analysis has applied techniques of contemporary literary criticism to a Hebrew poetic text. Such an approach, admittedly still a newcomer among exegetical methods, has pointed to an actual literary unity of Jer 30-31, maintained by most exegetes though rarely demonstrated. It also has shown that literary devices and polysemy, besides having a function as unifying elements, offer solutions to many text-critical problems which call for text emendation when approached by historical-critical methodologies.

Using an essentially synchronic approach, this study has shown that a literary analysis need not fall into ahistoricism or fundamentalism but must take into account the socio-historical context out of which the text has come. As a valid exegetical method, it considers as many aspects of the text as possible including verbal elements, literary devices and the structure of the text as bearers of meaning. As literary analysis, it does not deny a redactional process for composition; it rather focuses on the final product as an intelligible work, presupposing that redactional activity is meaningful and not haphazard.

It also points out how a single motif or grammatical construction (e.g., the use of the feminine image and address), when subjected to careful study can focus attention on the content and message of the text.

A study such as this one may also indicate some directions for further work on this or similar texts.

While certain poetic and stylistic devices present in Jer 30-31 have been indicated, the Little Book of Consolation bears study using stricter poetic analysis, focusing specifically on text aesthetics as conveying meaning. Also, because of the intertwining of prose and poetry, Jer 30-31 appears to be fertile ground for a study which seeks to determine the relationship between these two, either in the theoretical sense of how to distinguish one from the other, or in the specific Jeremianic context of how the one functions in regard to the other.

This analysis gives some indication of the relationship between contemporary exegesis and a literary reading, but it would be interesting to compare the results of a literary approach with that of patristic and other pre-critical exegesis.

The feminine imagery which has been considered in its literary, historical and psychological contexts bears further investigation and validation in a study of the rest of prophetic literature.

Only with careful exegesis can one hope to arrive at a valid theology. This is but one step on that road. Much has been done, but much is left to do. The Little Book of Consolation contains a wealth and depth of insight which can always be plumbed yet further. It is hoped that this study has revealed a few aspects not previously brought to light and opened the way to deeper understanding of this important text.

BIBLIOGRAPHY

Abrams, M.H. *A Glossary of Literary Terms*. New York, Chicago, San Francisco, Dallas, Montreal, Toronto, London and Sydney: Holt, Rinehart and Winston, 4th ed., 1981.

Ackroyd, P.R. "Hosea and Jacob" *VT* 13 (1963) 245-59.

Ahlström, G.W. "*'dyr*," *TWAT* I, 78-81.

Aletti, J.-N. et Trublet, J. *Approche poétique et théologique des Psaumes*. Paris: Editions du Cerf, 1983.

Alonso Schökel, L. "Tres imágenes de Isaías" *Est Bib* 15 (1956) 63-84.

———. "Dos poemas a la paz: Estudio estilístico de Is 8,23-9,6 y 11,1-16" *Est Bib* 18 (1959) 149-69.

———. "Is 10,28-32: Análisis estilístico" *Bib* 40 (1959) 230-36.

———. *Estudios de poética hebrea*. Barcelona: Juan Flores, Editor, 1963.

———. "Poésie hébraique" in *DBS* VIII, 47-90.

———. "Poetic Structure of Ps 42-43" *JSOT* 1 (1976) 4-11 (trans. from 1972 Spanish original).

———. *Trienta Salmos: Poesía y oración*. Valencia: Institución San Jerónimo, 1981.

———. *Manual de poética hebrea*. Academia Christiana 41. Madrid: Ediciones Cristiandad, 1987.

Alonso Schökel, L. y Sicré Diaz, J.L. *Profetas* I. Nueva Biblia Española. Madrid: Ediciones Cristiandad, 1980.

Alter, R. *The Art of Biblical Narrative*. New York: Basic Books, Inc., 1981.

———. *The Art of Biblical Poetry*. New York: Basic Books, Inc., 1985.

Amsler, S. "La sagesse de la femme" in M. Gilbert, ed., *La Sagesse de l'Ancien Testament*. BEThL 51. Gembloux: Editions Duculot et Leuven: Leuven University Press, 1979, 112-16.

Anderson, B.W. "The New Covenant and the Old" in B.W. Anderson, ed., *The Old Testament and Christian Faith*. London: SCM Press, 1964, 225-42.

———. "'The Lord Has Created Something New,' A Stylistic Study of Jer 31:15-22" *CBQ* 40 (1978) 463-78.

Auffret, P. *The Literary Structure of Psalm 2*, trans. from the French by D.J.A. Clines. JSOTS 3. Sheffield: JSOT Press, 1977.

Avishur, Y. "Pairs of Synonymous Words in the Construct State (and in Appositional Hendiadys) in Biblical Hebrew" *Semitics* 2 (1971) 17-81.

Babylonian Talmud. I. Epstein, ed. London: The Soncino Press, 1935-1952.

Bach, D. "Rites et paroles dans l'Ancien Testament. Nouveaux éléments apportés par l'étude de *Todah*" *VT* 28 (1978) 10-19.

Bach, R. "Bauen und Pflanzen" in R. Rendtorff und K. Koch, ed., *Studien zur Theologie der alttestamentlichen Uberlieferungen*. Fs. G. von Rad. Neukirchen Kreis Moers: Neukirchener Verlag, 1961, 7-32.

Baltzer, K. *The Covenant Formulary in Old Testament, Jewish and Early Christian Writings*, trans. from German by D.E. Green. Philadelphia: Fortress Press, 1971.

Baly, D. *The Geography of the Bible*. New York, London: Harper and Row Publishers, 1974.

Baron, S. W. *A Social and Religious History of the Jews*, 15 vols., 2nd rev. ed. New York: Columbia University Press, 1952.

Barr, J. *The Scope and Authority of the Bible*. Explorations in Theology 7. London: SCM Press, 1980.

Barth, Ch. "*nts*," *TWAT* V, 713-19.

Barthélemy, D. *Critique textuelle de l'Ancien Testament* II. OBO 50/2. Fribourg: Editions Universitaires; Göttingen: Vandenhoeck & Ruprecht, 1986.

Batto, B. F. *Studies on Women at Mari*. Baltimore and London: The Johns Hopkins University Press, 1974.

Baumann, A. "*ḥrd*," *TWAT* III, 176-82.

Baumann, E. L. "*šwb šbwt*, eine exegetische Untersuchung" *ZAW* 47 (1929) 17-44.

Becker, J. *Gottesfurcht im Alten Testament*. AnBib 25. Rome: Biblical Institute Press, 1965.

Begrich, J. "Das priesterliche Heilsorakel" *ZAW* 52 (1934) 81-92.

Berlin, A. *Poetics and Interpretation of Biblical Narrative*. Bible and Literature Series 9. Sheffield: The Almond Press, 1983.

———. *The Dynamics of Biblical Parallelism*. Bloomington: Indiana University Press, 1985.

Bertram, G. "*suntribō*," *TDNT* VII, 919-925.

Beuken, W. A. M. "Isaiah LIV: The Multiple Identity of the Person Addressed" in *Language and Meaning. Studies in Hebrew Language and Biblical Exegesis*. OTS 19. Leiden: E. J. Brill, 1974, 29-70.

Beuken, W. A. M. and van Grol, H. W. M. "Jeremiah 14,1-15,9: A Situation of Distress and Its Hermeneutics; Unity and Diversity of Form — Dramatic Development" in P.-M. Bogaert, ed., *Le livre de Jérémie: Le prophète et son milieu, les oracles et leur transmission*. BEThL 54. Leuven: Leuven University, 1981, 297-342.

Beyerlin, W. *"Wir Sind wie Träumende." Studien zur 126. Psalm*. SBS 89. Stuttgart: Verlag Katholisches Bibelwerk GmbH, 1978.

Bird, P. "Images of Women in the Old Testament" in R. R. Ruether, ed., *Religion and Sexism. Images of Women in the Jewish and Christian Traditions*. New York: Simon and Schuster, 1974, 41-88.

Blank, S. H. "Irony by Way of Attribution" *Semitics* 1 (1970) 1-6.

Boadt, L. "Is 41:8-13: Notes on Poetic Style and Structure" *CBQ* 35 (1973) 20-34.

Bodkin, M. *Archetypal Patterns in Poetry. Psychological Studies of Imagination*. New York: Vintage Books, 1958.

Böhmer, S. *Heimkehr und neuer Bund: Studien zu Jeremiah 30-31*. Göttingen: Vandenhoeck & Ruprecht, 1976.

Boman, T. *Das hebräische Denken im Vergleich mit dem griechischen*, 4. Aufl. Göttingen: Vandenhoeck & Ruprecht, 1965.

Bottéro, J. "La femme dans l'Asie occidentale ancienne: Mésopotamie et Israël" in P. Grimal, ed., *Histoire mondiale de la femme*, Vol. I: *Préhistoire et antiquité*. Paris: Nouvelle Libraire de France, 1965, 156-247.

———. *Mésopotamie. L'écriture, la raison et les dieux*. Paris: Editions Gallimard, 1987.
Boulding, E. *The Underside of History. A View of Women through Time*. Boulder, Colo.: Westview Press, 1976.
Bracke, J.M. *The Coherence and Theology of Jeremiah 30-31*. Ann Arbor: University Microfilms International, 1983.
———. "*šwb šbwt*: A Reappraisal" *ZAW* 97 (1985) 233-44.
Branson, R.D. "*ysr*," *TWAT* III, 688-97.
Bretón, S. *Vocación y misión: Formulario profético*. AnBib 111. Rome: Biblical Institute Press, 1987.
Breyfolge, C. "The Social Status of Woman in the Old Testament" *BW* 35 (1910) 106-16.
———. "The Religious Status of Woman in the Old Testament" *BW* 35 (1910) 405-19.
Bright, J. *Jeremiah*. AB 21. Garden City: Doubleday, 1965.
Brooks, C. *The Well Wrought Urn. Studies in the Structure of Poetry*. New York: Harcourt, Brace and World, 1947.
Brooks, C. and Warren, R. *Understanding Poetry*, 3rd ed. New York, Chicago, San Francisco, Toronto: Holt, Rinehart and Winston, 1960.
Brueggemann, W. "Jeremiah's Use of Rhetorical Questions" *JBL* 92 (1973) 358-74.
———. "The Book of Jeremiah: Portrait of the Prophet" *Int* 37 (1983) 130-45.
———. "The 'Uncared For' Now Cared For (Jer 30:12-17): A Methodological Consideration" *JBL* 104 (1985) 419-28.
———. "A Shape for Old Testament Theology II: Embrace of Pain" *CBQ* 47 (1985) 395-415.
Buchanan, G.W. "Eschatology and the 'End of Days'" *JNES* 20 (1961) 188-93.
Buis, P. *La notion d'alliance dans l'Ancien Testament*. Lectio Divina 88. Paris: Editions du Cerf, 1976.
———. "La nouvelle alliance" *VT* 18 (1968) 1-15.
Caird, G.B. *The Language and Imagery of the Bible*. London: Duckworth, 1980.
Caquot, A. *Les danses sacrées*. Sources Orientales 6. Paris: Editions du Seuil, 1963.
Carroll, R. *From Chaos to Covenant*. New York: The Crossroad Publishing Company, 1981.
———. *Jeremiah*. London: SCM Press, Ltd., 1986.
Cassuto, U. *The Goddess Anath*, trans. from Hebrew by I. Abrahams. Jerusalem: Magnes Press, 1971.
Castellino, G.R. "Observations on the Literary Structure of Some Passages in Jeremiah" *VT* 30 (1980) 398-408.
Ceresko, A. "The Function of Chiasmus in Hebrew Poetry" *CBQ* 40 (1978) 1-9.
———. "Poetic Analysis of Ps. 105, with Attention to Its Use of Irony" *Bib* 64 (1983) 20-46.
Childs, B.S. *Myth and Reality in the Old Testament*. SBT 27. London: SCM Press, 1960.
Clements, R.E. "The Unity of the Book of Isaiah" *Int* 36 (1982) 117-29.
Clements, R.E. and Botterweck, G. "*gwy*," *TWAT* I, 965-73.
Clifford, R. "The Use of *Hôy* in the Prophets" *CBQ* 28 (1966) 458-64.
———. "Style and Purpose in Psalm 105" *Bib* 60 (1979) 420-27.

———. *Fair Spoken and Persuading: An Interpretation of Second Isaiah*. New York, Ramsey and Toronto: Paulist Press, 1984.
Clines, D. J. A. *I, He, We and They: A Literary Approach to Isaiah 53*. JSOTS 1. Sheffield: University of Sheffield, 1976.
———. "Hosea 2: Structure and Interpretation" in E. A. Livingstone, ed., *Studia Biblica 1978. I. Papers on Old Testament and Related Themes. Sixth International Congress on Biblical Studies. Oxford, 3-7 April 1978*. JSOTS 11. Sheffield: JSOT Press, 1978, 83-103.
———. *The Theme of the Pentateuch*. JSOTS 10. Sheffield: JSOT Press, 1978.
Cluysenaar, A. *Introduction to Literary Stylistics. A Discussion of Dominant Structures in Verse and Prose*. London: B. T. Batsford, Ltd., 1976.
Cody, A. "When Is the Chosen People Called a *gôy*?" *VT* 14 (1964) 1-6.
Cohen, S. S. "Torah," *Universal Jewish Encyclopedia* X, I. Landman, *et al*., eds. New York: Universal Jewish Encyclopedia, Inc., 1948, 267-69.
Collins, T. *Line Forms in Hebrew Poetry. A Grammatical Approach to the Stylistic Study of the Hebrew Prophets*. Studia Pohl: Series Maior 7. Rome: Biblical Institute Press, 1978.
Condamin, A. *Le livre de Jérémie*, 3me édition corrigée. Paris: J. Gabalda et Cie., Editeurs, 1936.
Conrad, J. "*zqn*," *TWAT* II, 639-50.
Conroy, C. *Absalom Absalom!* AnBib 81. Rome: Biblical Institute Press, 1978.
Coogan, M. D. "A Structural and Literary Analysis of the Song of Deborah" *CBQ* 40 (1978) 143-66.
Cornill, C. H. *Das Buch Jeremia*. Leipzig: Chr. Herm. Tauchnitz, 1905.
Crane, R. S. *The Languages of Criticism and the Structure of Poetry*. Toronto: University of Toronto Press, 1953.
Craven, T. *Artistry and Faith in the Book of Judith*. SBLDS 70. Chico: Scholars Press, 1983.
Crenshaw, J. "A Living Tradition: the Book of Jeremiah in Current Research" *Int* 37 (1983) 117-29.
Croatto, J. S. and Soggin, J. A. "Die Bedeutung von *šdmwt* im AT" *ZAW* 74 (1962) 44-60.
Cross, F. M. "The Development of the Jewish Scripts" in G. E. Wright, ed., *The Bible and the Ancient Near East*. Fs. W. F. Albright. Garden City, N. Y.: Doubleday and Co., Inc., 1961, 133-202.
———. *Canaanite Myth and Hebrew Epic. Essays in the History of the Religion of Israel*. Cambridge: Harvard University Press, 1973.
Culley, R. C. *Oral Formulaic Language in Biblical Psalms*. Toronto: University of Toronto Press, 1967.
Dahood, M. "Philological Notes on Jer 18:14-15" *ZAW* 74 (1962) 207-09.
———. "Ugaritic Studies and the Bible" *Greg* 43 (1962) 55-79.
———. *Psalms* III, 101-150. AB 17A. Garden City: Doubleday and Company, Inc., 1970.
———. "Northwest Semitic Texts and Textual Criticism of the Hebrew Bible" in C. Brekelmans, ed., *Questions disputées d'Ancien Testament. Méthode et Théologie*. BEThL 33. Leuven: Leuven University Press, 1974, 11-37.
———. "Ugaritic-Hebrew Parallel Pairs" in L. Fisher, ed., *Ras Shamra Parallels. The Texts from Ugarit and the Hebrew Bible* Vol. II. AnOr 50. Rome: Biblical Institute Press, 1975, 1-33.

———. "The Word Pair *'ākal* // *kālāh* in Jer XXX:16" *VT* 27 (1977) 482.
Daiches, D. *Critical Approaches to Literature*. New York: W. W. Norton and Co., 1956.
Dalman, G. *Arbeit und Sitte in Palästina*, Band I. Gütersloh: C. Bertelsmann, 1928.
Danziger, M. K. and Johnson, W. S. *An Introduction to Literary Criticism*. Boston: D. C. Heath and Company, 1961.
Daube, D. *Studies in Biblical Law*. Cambridge: University Press, 1947.
de Boer, P. A. H. *Fatherhood and Motherhood in Israelite and Judean Piety*. Leiden: E. J. Brill, 1974.
Delekat, L. "Zum hebräischen Wörterbuch" *VT* 14 (1964) 7-66.
de Robert, P. *Le berger d'Israël*. Cahiers Théologiques 57. Neuchâtel: Delachaux et Niestlé, 1968.
de Vaux, R. *Les institutions de l'Ancien Testament* I. Paris: Editions du Cerf, 1958.
Diepold, P. *Israels Land*. BWANT 95. Stuttgart, Berlin, Köln, Mainz: W. Kohlhammer Verlag, 1972.
Dietrich, E. L. *šwb šbwt. Die endzeitliche Wiederherstellung bei den Propheten*. BZAW 40. Giessen: Alfred Töpelmann, 1925.
Dragin, I. *Targum Onkelos to Deuteronomy. An English Translation of the Text with Analysis and Commentaries*. (New York): KTAV Publishing House, Inc, 1982.
Dreyfus, F. "Le thème de l'héritage dans l'Ancien Testament" *RSPhTh* 42 (1958) 3-49.
———. "Reste d'Israël," *DBS* X, 414-37.
Driver, G. R. "Hebrew Roots and Words" *Die Welt des Orients* 1 (1950) 406-15.
Ducrot, O. et Todorov, T. *Dictionnaire encyclopédique des sciences du langage*. Paris: Editions du Seuil, 1972.
Duhm, B. *Das Buch Jeremia*. KHAT XI. Tübingen und Leipzig: J. C. B. Mohr (Paul Siebeck), 1901.
Durand, G. *Les structures anthropologiques de l'imaginaire*. Collection Etudes Supérieures. Poitiers: Bordas, 1969.
Ebeling, E. s.v. "Frau," *Reallexikon der Assyriologie und Vorderasiatischen Archaëologie* III. Berlin und New York: Walter de Gruyter, 1971, 100-04.
Eising, H. "*zkr*," *TWAT* II, 571-93.
Eissfeldt, O. "Jahwe Zebaoth" in R. Sellheim und F. Maass, Hrsg., *Kleine Schriften*, 3. Band. Tübingen: J. C. B. Mohr (Paul Siebeck), 1966, 103-23.
Eitan, I. "Hebrew and Semitic Particles" (con.) Comparative Studies in Semitic Philology, *AJSL* 45 (1928-29) 48-63.
Ellison, H. L. "The Prophecy of Jeremiah" (con.) *EvQ* 36 (1964) 92-99.
Exum, J. C. "Isaiah 28-32: A Literary Approach" in *SBL 1979 Seminar Papers*, Vol. II. Missoula: Scholars Press, 1979, 123-51.
———. "Of Broken Pots, Fluttering Birds and Visions in the Night: Extended Simile and Poetic Techniques in Isaiah" *CBQ* 43 (1981) 331-52.
Feldman, A. *The Parables and Similes of the Rabbis, Agricultural and Pastoral*. Cambridge: Cambridge University Press, 1924.
Feuillet, A. "Note sur la traduction de Jer xxxi, 3c" *VT* 12 (1962) 122-24.
Fishbane, M. *Text and Texture: Close Readings of Selected Biblical Texts*. New York: Schocken Books, 1979.

Fitzgerald, A.F. "The Mythological Background for the Presentation of Jerusalem as Queen and False Worship as Adultery in the OT" *CBQ* 34 (1972) 403-16.

———. "*BTWLT* and *BT* as Titles for Capital Cities" *CBQ* 37 (1975) 167-83.

Fohrer, G. "Twofold Aspects of Hebrew Words" in P. Ackroyd and B. Lindars, eds., *Words and Meanings*. Fs. D.W. Thomas. Cambridge: Cambridge University Press, 1968, 95-103.

———. *Introduction to the Old Testament*, trans. from German by D. Green. London: SPCK, 1970.

———. "Der Israel-Prophet in Jeremia 30-31" in A. Caquot et M. Delcor, éds., *Mélanges bibliques et orientaux en l'honneur de M. Henri Cazelles*. AOAT 212. Kevelaer: Butzon & Berker; Neukirchen-Vluyn: Neukirchener Verlag, 1981, 135-48.

Fohrer, G. and Lohse, E. "*Siōn*," *TDNT* VII, 292-319.

Fokkelman, J.P. *Narrative Art in Genesis: Specimens of Stylistic and Structural Analysis*. Studia Semitica Neerlandica 17. Assen/Amsterdam: Van Gorcum, 1975.

Follis, E. "The Holy City as Daughter" in E. Follis, ed., *Directions in Biblical Hebrew Poetry*. JSOTS 40. Sheffield: JSOT Press, 1987, 173-84.

Freedman, D.N. "The Twenty-third Psalm" in L.L. Orlin, *et al.*, eds., *Michigan Oriental Studies in Honor of George G. Cameron*. Ann Arbor: Department of Near Eastern Studies, University of Michigan, 1976, 139-66.

———. "Pottery, Poetry and Prophecy: An Essay on Biblical Poetry" *JBL* 96 (1977) 5-26.

Freedman, D.N. and Willoughby, B.E. "*nś'*," *TWAT* V, 626-42.

Freedman, H. *Jeremiah*. Soncino Books of the Bible. London, Jerusalem and New York: The Soncino Press, 1985.

Frost, S.B. "Eschatology and Myth" *VT* 2 (1952) 70-80.

Frye, N. *The Great Code: The Bible and Literature*. London, Melbourne, and Henley: Routledge & Kegan Paul, 1981.

Fuhs, H.F. "*yr'*," *TWAT* III, 870-93.

Furlani, G. *La civiltà Babilonese e Assira*. Roma: Istituto per l'Oriente, 1929.

Garelli, P. et Nikiprowetzky, V. *Le Proche-Orient Asiatique. Les empires Mésopotamiens. Israël*. L'histoire et ses problèmes, 2 bis. Paris: Presses Universitaires de la France, 1974.

Gelin, A. "Le sens du mot 'Israël' en Jer 30/31" in *Memorial J. Chaine*. Bibliothèque de la Faculté Catholique de Théologie de Lyon 5. Lyon: Facultés Catholiques, 1950.

Geller, S. *Parallelism in Early Biblical Poetry*. HSM 20. Missoula: Scholars Press, 1979.

Gesenius, W. *Hebräisches und aramäisches Handwörterbuch über das Alte Testament*, bearbeitet von F. Buhl, 17. Aufl. Leipzig: Verlag von F.C.W. Vogel, 1921.

Gibson, W. "Authors, Speakers, Readers, and Mock Readers" in J.P. Tompkins, ed., *Reader-Response Criticism. From Formalism to Post-Structuralism*. Baltimore and London: Johns Hopkins University Press, 1980, 1-6.

Giesebrecht, F. *Das Buch Jeremia*, 2. völlig umgearbeitete Aufl. HKAT. Göttingen: Vandenhoeck & Ruprecht, 1907.

Ginzberg, L. *The Legends of the Jews*, 7 vols., trans. from German by H. Szold. Philadelphia: The Jewish Publication Society of America, 1909-1938.

Gitay, Y. *Prophecy and Persuasion: A Study of Isaiah 40-48*. Forum Theologiae Linguisticae 14. Bonn: Linguistica Biblica, 1981.

Good, E. *Irony in the Old Testament*, 2nd ed. Bible and Literature Series, 3. Sheffield: The Almond Press, 1981.

Gordis, R. "Democratic Origins in Ancient Israel – the Biblical *ʿedah*" in S. Lieberman, ed., *Alexander Marx Jubilee Volume*. New York: The Jewish Theological Assembly of America, 1950, 369-88.

———. "The Structure of Biblical Poetry" in *Prophets, Poets and Sages: Essays in Biblical Interpretation*. Bloomington and London: Indiana University Press, 1971, 61-94.

Gordon, C. "The Status of Woman Reflected in the Nuzi Tablets" *ZA* 43 (1936) 147-69.

Graf, K. H. *Der Prophet Jeremia*. Leipzig: T. O. Weigel, 1862.

Gray, G. B. *The Forms of Hebrew Poetry*. New York: KTAV Publishing House, 1972. Reprint of 1915 edition, with prolegomenon by D. N. Freedman.

Greenstein, E. L. "How Does Parallelism Mean?" in *A Sense of Text. The Art of Language in the Study of Biblical Literature*. JQR Suppl. 1982. Winona Lake: Eisenbrauns, 1983, 41-70.

Grether, O. *Name und Wort Gottes im Alten Testament*. BZAW 64. Giessen: Alfred Töpelmann, 1934.

Gros Louis, K. R. R., *et al.*, eds. *Literary Interpretations of Biblical Narratives*, 2 vols. Nashville: Abingdon Press, 1977/1982.

Gross, H. "*mšl*" II, *TWAT* V, 73-77.

Gruber, M. I. *Aspects of Non-Verbal Communication in the Ancient Near East*. Studia Pohl 12. Rome: Biblical Institute Press, 1980.

Gugenheim, M. et Mme. E., trans. *Le Deutéronome, Commentaire de Rachi, Le Pentateuque*, Tome V. Paris: Fondation Odette S. Levy, 1968.

Habets, G. "Die Eschatologie der alttestamentlichen Propheten" *St Miss* 32 (1983) 251-71.

Hamp, V. "*bkh*," *TWAT* I, 638-43.

Harris, R. "The *nadītu* Woman" in R. D. Briggs and J. A. Brinkman, eds., *Studies Presented to A. Leo Oppenheim*. Chicago: University of Chicago Press, 1964, 106-35.

———. Review of *Histoire mondiale de la femme* in *JESHO* 9 (1966) 308-09.

———. "Woman in the Ancient Near East," *IDBS*, 960-63.

Hastings, J., ed. *A Dictionary of the Bible Dealing with Its Language, Literature, and Contents*, 5 vols. Edinburgh: T. & T. Clark; New York: Chas. Scribner's Sons, 1898-1904.

Hausmann, J. "*ntš*," *TWAT* V, 727-30.

Hayward, C. T. R. *The Targum of Jeremiah*. The Aramaic Bible 12. Edinburgh: T. & T. Clark Ltd., 1987.

Heaton, E. W. "The Root *š'r* and the Doctrine of the Remnant" *JThSt* NS 3 (1952) 27-39.

Heilige Schrift Familienbibel, Die, Einheitsübersetzung. Leipzig: St Benno-Verlag GmbH, 1983.

Held, M. "The Action-Result (Factitive-Passive) Sequence of Identical Verbs in Biblical Hebrew and Ugaritic" *JBL* 84 (1965) 272-82.

Helfmeyer, F.J. "*klh*," *TWAT* IV, 166-74.

Hempel, J. "Heilung als Symbol und Wirklichkeit im biblischen Schrifttum" *Nachrichten der Akademie der Wissenschaften im Göttingen* 3 (1958) 237-314.

Herntrich, V. u. Büchsel, F. "*krinō*," *TDNT* III, 921-33.

Herrmann, S. *Die prophetischen Heilserwartungen im Alten Testament*. BWANT 5. Stuttgart: W. Kohlhammer Verlag, 1965.

———. "Forschung am Jeremiabuch: Probleme und Tendenzen ihren neueren Entwicklung" *ThL* 102 (1977) 481-90.

Hillers, D. *Treaty Curses and the Old Testament Prophets*. BibOr 16. Rome: Pontifical Biblical Institute, 1964.

Holladay, W. *The Root ŠÛBH in the Old Testament with Particular References to Its Usage in Covenantal Contexts*. Leiden: E.J. Brill, 1958.

———. "Prototype and Copies: A New Approach to the Poetry-Prose Problem in the Book of Jeremiah" *JBL* 79 (1960) 351-67.

———. "Style, Irony and Authenticity in Jeremiah" *JBL* 81 (1962) 44-54.

———. "The Recovery of the Poetic Passages of Jeremiah" *JBL* 85 (1966) 401-35.

———. "Jeremiah 31:22b Reconsidered: The Woman Encompasses the Man" *VT* 16 (1966) 236-39.

———. *Jeremiah: Spokesman Out of Time*. Philadelphia: United Church Press, 1974.

———. *The Architecture of Jeremiah 1-20*. Cranberry, N.J., and London: Associated University Presses, 1976.

———. *Jeremiah 1. A Commentary on the Book of the Prophet Jeremiah Chapters 1-25*. Hermeneia. Philadelphia: Fortress Press, 1986.

Holy Bible: New International Version. Grand Rapids: Zondervan, 1978.

Humbert, P. "Maladie et médecine dans l'Ancien Testament" *RevHPhRel* 44 (1964) 1-29.

Hvidberg, F.F. *Weeping and Laughter in the Old Testament. A Study of Canaanite-Israelite Religion*. Leiden: E.J. Brill, 1962.

Hyatt, J.P. "The Book of Jeremiah," *IB* V. New York and Nashville: Abingdon Press, 1956, 777-1142.

Irwin, W.H. *Isaiah 28-33. Translation and Philological Notes*. BibOr 30. Rome: Biblical Institute Press, 1977.

———. "Syntax and Style in Isaiah 26" *CBQ* 41 (1979) 240-61.

Isbell, C. and Jackson, M. "Rhetorical Criticism and Jeremiah VII 1-VIII 3" *VT* 30 (1980) 20-26.

Jacob, E. "Féminisme ou Messianisme? A propos de Jérémie 31:22" in H. Donner, *et al.*, eds., *Beiträge zur alttestamentlichen Theologie*. Fs. W. Zimmerli. Göttingen: Vandenhoeck und Ruprecht, 1977, 179-84.

Janzen, J.G. *Studies in the Text of Jeremiah*. HSM 6. Cambridge: Harvard University Press, 1973.

Jefferson, A. and Robey, D., eds. *Modern Literary Theory. A Comparative Introduction*. London: Batsford Academic and Educational, Ltd., 1982.

Jenni, E. "Eschatology of OT," *IDB* II, 126-33.
———. "*'dyr*," *THAT* I, 38-41.
———. "*'hb*," *THAT* I, 60-73.
Jobling, D. "The Quest of the Historical Jeremiah: Hermeneutical Implications of Recent Literature" in L. G. Perdue and B. W. Kovacs, eds., *A Prophet to the Nations: Essays in Jeremiah Studies*. Winona Lake: Eisenbrauns, 1984, 285-98.
Johnson, A. R. *The Vitality of the Individual in the Thought of Ancient Israel*. Cardiff: University of Wales Press, 1949.
Johnson, B. "*mšpṭ*," *TWAT* V, 93-107.
Joüon, P. *Grammaire de l'hébreu biblique*. Rome: Biblical Institute Press, 1923.
———. "Crainte et peur en hébreu biblique. Etude de lexicographie et de stylistique" *Bib* 6 (1925) 174-79.
Jung, C. G. *The Archetypes and the Collective Unconscious*. The Collected Works of C. G. Jung, vol. 9.1, R. F. C. Hull, trans. Bollingen Series XX. Princeton: Princeton University Press, 1959.
———. *Psychology and Religion: West and East*. The Collected Works of C. G. Jung, vol. 11, R. F. C. Hull, trans. Bollingen Series XX (2nd ed.). Princeton: Princeton University Press, 1969.
———. *The Structure and Dynamics of the Psyche*. The Collected Works of C. G. Jung, vol. 8, R. F. C. Hull, trans. Bollingen Series XX. Princeton: Princeton University Press, 1969.
———. *Psychological Types*. The Collected Works of C. G. Jung, vol. 6, Revision by R. F. C. Hull of a translation by H. G. Baynes. Bollingen Series XX. Princeton: Princeton University Press, 1971.
Kalluveettil, P. *Declaration and Covenant. A Comprehensive Review of Covenant Formulae from the Old Testament and the Ancient Near East*. AnBib 88. Rome: Biblical Institute Press, 1982.
Keil, C. F. *The Prophecies of Jeremiah* II, trans. from German by J. Kennedy. Grand Rapids: Wm. B. Eerdmans, 1980 (reprint date; original date not given).
Kellermann, D. "*mškn*," *TWAT* V, 62-69.
Kennicott, B., ed. *Vetus Testamentum Hebraicum cum variis lectionibus*, 2 tom. Oxonii: Clarendoniano, 1776.
Kessler, M. "Inclusio in the Hebrew Bible" *Semitics* 6 (1978) 44-49.
King, L. W. *Babylonian Magic and Sorcery being "The Prayers of the Lifting of the Hand."* London: Luzac and Co., 1896.
Koch, K. "*ḥṭ'*," *TWAT* II, 857-70.
Köhler, L. *Der hebräische Mensch*. Tübingen: J. C. B. Mohr (Paul Siebeck), 1953.
König, E. *Hebräisches und aramäisches Wörterbuch zum Alten Testament*, 5. vermehrte Aufl. Leipzig: Dieterich'sche Verlagsbuchhandlung, 1931.
Kosmala, H. "'At the End of the Days'" *ASTI* 2 (1963) 27-37.
———. "Form and Structure in Ancient Hebrew Poetry (A New Approach)" *VT* 14 (1964) 423-45.
———. "Form and Structure in Ancient Hebrew Poetry" *VT* 16 (1966) 152-80.
Krašovec, J. *Der Merismus im Biblisch-Hebräischen und Nordwestsemitischen*. BibOr 33. Rome: Biblical Institute Press, 1977.

———. "Merism – Polar Expressions in Biblical Hebrew" *Bib* 64 (1983) 231-39.
———. *Antithetic Structure in Biblical Hebrew Poetry*. SVT 35. Leiden: E. J. Brill, 1984.
Kraus, H. J. *Worship in Israel. A Cultic History of the Old Testament*, trans. fr. German by G. Buswell. Oxford: Basil Blackwell, 1966.
Krause, H.-J. "*hôj* als profetische Leichenklage über das eigene Volk im 8. Jahrhundert" *ZAW* 85 (1973) 15-46.
Kselman, J. S. "Design and Structure in Hebrew Poetry" *SBL 1980 Seminar Papers*. Chico: Scholars Press, 1980, 1-16.
Kugel, J. *The Idea of Biblical Poetry. Parallelism and Its History*. New Haven: Yale University Press, 1983.
Kühlewein, J. "*yld*," *THAT* I, 732-36.
———. "*rḥq*," *THAT* II, 768-71.
Kutsch, E. "Gottes Zuspruch und Anspruch. *b^erît* in der alttestamentlichen Theologie" in C. Brekelmans, ed., *Questions disputées d'Ancien Testament. Méthode et Théologie*. BEThL 33. Gembloux: J Duculot; Leuven: Leuven University Press, 1974, 71-90.
———. "*ḥrp*" II, *TWAT* III, 223-29.
Labuschagne, C. J. "The Emphasizing Particle *gam* and Its Connotations" in W. C. van Unnik and A. S. van der Woude, eds., *Studia Biblica et Semantica*. Fs. T. C. Vriezen. Wageningen: H. Veenman & Zonen, 1966, 193-203.
Lambdin, T. O. *Introduction to Biblical Hebrew*. London: Darton, Longman and Todd, 1973.
Lehmann, M. "A New Interpretation of the Term *šdmwt*" *VT* 3 (1953) 361-71.
Lemke, W. "Jeremiah 31:31-34" *Int* 37 (1983) 183-87.
Levin, C. *Die Verheissung des neuen Bundes in ihrem theologiegeschichtlichen Zusammenhang ausgelegt*. FRLANT 137. Göttingen: Vandenhoeck & Ruprecht, 1985.
Levin, S. *Linguistic Structures in Poetry*. Janua Linguarum, Series Minor 23. The Hague, Paris, New York: Mouton Publishers, 1962.
Liddell, H. G. and Scott, R. *A Greek-English Lexicon*, Revised and Augmented by H. S. Jones, 9th ed. Oxford: Clarendon Press, 1968.
Liedke, G. "*špṭ*," *THAT* II, 999-1009.
Lindars, B. "Rachel Weeping for Her Children — Jeremiah 31:15-22" *JSOT* 12 (1979) 47-62.
Lindblom, J. "Gibt es eine Eschatologie bei den alttestamentlichen Propheten?" *Studia Theologica* 7 (1952) 79-114.
Lindhagen, C. *The Servant Motif in the Old Testament. A Preliminary Study to the 'Ebed-Yahweh Problem' in Deutero-Isaiah*. Uppsala: Lundequistska Bokhandeln, 1950.
Loewe, R. *The Position of Women in Judaism*. London: SPCK, 1966.
Lofthouse, W. F. "Ḥen and Ḥesed in the Old Testament" *ZAW* 51 (1933) 29-35.
Lohfink, N. "Der junge Jeremia als Propagandist und Poet. Zum Grundstock von Jer 30-31" in P.-M. Bogaert, ed. *Le livre de Jérémie: Le prophète et son milieu, les oracles et leur transmission*. BEThL 54. Leuven: Leuven University, 1981, 351-68.

———. "Der Gotteswortverschachtelung in Jer 30-31" in L. Ruppert, *et al.*, Hrsg., *Künder des Wortes*. Fs. Josef Schreiner. Würzburg: Echter Verlag, 1982, 105-20.

———. "*yrš*," *TWAT* III, 953-85.

Long, B. O. "The Stylistic Components of Jeremiah 3:1-5" *ZAW* 88 (1976) 386-90.

Longman, T. "A Critique of Two Recent Metrical Systems" *Bib* 63 (1982) 230-54.

Lord, A. B. *The Singer of Tales*. Harvard Studies in Comparative Literature 24. Cambridge: Harvard University Press, 1960.

Lundbom, J. *Jeremiah: A Study in Ancient Hebrew Rhetoric*. SBLDS 18. Missoula: Scholars Press, 1975.

Lust, J. "'Gathering and Return' in Jeremiah and Ezechiel" in P.-M. Bogaert, ed., *Le livre de Jérémie. Le prophète et son milieu, les oracles et leur transmission*. BEThL 54. Leuven: Leuven University Press, 1981, 119-42.

Luyster, R. "Wind and Water: Cosmogonic Symbolism in the Old Testament" *ZAW* 93 (1981) 1-10.

Lys, D. *Nèpèsh. Histoire de l'âme dans la révélation d'Israël au sein des religions proches-orientales*. Etudes d'Histoire et de Philosophie Religieuses 50. Paris: Presses Universitaires de France, 1958.

McCarter, P. K. *II Samuel*. AB 9. Garden City, N. Y.: Doubleday and Co., Inc, 1984.

McCarthy, D. J. "*B^erît* and Covenant in the Deuteronomistic History" in G. W. Anderson, *et al.*, ed., *Studies in the Religion of Ancient Israel*. SVT 23. Leiden: E. J. Brill, 1972, 65-85.

———. *Treaty and Covenant* (rev. ed.). AnBib 21A. Rome: Biblical Institute Press, 1978.

McKane, W. "Relations between Poetry and Prose in the Book of Jeremiah with Special Reference to Jeremiah III 6-11 and XII 14-17" in J. A. Emerton, ed., *Congress Volume: Vienna 1980*. SVT 32. Leiden: E. J. Brill, 1981, 220-37.

Martin-Achard, R. "Quelques remarques sur la nouvelle alliance chez Jérémie (Jérémie 31,31-34)" in C. Brekelmans, ed., *Questions disputées d'Ancien Testament. Méthode et Théologie*. BEThL 33. Gembloux: J. Duculot; Leuven: Leuven University Press, 1974, 141-64.

May, H. G. "Individual Responsibility and Retribution" *HUCA* 32 (1961) 107-20.

Mayer, G., *et al.* "*ydh*," *TWAT* III, 455-74.

Meissner, B. *Babylonien und Assyrien* 1. Band. Heidelberg: Carl Winters Universitätsbuchhandlung, 1920.

Mejía, J. "La problématique de l'Ancienne et de la Nouvelle Alliance dans Jérémie xxxi 31-34 et quelques autres textes" in J. A. Emerton, ed., *Congress Volume: Vienna 1980*. SVT 32. Leiden: E. J. Brill, 1981, 263-77.

Mendenhall, G. *Law and Covenant in Israel and the Ancient Near East*. Pittsburgh: The Biblical Colloquium, 1955.

Midrash on Psalms. W. G. Braude, trans. Yale Judaica Series XIII. New Haven: Yale University Press, 1959.

Midrash Rabbah: Exodus. S.M. Lehrman, trans. London: The Soncino Press, 1939.

Midrash Rabbah: Genesis II. H. Freedman, trans. London: The Soncino Press, 1939.

Milgrom, J., *et al.* "*'dh*," *TWAT* V, 1079-92.

Miller, P.D. *Genesis 1-11: Studies in Structure and Theme*. JSOTS 8. Sheffield: University of Sheffield, 1978.

———. "The Gift of God, The Deuteronomic Theology of the Land" *Int* 23 (1969) 451-65.

Mishnah, The. H. Danby, trans. Oxford: The Clarendon Press, 1933.

Moberly, R.W.L. *At the Mountain of God. Story and Theology in Exodus 32-34*. JSOTS 22. Sheffield: JSOT Press, 1983.

Morgenstern, J. *Rites of Birth, Marriage, Death and Kindred Occasions Among the Semites*. Cincinnati: Hebrew Union College Press and Chicago: Quadrangle Books, 1966.

Mosca, P.G. "Psalm 26: Poetic Structure and the Form-Critical Task" *CBQ* 47 (1985) 212-37.

Movers, C.F. *De Utriusque Recensionis Vaticiniorum Ieremias, Graecae Alexandrinae et Hebraicae Masorethicae, Indole et Origine Commentatio Critica*. Hamburgi: Fridericum Perthes, 1837.

Mowinckel, S. *Zur Komposition des Buches Jeremia*. Kristiania: Jacob Dybwad, 1914.

———. *He That Cometh*, trans. from the Norwegian by G.W. Anderson. Oxford: Basil Blackwell, 1956.

Mowvley, H. "The Concept and Content of 'Blessing' in the Old Testament" *BT* 16 (1965) 74-80.

Muilenburg, J. "A Study in Hebrew Rhetoric: Repetition and Style," *Congress Volume: Copenhagen 1953*. SVT 1. Leiden: E.J. Brill, 1953, 97-111.

———. "The Linguistic and Rhetorical Usages of the Particle *ky* in the Old Testament" *HUCA* 32 (1961) 135-60.

———. "Terminology of Adversity in Jeremiah" in H.T. Frank and W.L. Reed, eds., *Translating and Understanding the Old Testament*. Fs. H. May. New York: Abingdon Press, 1970, 42-63.

Münderlein, G. "*hrs*," *TWAT* II, 499-501.

Muraoka, T. *Emphatic Words and Structures in Biblical Hebrew*. Jerusalem: The Magnes Press, 1985.

Negoiță, A. and Ringgren, H. "*dšn*," *TWAT* II, 331-34.

Neufeld, E. *Ancient Hebrew Marriage Laws with Special References to General Semitic Laws and Customs*. London, New York, Toronto: Longmans, Green and Co., 1944.

Neumann, E. *The Great Mother. An Analysis of the Archetype*, trans. from the German by R. Manheim. Bollingen Series XLVII, 2nd ed. Princeton: Princeton University Press, 1963.

Neumann, P.K.D. "Das Wort, das geschehen ist... Zum Problem der Wortempfangsterminologie in Jer I-XXV" *VT* 23 (1973) 171-217.

Nicholson, E.W. *Jeremiah 26-52*. CBC. Cambridge: Cambridge University Press, 1975.

———. "Covenant in a Century of Study since Wellhausen" in *Crises and Perspectives: Studies in Ancient Near Eastern Polytheism, Biblical Theology, Palestinian Archaeology and Intertestamental Literature*. OTS 24. Leiden: E. J. Brill, 1986, 54-63.
Nötscher, F. "Zum emphatischen Lamed" *VT* 3 (1953) 372-80.
Nova Vulgata Bibliorum Sacrorum. Città del Vaticano: Libreria Editrice Vaticana, 1986.
O'Connor, M. *Hebrew Verse Structure*. Winona Lake: Eisenbrauns, 1980.
Oepke, A. "*iaomai*," *TDNT* III, 194-215.
Oesterley, W. O. E. *The Sacred Dance. A Study in Comparative Folklore*. Cambridge: The University Press, 1923.
Olmstead, A. T. *History of Assyria*. Chicago: University of Chicago Press, 1951.
Oppenheim, A. L. *Ancient Mesopotamia. Portrait of a Dead Civilization*. Chicago and London: University of Chicago Press, 1964.
Otzen, B. "*'bd*," *TWAT* I, 20-24.
Overholt, T. W. "The Falsehood of Idolatry: An Interpretation of Jer. X. 1-16" *JThS* N. S. 16 (1965) 1-12.
Oxford Latin Dictionary. P. W. G. Glare, *et al*., eds. Oxford: Clarendon Press, 1968-1982.
Parunak, H. Van Dyke. "A Semantic Study of NḤM" *Bib* 56 (1975) 512-32.
Paul, S. "Amos 1:3-2:3: A Concatenous Literary Pattern" *JBL* 90 (1971) 397-403.
Pedersen, J. *Israel. Its Life and Culture I-II*, trans. by A. Møller. London: Oxford University Press: 1926.
Perdue, L. G. "Jeremiah in Modern Research: Approaches and Issues" in L.G. Perdue and B. W. Kovacs, eds., *A Prophet to the Nations: Essays in Jeremiah Studies*. Winona Lake: Eisenbrauns, 1984, 1-32.
Peritz, I. J. "Woman in the Ancient Hebrew Cult" *JBL* 17 (1898) 111-48.
Plöger, J. *Literarkritische formgeschichtliche und stilkritische Untersuchungen zum Deuteronomium*. BBB 26. Bonn: Peter Hanstein Verlag, 1967.
Polan, G. *In the Ways of Justice Toward Salvation: A Rhetorical Analysis of Isaiah 56-59*. American University Studies, Series VII: Theology and Religion, Vol. 13. New York, Berne, Frankfurt am Main: Peter Lang, 1986.
Polk, T. *The Prophetic Persona: Jeremiah and the Language of the Self*. JSOTS 32. Sheffield: JSOT Press, 1984.
Pope, M. "'Pleonastic' *Waw* before Nouns in Ugaritic and Hebrew" *JAOS* 73 (1953) 95-98.
Potter, H. D. "The New Covenant in Jer xxxi:31-34" *VT* 33 (1983) 347-57.
Preuschen, E. "Die Bedeutung von *šwb šbwt* im Alten Testament" *ZAW* 15 (1895) 1-74.
Preuss, H. D. "*zr'*," *TWAT* II, 663-86.
Procksch, O. and Büchsel, F. "*luō*," *TDNT* IV, 328-35.
Rabin, C. "*noṣerim*" *Textus* 5 (1966) 44-52.
Rainey, A. "Woman," *Enc Jud* XVI, 623-30.
Raitt, T. M. *A Theology of Exile. Judgment/Deliverance in Jeremiah and Ezechiel*. Philadelphia: Fortress Press, 1977.
Ramban (Nachmanides). *Commentary of the Torah: Genesis*, C. B. Chavel, trans. and ed. New York: Shilo Publishing House, 1971.

Ramsey, G. "Speech-Forms in Hebrew Law and Prophetic Oracles" *JBL* 96 (1977) 43-58.

Reallexikon der Assyriologie und Vorderasiatischen Archäologie. 6 Bde. Begründet von E. Ebeling u. B. Meissner; O.D. Dietz, Hrsg. Berlin und Leipzig: Walter de Gruyter & Co., 1932-1983.

Reider, J. "Etymological Studies in Biblical Hebrew" *VT* 4 (1954) 276-95.

Rengstorf, K.H. "*klaiō*," *TDNT* III, 722-26.

Reymond, P. *L'eau, sa vie, et sa signification dans l'Ancien Testament*. SVT 6. Leiden: E.J. Brill, 1958.

Riesener, I. *Der Stamm ʿbd im Alten Testament. Eine Wortuntersuchung unter Berücksichtigung neurer sprachwissenschaftlicher Methoden*. BZAW 149. Berlin, New York: Walter de Gruyter, 1979.

Rinaldi, G. "Alcuni termini ebraici relativi alla letteratura" *Bib* 40 (1959) 267-89.

Ringgren, H. "*yṣhr*," *TWAT* III, 825-26.

———. "*nwh*," *TWAT* V, 293-97.

Ringgren, H., *et al.* "*ʿbd*," *TWAT* V, 985-1012.

Rosenbaum, M. and Silberman, A.M., trans. *Pentateuch with Targum Onkelos, Haphtaroth and Rashi's Commentary. Deuteronomy*. New York: Hebrew Publishing Company, s.d.

Rost, L. *Die Damaskusschrift*. Kleine Texte für Vorlesungen und Übungen. Berlin: Walter de Gruyter & Co., 1933.

———. "Die Schuld der Väter" in *Studien zum Alten Testament*. BWANT 101. Stuttgart, Berlin, Köln, Mainz: W. Kohlhammer, 1974, 66-71.

Rowley, H.H. *Worship in Ancient Israel. Its Form and Meaning*. London: SPCK, 1967.

Rudolph, W. *Jeremia*, 3., verbesserte Aufl. HAT 12. Tübingen: J.C.B. Mohr (Paul Siebeck), 1968.

Ruprecht, E. "*śmḥ*," *THAT* II, 828-35.

Sakenfeld, K.D. *The Meaning of Ḥesed in the Hebrew Bible. A New Inquiry*. HSM 17. Missoula: Scholars Press, 1978.

Savage, M. "Literary Criticism and Biblical Studies: A Rhetorical Analysis of the Joseph Narrative" in C.D. Evans, *et al.*, eds., *Scripture in Context. Essays on the Comparative Method*. Pittsburgh Theological Monograph Series 34. Pittsburgh: The Pickwick Press, 1980, 79-100.

Saydon, P. "Assonance in Hebrew as a Means of Expressing Emphasis" *Bib* 36 (1955) 36-50, 287-304.

Scharbert, J. *Der Schmerz im Alten Testament*. BBB 8. Bonn: Peter Hanstein Verlag, 1955.

Schechter, S., trans. and ed. *Documents of Jewish Sectaries I: Fragments of a Zadokite Work*. (New York): KTAV Publishing House, 1970.

Schedl, C. "'Femina circumdabit virum' oder 'Via Salutis'? Textkritische Untersuchung zu Jer 31,22" *ZKTh* 83 (1961) 431-42.

Schmid, H.H. *šālōm. "Frieden" im alten Orient und im Alten Testament*. SBS 51. Stuttgart: Verlag Katholisches Bibelwerk GmbH, 1971.

Schmidt, K.L. "*ekklēsia*," *TDNT* III, 501-36.

Schmitt, J.J. "The Gender of Ancient Israel" *JSOT* 26 (1983) 115-25.

———. "The Motherhood of God and Zion as Mother" *RB* 92 (1985) 557-69.

Schottroff, W. "*ydʿ*," *THAT* I, 682-701.

Schramm, G. "Poetic Patterning in Biblical Hebrew" in L. L. Orlin, *et al.*, eds., *Michigan Oriental Studies in Honor of George G. Cameron*. Ann Arbor: Department of Near Eastern Studies, University of Michigan, 1976, 167-91.

Schreiner, J. "*yld*," *TWAT* III, 633-39.

Schröter, U. "Jeremias Botschaft für das Nordreich, zu N. Lohfink's Überlegungen zum Grundbestand von Jeremia xxx-xxxi" *VT* 35 (1985), 312-29.

Scott, C. T. "Typography, Poems, and the Poetic Line" in M. A. Jazayery, *et al.*, eds., *Linguistic and Literary Studies*. Fs. A. A. Hill. Linguistic and Literary Studies IV: Trends in Linguistics 10. The Hague, Paris, New York: Mouton Publishers, 1979, 153-60.

Scott, W. S. *Five Approaches of Literary Criticism. An Arrangement of Contemporary Critical Essays*. New York: Collier Books, 1962.

Seidl, Th. "Die Wortereignisformel in Jeremia. Beobachtungen zu den Formen der Redeeröffnung in Jeremia, im Anschluss an Jer 27,1.2" *BZ* (N. F.) 23 (1979) 20-47.

Seybold, K. and Mueller, U. B. *Sickness and Healing*, trans. from the German by D. W. Scott. Biblical Encounter Series. Nashville: Abingdon Press, 1981.

Shipley, J. T. *Dictionary of World Literary Terms* (rev. ed.). London: George Allen & Unwin Ltd., 1970.

Simian-Yofre, H. "*nḥm*," *TWAT* V, 366-84.

Simons, J. *Jerusalem in the Old Testament. Researches and Theories*. Leiden: Nederlandsch Archaeologisch-Philologisch Instituut voor het Nabije Oosten, 1952.

Ska, J.-L. *Le passage de la mer: Etude de la construction, du style et de la symbolique d'Ex 14,1-31*. AnBib 109. Rome: Biblical Institute Press, 1986.

Smith, G. A. *The Historical Geography of the Holy Land*, 25th ed., rev. London: Hodder & Stoughton, 1931.

Soderlund, S. *The Text of Jeremiah: A Revised Hypothesis*. JSOTS 47. Sheffield: JSOT Press, 1985.

Sperber, A., ed. *The Prophets according to Codex Reuchlinianus*. Leiden: E. J. Brill, 1969.

Stamm, J. J. "*g'l*," *THAT* I, 383-94.

———. "*pdh*," *THAT* II, 389-406.

Stenmans, P., *et al.* "*kbd*," *TWAT* IV, 13-23.

Sternberg, M. *The Poetics of Biblical Narrative: Ideological Literature and the Drama of Reality*. Bloomington: Indiana University Press, 1985.

Stinespring, W. F. "Zion, Daughter of," *IDBS*, 985.

Stoebe, H. J. "*ḥnn*," *THAT* I, 587-97.

———. "*nḥm*," *THAT* II, 59-66.

———. "*rḥm*," *THAT* II, 761-68.

———. "*r*ʿ," *THAT* II, 794-803.

Stolz, F. "*'bl*," *THAT* I, 27-31.

Strack, H. L., ed. *The Hebrew Bible. The Latter Prophets*. The Babylonian Codex of Petrograd. New York: KTAV Publishing House, Inc., 1971.

Thompson, J. A. "Israel's 'Lovers'" *VT* 27 (1977) 475-81.

———. *The Book of Jeremiah*. NICOT. Grand Rapids: Wm. B. Eerdmans Publishing Co., 1980.
Tidwell, N. "A Road and a Way. A Contribution to the Study of Word-Pairs" *Semitics* 7 (1980) 50-80.
Torrey, C.C. "Studies in the Aramaic of the First Century A.D." *ZAW* 65 (1953) 228-47.
Tosato, A. *Il matrimonio israelitico. Una teoria generale*. AnBib 100. Rome: Biblical Institute Press, 1982.
Tov, E. *The Septuagint Translation of Jeremiah and Baruch: A Discussion of an Early Revision of the LXX of Jeremiah 29-52 and Baruch 1:1-3:8*. HSM 8. Missoula: Scholars Press, 1976.
Trible, P. *God and the Rhetoric of Sexuality*. Overtures to Biblical Theology. Philadelphia: Fortress Press, 1978.
———. "Woman in the Old Testament," *IDBS*, 963-66.
Tromp, N.J. "Amos V 1-17. Towards a Stylistic and Rhetorical Analysis" in A.S. van der Woude, ed., *Prophets, Worship and Theodicy*. OTS 23. Leiden: E.J. Brill, 1984, 56-84.
Tsevat, M. "Rachel's Tomb," *IDBS*, 724-25.
———. "*bkwr*," *TWAT* I, 643-50.
Ulanov, A.B. *The Feminine in Jungian Psychology and in Christian Theology*. Evanston: Northwestern University Press, 1971.
Universal Jewish Encyclopedia, 10 vols. I. Landman, *et al.*, eds. New York: Universal Jewish Encyclopedia Co., Inc., 1948.
van der Ploeg, J. "Studies in Hebrew Law" *CBQ* 12 (1950) 248-59.
van der Woude, A.S. "*ṣb'*," *THAT* II, 498-507.
Volz, P. *Der Prophet Jeremia*. KAT X. Leipzig: A. Deichertsche Verlagsbuchhandlung, 1922.
von Rad, G. *Old Testament Theology* 2 vol., trans. from the German by D. Stalker. New York, Evanston, San Francisco and London: Harper and Row Publishers: 1965.
———. *Das 5. Buch Mose. Deuteronomium*, 3., unveränd. Aufl. ATD 8. Göttingen: Vandenhoeck & Ruprecht, 1978.
von Rad, G. and Delling, G. "*hēmera*," *TDNT* II, 943-47.
Vos, C. *Woman in Old Testament Worship*. Delft: Judels & Brinkman, s.d.
Vriezen, Th. "Prophecy and Eschatology," *Congress Volume: Copenhagen 1953*. SVT 1. Leiden: E.J. Brill, 1953, 199-229.
Wagner, S. "*ygh*," *TWAT* III, 406-12.
———. "*yqr*," *TWAT* III, 855-65.
Wallis, G., *et al*. "*'hb*," *TWAT* I, 108-28.
Walton, B. *Biblia Sacra Polyglotta*, 6 tom. London: Thomas Roycroft, 1656.
Wambacq, B. *L'épithète divine Jahvé Ṣ^{e}ba'ôt. Etude philologique, historique et exégétique*. Brugge: Desclée De Brouwer, 1947.
Wanke, G. "*phobeō*," *TDNT* IX, 197-205.
Watson, W.G.E. *Classical Hebrew Poetry: A Guide to Its Techniques*. JSOTS 26. Sheffield: JSOT Press, 1984.
———. "Internal Parallelism in Classical Hebrew Verse" *Bib* 66 (1985) 365-84.
Weinfeld, M. "The Covenant of Grant in the Old Testament and in the Ancient Near East" *JAOS* 90 (1970) 184-203.

———. "*Berît* — Covenant vs. Obligation" (Review article of Kutsch's *Verheissung und Gesetz*) *Bib* 56 (1975) 120-28.
Weippert, H. "Das Wort vom neuen Bund im Jeremia xxxi 31-34" *VT* 29 (1979) 336-51.
Weiser, A. *Das Buch Jeremia. Kapitel 25,15-52,34.* ATD 21. Göttingen: Vandenhoeck & Ruprecht, 1966.
Weiss, M. *The Bible from Within: The Method of Total Interpretation.* Jerusalem: The Magnes Press, 1984.
Wellek, R. *The Attack on Literature and Other Essays.* Chapel Hill: University of North Carolina Press, 1982.
Wellek, R. and Warren, A. *Theory of Literature*, 3rd ed. San Diego, New York, London: Harcourt Brace Jovanovich, 1977.
Wellhausen, J. *Prolegomena to the History of Ancient Israel.* Gloucester, Mass.: Peter Smith, 1973 (reprint of 1957 ed.).
Wernberg-Møller, P. "A Note on *zwr* 'to Stink'" *VT* 4 (1954) 322-25.
———. "'Pleonastic' *Waw* in Classical Hebrew" *JSS* 3 (1958) 321-26.
Westermann, C. *Grundformen prophetischer Rede.* BEvTh 31. München: Chr. Kaiser Verlag, 1960.
———. *Das Buch Jesaja. Kapitel 40-66.* ATD 19. Göttingen: Vandenhoeck & Ruprecht, 1966.
———. "*ydh*," *THAT* I, 674-82.
———. "*kbd*," *THAT* I, 794-812.
———. "*ʿbd*," *THAT* II, 182-200.
Wheelwright, P. *Metaphor and Reality.* Bloomington and London: Indiana University Press, 1962.
Wildberger, H. "Israel und sein Land" *EvTh* 16 (1956) 404-22.
Wolff, H. W. *Anthropology of the Old Testament*, trans. from the German by M. Kohl. London: SCM Press, Ltd; Philadelphia: Fortress Press, 1974.
Zevit, Z. "The Linguistic and Contextual Arguments in Support of a Hebrew 3 ms Suffix *-y*" *UF* 9 (1977) 315-28.
"Zion," *EncJud* 16, 1030-31 (ed. staff).
Zlotowitz, M. *BEREISHIS. Genesis: A New Translation with a Commentary Anthologized from Talmudic, Midrashic and Rabbinic Sources.* New York: Mesorah Publications, 1977.
Zobel, H.-J. "*ḥsd*," *TWAT* III, 48-71.
———. "*yʿq(w)b*," *TWAT* III, 752-77.
———. "*mʿt*," *TWAT* IV, 1030-36.
Zorell, F., *et al. Lexicon Hebraicum Veteris Testamenti.* Rome: Biblical Institute Press, 1984.
Zurro, E. *Procedimientos iterativos en la poesía ugarítica y hebrea.* BibOr 43. Rome: Biblical Institute Press, 1987.

AUTHOR INDEX

Finito di stampare il 26 luglio 1991
Tipografia Poliglotta della Pontificia Università Gregoriana
Piazza della Pilotta, 4 – 00187 Roma